D0103445

Contents

Introduction

In the late Middle Ages, Bruges was one of the leading cities of Europe, an international and cosmopolitan trading centre with a web of connections stretching to the Mediterranean, the Middle East and North Africa. It had resident bankers from Renaissance Italy, and hosted traders from Spain, Portugal, England, Scotland and Hanseatic Germany. Its ruling family, the Dukes of Burgundy, could boast close family links to the French and English crowns. With all this wealth and prestige, Bruges became a major centre of patronage for art and learning; it was also famous – notorious even – for its visible wealth and luxury, and its glorious feasts.

But in the late 15th century, nature and politics conspired to send Bruges spiralling into decline. For the next 400 years Bruges coasted along, changing little of its medieval fabric, but losing little of it either. It became a pious city of monasteries and convents, and good works: the well-to-do endowed numerous almshouses to shelter the less fortunate. The Industrial Revolution virtually passed Bruges by; instead, Bruges's womenfolk produced handmade lace. In the middle of the 19th century, when things medieval and Gothic came back into vogue, artists and antiquarians realized that Bruges was an authentic gem – a genuine medieval city fixed in time. The churches, civic buildings and patrician mansions were renovated and spruced up by neogothic enthusiasts, and visitors began to flock in – marking the beginnings of Bruges's new life as a centre for tourism.

Today Bruges prospers again, as one of the most visited cities in Europe. There was perhaps a danger that it could become a sterile museum city, a cash cow for cynical residents. Not a bit of it. Centuries-old traditions of hospitality, artistic ingenuity and a mercantile quest for comfort and well-being have come together to make Bruges one of the most pleasurable and rewarding places to visit. Here is a city with world-class attractions, yet small and intimate enough to visit entirely on foot – and it has a basketful of welcoming and charming hotels, plus excellent restaurants and cafés.

Bruges's new-found dynamism was perfectly expressed when it was chosen to be a Cultural Capital of Europe for 2002. It rose to the occasion, proudly renovating, polishing and re-gilding its old monuments, and building a magnificent new concert hall that promises to place Bruges firmly on the cultural map of Northern Europe. The bustling activity, the scaffolding and cranes pricking the skyline, the roster of art exhibitions and concerts, produced a satisfying resonance with the past. Bruges in its medieval heyday must have felt something like this.

The Neighbourhoods

10 Market day, p.189

1 The view from the Belfort, p.70

3 The Stadhuis, p.73

Northeastern Bruges

Western Bruges

Central Bruges

9 The modest charms of the almshouses, p.113

8 The calm beauty of the Begijnhof, p.89

7 Walking the medieval streets, p.119

5 Visiting a local brewery, p.181

4 Delicious Flemish food, p.169

Southern Bruges

6 A trip on the canals, p.56

2 Medieval art in the Groeningemuseum and Memlingmuseum, p.82 and p.88

In this guide the city has been divided into four neighbourhoods, outlined on the map above, each with its own sightseeing chapter. This map also shows our suggestions for the Top Ten activities and places to visit in Bruges.

Days Out in Bruges

Couples' City p.6

Beer p.8

Venice of the North p.9

Almshouses and Old Lace p.10

Bruges-la-Morte p.14

Neo-medieval City p.12

COUPLES' CITY

There could hardly be a more romantic city than Bruges. Its intimate scale, its relaxed atmosphere, its alluring combination of hospitable, super-comfortable hotels and stylish restaurants, create a magical formula. This is the place to do lots and fill your days, visiting, walking, shopping, talking – or to do extraordinarily little, ambling the medieval streets, sitting on a bench, absorbing the sheer beauty of the place.

One

Start: At your hotel.
Breakfast: Enjoy the copious breakfast that virtually all the good hotels offer.
Morning: Take a **horse-drawn carrlage ride** from the Markt to the **Begijnhof** and back.
Lunch: A light lunch at **Salade Folle**.
Afternoon: Wander around the **Minnewater**, the so-called 'Lake of Love', then visit the **Onze-Lieve-Vrouwekerk** to see Michelangelo's *Madonna and Child*.
Dinner: Relish the supreme cooking and comforts of **De Snippe**.
Evening: Wander back to the centre to enjoy the changing light on the canals, then head home to your hotel.

Two

Start: The Markt.

Breakfast: At **Prestige**, for the delicious confections of a master pâtissier.

Morning: Visit the **Burg**, the medieval centre – look out for the statue of *The Lovers*. Head for the lively **Vismarkt** (*photo below*) and walk along the canals on the **Groenerei, Rozenhoedkaai and Dijver**.

Lunch: Excellent fish at **Den Gouden Karpel**.

Afternoon: The **Memlingmuseum** for a glimpse of medieval beauty. Then walk up to the **Sint-Salvatorskathedraal** and do some **shopping** in and around Steenstraat and the Zilverpand.

Dinner: **Den Amand**, for superb food in a tiny, sympathetic restaurant.

Evening: A drink at **La Plaza**, a super-luxurious and stylish bar.

BEER

Belgian beer is world famous, and Bruges is a centre of excellence with two breweries producing several brands of national celebrity, such as Brugs Tarwebier and Straffe Hendrik. The city can even claim a direct link with St Arnold, the patron saint of beer, who discovered that the amber nectar could cure the plague. Beer-lovers can visit the breweries, imbibe their wares, drink in a veritable university of Belgian beer – and they can even have all their food cooked in beer.

Three

Start: The Markt.
Breakfast: **Het Dagelijks Brood**, to line the stomach with country bread.
Morning: Visit **Huisbrouwerij De Halve Mann**, brewery and home of Straffe Hendrik.
Lunch: **Den Dyver**, which specializes in beer-cooking.
Afternoon: After a rest, head for **'t Brugs Beertje** (opens at 4pm; closed Wed), the famous specialist beer pub.
Dinner: At **Bierbistro Erasmus**, for more beer-cookery, and more Belgian beer.
Evening: **Café 'De Versteende Nacht'**, for some jazz, and a beer or two.

Food and Drinks
Bierbistro Erasmus, p.172
Het Dagelijks Brood, p.173
Den Dyver, p.172

Sights and Activities
't Brugs Beertje, p.181
Huisbrouwerij De Halve Mann, p.91
Nightlife
Café 'De Versteende Nacht', p.182

VENICE OF THE NORTH

It may make your heart sink to hear this cliché, but Bruges can justifiably be compared to Venice. Not because of the canals – there aren't enough of them for that – but because in late medieval times Bruges was a trading city to rival Venice. This could be measured in the sheer volume, value and variety of goods that passed through its customs house and trading halls: silk, jewels, precious woods, perfumes, spices, exotic fruits and animals, as well as wool, wine, salt and timber.

Four

Start: The Burg.

Breakfast: **Restaurant-Tearoom Hennon**, for a modern breakfast beneath ancient beams.

Morning: Climb the **Belfort** for an overview of the city, then take a **canal trip** around the centre of town. Head for the **Groeningemuseum** to admire the wealth of medieval Bruges.

Lunch: Opt for a light lunch at **De Medici Sorbetière** (for the Italian connection).

Afternoon: Walk along Naaldenstraat to see the **Hof Bladelin** (Medici residence), then head for Vlamingstraat and the **Huis Ter Beurze** (the original stock exchange). Wander around the old trading centre, either side of the Spiegelrei, and up to the **Sint-Gilliskerk**.

Dinner: A splendid dinner at **De Witte Poorte**.

Evening: A stroll along the Sint-Annarei and **Groenerei**, and have a drink at **De Kogge** (named after a type of sailing ship).

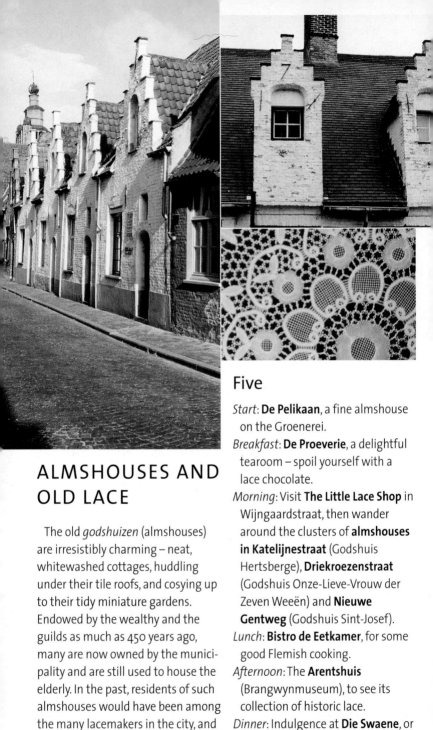

ALMSHOUSES AND OLD LACE

The old *godshuizen* (almshouses) are irresistibly charming – neat, whitewashed cottages, huddling under their tile roofs, and cosying up to their tidy miniature gardens. Endowed by the wealthy and the guilds as much as 450 years ago, many are now owned by the municipality and are still used to house the elderly. In the past, residents of such almshouses would have been among the many lacemakers in the city, and it is fitting that the Kantcentrum (lace museum) is housed in a set of old almshouses.

Five

Start: **De Pelikaan**, a fine almshouse on the Groenerei.

Breakfast: **De Proeverie**, a delightful tearoom – spoil yourself with a lace chocolate.

Morning: Visit **The Little Lace Shop** in Wijngaardstraat, then wander around the clusters of **almshouses in Katelijnestraat** (Godshuis Hertsberge), **Driekroezenstraat** (Godshuis Onze-Lieve-Vrouw der Zeven Weeën) and **Nieuwe Gentweg** (Godshuis Sint-Josef).

Lunch: **Bistro de Eetkamer**, for some good Flemish cooking.

Afternoon: The **Arentshuis** (Brangwynmuseum), to see its collection of historic lace.

Dinner: Indulge at **Die Swaene**, or something lighter at **L'Imprévu**.

Evening: A drink at the old pub **De Garre**.

Six

Start/breakfast: At your hotel (there's not much opportunity for breakfast in northeast Bruges).

Morning: Visit **Onze-Lieve-Vrouw ter Potterie** church and museum, for a glimpse of the pious world from which almshouses evolved.

Lunch: **Taverne De Verloren Hoek**, for a light, Flemish-style lunch.

Afternoon: The **Kantcentrum** (lace museum) for a demonstration. Then move on to the **Museum voor Volkskunde** (*photo above*) for an insight into daily life in the past, in converted almshouses. Head across town to another almshouse area in the west, around Kreupelenstraat and **Onze-Lieve-Vrouw van de Blindekens**.

Dinner: At the pasta-bistro **Het Andere Idee**.

Evening: Drink at one or both of the welcoming, friendly bars **Lokkedize** and **Joey's Café**.

NEO-MEDIEVAL CITY

In the late 19th century, Bruges was recognized for what it was: a medieval city preserved virtually intact. It was also still a pious city of churches and convents, fervently Roman Catholic. This was a time when neo-medievalism was all the rage. Wealthy landowners were building mansions in medieval style, and artists of the Pre-Raphaelite Brotherhood in England sought to re-create the medieval world in their paintings. Gothic was considered the only truly Christian architecture. In Bruges, medieval enthusiasts – many of them British – set about preserving, restoring and enhancing Bruges's medieval heritage. In truth, they may have gone too far: much of Bruges's medieval countenance is in fact 19th century, but this is worthy of admiration in itself.

Seven

Start: The Burg.

Breakfast: At **Tom Pouce**, with a view out over the Burg.

Morning: Visit the **Stadhuis** (*photos above middle and bottom right*), for its neo-medieval murals, and the **Heilig-Bloedbasiliek**. Take in the **Renaissancezaal van het Brugse Vrije**, for some authentic 16th-century décor.

Lunch: High style in the **Duc de Bourgogne**, part of a former palace.

Afternoon: In the Markt, admire the neogothic **Provinciaal Hof**. Then walk up Vlamingstraat to see the heavily restored **Poortersloge** and the **Oud Tolhuis** (*photo below left*).

Dinner/evening: An evening of neo-medieval feasting at **Brugge Anno 1468/Bruges Celebrations**.

Eight

Start: The Markt.

Breakfast: At **Craenenburg**, site of the imprisonment of Archduke Maximilian.

Morning: The neogothic **Sint-Magdalenakerk**, then the **Gruuthusemuseum** (*photo below middle*), one of the earliest restoration projects, designed to house the antiquarians' collections of artefacts.

Lunch: Good Flemish fare at the neo-somethinghistoric **Marieke van Brugghe**.

Afternoon: Visit the Brangwyn-museum in the **Arentshuis**, to pay homage to Frank Brangwyn and his father, the neogothic architect William Curtis Brangwyn.

Dinner: At **'t Nieuw Museum**, to enjoy a contemporary equivalent of a medieval Flemish tavern.

Evening: Walk along the canals for a drink at the old **Café Vlissinghe**.

BRUGES-LA-MORTE

Georges Rodenbach's experimental Symbolist novella, published in 1892, is a work of delicious melancholy and gloom – a tale of death and morbidity, of forbidden and doomed love. For Rodenbach, Bruges was the perfect setting: misty, shadowy, with its medieval houses crumbling into rank canals, and a prevailing atmosphere of sanctimonious piety and disapproval. The people of Bruges did not much appreciate his portrayal of their city as 'dead', but begrudgingly had to thank Rodenbach for the tourist trade that arrived in the wake of the novel's success. Bruges is no longer like this, but it is still fun to seek out the kinds of places that inspired Rodenbach's vision of the city, and which evoke the novel's *fin-de-siècle* mood.

Nine

Start: The Markt.

Breakfast: **Tearoom Verdi**, for that silence and propriety with which the widowed Hugues Viane (the main character) would have felt at home.

Morning: Take a look at the **Stadsschouwburg**, where Jane Scott, Hugues Viane's lover, danced. Then head for the **Rozenhoedkaai**, where Hugues lived. Continue on to the **Onze-Lieve-Vrouwekerk** to pay homage to the tomb of Mary of Burgundy, as Hugues regularly did.

Lunch: Buy a picnic at **De Trog**, and eat it on a lonely bench overlooking the **Minnewater** (*photo above*).

Afternoon: Haunt the gloomy recesses of the **Sint-Salvatorskathedraal**, then head along the backwaters of the Speelmansrei and Moerstraat to the **Sint-Jacobskerk** (open July–Aug only), to admire the tombs.

Dinner: You can take this melancholy too far! Cast away the gloom with a meal at the dynamic restaurant **Rock Fort**, and see just how alive Bruges really is.

Evening: Raise a glass to Hugues Viane, the misery-guts, at the fine old pub near his home, **L'Estaminet**.

Other Great
Belgian Cities

Ghent p.17

Brussels p.16

Antwerp p.18

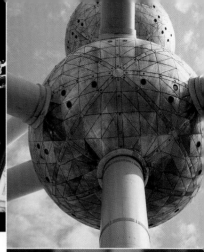

Brussels

Brussels is a remarkably unpretentious city, given its role as 'Capital of Europe' – perhaps its long heritage enables it to take its new-found status in its stride. Brussels' historic importance and prosperity can be measured in the glittering elegance of the guildhouses in its centrepiece, the Grand' Place, and also in its museums and galleries. You can see what Rubens was really about in the Musées Royaux des Beaux-Arts, and relish the outstanding collection of Belgian Symbolist painting. Anyone with the slightest feeling for Art Nouveau should visit the Musée Horta, a masterpiece in design. Tintin fans will make tracks to the comic-book museum, the Centre Belge de la Bande Dessinée. But Brussels also makes a good day out because it is so eminently walkable – it's easy to get a feel for the place by wandering the medieval web of streets in the centre. A fine Brussels beer in one of its trusty pubs, and a meal in one of its first-rate restaurants, will also give you a reliable insight into what makes this great city tick.

From top: Grand' Place, Atomium, Centre Belge de la Bande Dessinée, Musées Royaux des Beaux-Arts.

Brussels

Ghent

Dignified splendour sets this great Flemish city apart from its neighbours and makes it a rewarding choice for a day trip from Bruges. Ghent's gilded spires, stately façades and tranquil canals reflect its noble past, reinvigorated today by the university. Textiles still dominate the city's industry and commerce flourishes in fashionable new boutiques. The city's cathedral is home to Jan van Eyck's masterpiece, *Adoration of the Mystic Lamb*, and its design and folk museums are the most impressive of their kind in Belgium.

From top: Canal-boat figurehead, Sint-Baafskathedraal (*twice*), Sint-Michielsbrug.

Ghent

Antwerp

There's a seductive energy in Antwerp, born of a proud, powerful past and a more recent adventurous rejuvenation. The old city centre exhibits the traditional Belgian charms of delicate spires, a fine cathedral and an impressive Grote Markt flanked by ornate guildhouses. Antwerp's artistic heritage is evident in its richly endowed galleries, churches and museums. The international diamond trade thrives and industry retains a strong presence, but is largely removed from the city's medieval centre. Vibrant young clothes designers have added a fashionable edge to a city where the bars and clubs are buzzing with music and the literary cafés are alive with discussion.

Clockwise from top left: Diamond District, Onze Lieve Vrouwe Kathedraal, fountain in the Grote Markt, the Steen.

Antwerp
Day Trips chapter p.138
Hotels p.140 Restaurants p.140

Roots of the City

To 850: The Early Years

Way back in time, the North Sea washed in and out of these indeterminate flat lands, creating a patchwork of islands amid the marshes. The **Romans** first conquered Belgium in a bitter war that led Julius Caesar to declare: *'Horum popularum omnium fortissimi sunt Belgae'* ('Of all these people [the Celts or Gauls], the Belgae are the most courageous'). Remains of a Gallo-Roman settlement have been found in Bruges, but it was probably little more than an isolated trading outpost. After five centuries of stable rule, the Romans withdrew to defend their homelands from the Barbarians pushing in from the east. They ceded northern Europe to a Germanic tribe called the Franks. The Frankish leader, **Clovis I** (r. AD 481–511), founded the Christian Merovingian dynasty (c. 500–751), and Tournai became the hub of an empire covering much of France and Germany. It was during this era that Christian monks spread through the Frankish empire as missionaries. Among them was **Saint Eloi** (or Eligius, c. 588–660) from Limoges, and **Saint Amand** (c. 584–679) from Poitou, who are said to have brought the faith to Bruges. The development of Bruges still lay 100 years in the future, but events were afoot that would shape the destiny of Flanders, right down to the modern age.

The Merovingian kings ruled until 751, when they were ousted by **Pepin the Short**, who founded the Carolingian dynasty (751–987). Pepin the Short's son, born in Liège in 742, was one of the great kings of this transitional period of European history. He was called **Charlemagne** ('Charles the Great', r. 768–814), and under his rule the Moors were pushed back from northern Spain, and the Frankish kingdoms were extended into Italy and southern Germany.

Charlemagne saw himself as the heir to the Roman Empire, and the Pope obliged by crowning him Emperor of the West in 800. But after his death his heirs squabbled and the Frankish Empire splintered. Under the

Treaty of Verdun in 843, the River Scheldt (or Schelde), which flows across the middle of Belgium between Tournai and Antwerp, marked the border between lands assigned to rival grandsons of Charlemagne – the German king **Lothair I** (795–855) and the French king **Charles the Bald** (823–77). Charles took West Francia, to the west and north of the Scheldt, and Lothair took lands to the south and east. His kingdom became known as Lotharingia, later Lorraine.

The division of the Frankish empire along the Scheldt was not simply geographical, but was also linguistic. In late Roman times, when the Franks had settled in the north of Belgium, the south was occupied by Romanized Celts called the Wala – later the Walloons – whose language evolved out of Latin to become French. Hence, this was a political and linguistic divide which, broadly speaking, still exists today. The history of Belgium was now to follow two different threads for five centuries.

850–1280: Baldwin Iron-Arm

One catalyst for the collapse of the Frankish Empire was the growing frequency of raids by the Vikings. With their centralized power now dissipated, the Franks were unable to coordinate a response, and local warlords rose to fill the vacuum. One of these was Baldwin (d. 878), a man of such ruthless courage that he was nicknamed 'Iron-Arm'. He challenged the authority of the French

What's in a Name?

The origin and meaning of the name Bruges, or Brugge, remains a mystery. Although *brug* means bridge in Dutch, and there are plenty of these in the city, it is thought unlikely to be the true derivation. More favoured is the theory that it comes from the Norwegian Viking word *bryggja*, meaning a landing place, perhaps conflated with the old word for the River Reie, Rugja. The name Bruggia first appears in print on coins struck in AD 864.

king, Charles the Bald, and ran off with his daughter, Judith.

For her father, running off with Baldwin Iron-Arm was about the last straw. The couple had to seek refuge in Rome, where Pope Nicholas I managed to bring about a reconciliation. In 862 Charles gave Baldwin a rather back-handed reward: he put him in charge of the Viking-ridden northern territory, and created for him the title Count of Flanders. The long and testy relationship between the Counts of Flanders and their overlord, the French king, was to continue the way that it had been forged.

Baldwin built a castle, or *steen*, at Bruges, a large square island in the marshlands of the River Reie. He set up a palisade, dug a ring of canals around his island, and founded a chapel, the **Sint-Donaaskerk**, that was soon to be dedicated to St Donatian (or Donatus), a 4th-century Roman missionary in France whose remains were brought here. The shape of this island can still be discerned from the old canals and quays, with the Sint-Annarei in the east, the Spiegelrei to the north, the Groenerei to the south, and the Kraanrei (since drained) to the west.

Initially Baldwin Iron-Arm's Bruges was a stronghold against the Viking raiders, but it also grew as a trading outpost. The Counts of Flanders became rich by taxing trade. In return, merchants received their protection. Through trade, Bruges soon began to develop its web of international connections.

A series of Baldwins now ruled over Flanders. **Baldwin V**, who came to power in

1036, had a daughter called **Matilda.** The story goes that she caught the eye of **William, Duke of Normandy**, the future conqueror of England, on a visit to Bruges. She, however, fancied Brihtic, Earl of Gloucester, who was also in Bruges at the time, but spurned her. Furious also to be rejected, William grabbed Matilda in the street, spanked her on her bare bottom, threw her into the mud and then rode away. Such outrageous behaviour might have resulted in war, but Matilda would have none of it. Instead she insisted on marrying William, and a long and stable union was forged.

Although Bruges was made capital of the County of Flanders in 1093, the niceties of chivalry still lay some way off in the future. In 1127 **Count Charles the Good** was murdered while saying his prayers in the church of St Donatian. He was, it seems, a genuinely good man, who strove to protect the poor from exploitation. News of this savage death spread rapidly across northern Europe (such were Bruges's trading links already). His killers were the ambitious Erembald clan, whose powers he had striven to curtail. The result was a spate of reprisals, after which **Derick** (or Thierry) **of Alsace** was appointed the new Count in favour of the first choice of France, William Clito. It was a measure of Bruges's independence from France, which Derick affirmed by granting the city its first charter – a guarantee of its autonomy.

In around 1127 a new set of defensive walls was built around the city, covering an area now demarcated by the Sint-Annarei to the east, the Augustijnenrei to the north, the Dijver to the south and the Speelmansrei to the west. Bruges was already an established trading centre, but a stroke of luck

11th–12th Centuries
Heilig-Bloedbasiliek, St Basil's Chapel, built in 1099, p.73
Sint-Annarei, Augustijnenrei, Dijver, Speelmansrei, canals defining the city walls built in 1127, *see* maps at the back of this book

transformed its fortunes. In Roman times the town had direct access to the sea, but the coastal lowlands were constantly vulnerable to silt. By the late 11th century Bruges's access to the sea had become more or less blocked off by silt, largely the product of land reclamation which affected drainage. Bruges had begun to turn to overland trade. Then a mighty storm in 1134 caused massive inundation along the coast, and left behind a deep inlet called the Zwin. This provided Bruges with a natural harbour, accessible at Damme, 7km to the northeast. A canal between Bruges and Damme was dug in 1180, so that goods could be unloaded at Damme and transferred to barges and taken to the city centre.

By the 13th century Bruges was one of the wealthiest cities of northern Europe. It was a key player in the London Hansa (trade association) and had close links with the **Hanseatic League**, the powerful association of seventeen northern European (mainly German) trading cities. The city's merchants exchanged Flemish cloth for wool, lead, tin, coal and cheese from England; pigs from Denmark; wood and fish from Scandinavia; leather goods, oranges, lemons and pomegranates from Spain; wine from Germany and France; furs from Russia and Bulgaria; silks and oriental spices from Venice and Genoa; exotic animals from North Africa. Each year, from the third week after Easter to Whitsun, Bruges held a month-long trade fair, one of the great mercantile events of medieval Europe.

But the key trade of Flanders was **textiles**. Wool was imported and turned into cloth by the weavers of Bruges, Ghent and Ypres. There were over 4000 weavers in Bruges alone. The best wool came from England, and the deft skills of the Flemish weavers turned this into the finest cloth available. After 1282 only cloth made with English wool could be graded as first class. This trade created an interdependency between Flanders and England, much valued on both sides. It was also a political hot potato, because Flanders was a part of France, and England and France

were continually at loggerheads. And, because of its heavy dependence on one sole product, Flanders was always vulnerable to economic and political turmoil. In addition, because the merchants so closely controlled and regulated the weavers, this gave rise to a constant undercurrent of social friction.

By and large Flanders was left to its own devices, and Ghent, Bruges and Ypres became virtually independent city states. This often put the Counts of Flanders in an awkward position: on the one hand they owed their allegiance to France, and on the other hand the economic wealth of their people depended on the ability to control trade, and relationships with England. Power ebbed and flowed.

1280–1328: Revolt

By the late 13th century the French feared that Flanders was slipping from their grasp, and vigorously reasserted their authority. The patricians of Bruges supported this move and pledged their allegiance to the French king, but the craft guilds and the populace deeply resented the erosion of privileges and the presence of large numbers of French troops sent in to impose order. The city was split into two opposing factions: the patricians and supporters of French rule were called the *leliaerts* (after the *fleur de lis* or lily, the French royal emblem); the Flemish masses were called the *clauwaerts* (from the claws of the Flemish lion).

In 1280 a *clauwaert* uprising, the **Moerlemaye Revolt**, was brutally crushed. In 1297 the king of France, **Philip the Fair** (i.e good-looking rather than fair minded; r. 1285–1314) annexed Flanders, a move opposed by the Count of Flanders, **Guy de Dampierre**. As France reinforced its army, Bruges was fortified with a new and larger set of defensive walls and ramparts 7km long – the 'Brugse Vesten' – the line of which can be traced today by the outer oval ring of canals around the city.

On 29 May 1301, amid considerable tension, Philip the Fair came to Bruges on a state visit to reassert French authority. The nobility and wealthiest merchants turned out in their finery, the opulence of which surprised the French Queen, Joanna of Navarre, who commented famously: 'I thought I alone was Queen, but I see that I have 600 rivals here.'

To add insult to injury, the citizens of Bruges were asked to foot the bill for Philip's ostentatious reception. Bruges was seething. Two leaders emerged at the head of this *clauwaert* resentment: **Pieter de Coninck**, a weaver, and **Jan Breydel** (or Breidel), a butcher. Early in the morning of 18 May 1302 the rebels massacred all supporters of the French and French troops – and anyone who was unable to pronounce in convincing Flemish the shibboleth '*Schild en Vriend*' (shield and friend). Some 1500 died in what has been euphemistically called the '**Bruges Matins**' (Brugse Metten).

This revolt in Bruges stirred up a wide-spread rebellion in Flanders. Later that year, on 11 July, Flemish volunteers led by Jan Breydel took on the full might of the French army on the Groeninge Plain near Kortrijk (Courtrai). Bruges fielded the largest contingent of 2380 men. The French had massively superior and better equipped forces, led by a cavalry of gloriously caparisoned knights, the cream of French

> ## Battle of the Golden Spurs
>
> The Flemish 'national' holiday is 11 July, the anniversary of the Battle of the Golden Spurs in 1302. The battle struck a great and symbolic blow for Flemish independence, although power was clawed back by the French in subsequent decades. It remains a highly emotive symbol, but its significance has shifted: it is now taken as a symbol of Flemish autonomy from the French-speaking Belgians. Events commemorating the battle are often underscored by Flemish 'nation-alism', promoting a separatist agenda.

chivalry, but the Flemish prepared the marshy ground well, laying branches that acted as traps. The battle began with a devastating attack by the French archers. Thinking they were on the verge of victory, the heavily armoured French knights charged in, but soon became completely bogged down. Now helpless, they were picked off one by one by the Flemish pikemen, who took no prisoners. This humiliating rout became known as the **Battle of the Golden Spurs** (*Gulden Sporenslag*), because the Flemish victors collected 700 pairs of golden spurs, which they exhibited triumphantly in Kortrijk Cathedral.

As a result of this battle, Flanders enjoyed a brief spell of independence, but French forces mounted a counterattack which included the indecisive **Battle of Pevelenberg** in 1304, followed by the **Treaty of Athis-sur-Orge** in 1305, by which the Flemish had to pay reparations and disarm. The humiliation of the Battle of the Golden Spurs remained a sore wound for the French, and their victory over the Flemish at the **Battle of Cassel** in 1327 turned into a vengeful massacre. By 1329 Flanders was under French rule once more. The policy of crushing suppression ruthlessly led to a period of instability and confusion throughout Flanders, which coincided with the outbreak of the Hundred Years' War, and the emigration to England of large numbers of weavers.

> ## 13th Century
>
> **Belfort**, the watchtower, clocktower and civic symbol, first built in 1282, p.70
>
> **Brugse Vesten**, city walls built at the end of the 13th century and defined by the oval-shaped outer ring of canals, *see* maps at the back of this book
>
> **Halle**, the covered market of 1239, p.71
>
> **Huis Ter Beurze**, site of the world's first stock exchange, p.121
>
> **Onze-Lieve-Vrouwekerk**, a Gothic church, built over 200 years from 1220, p.85
>
> **Poortersloge**, the meeting place for leading merchants, p.122
>
> **Sint-Gilliskerk**, dating from 1277, p.97
>
> **Sint-Janshospitaal**, hospital buildings dating from the early 13th century, p.88
>
> **Sint-Salvatorskathedraal**, built mainly after 1275, p.110

1328–84: The Hundred Years' War (1337–1453)

English claims to French territory, plus their trading interests in Flanders, led to a protracted series of military confrontations with France known as the Hundred Years' War. The trigger was the death of the last French Capetian king in 1328, after which the English king **Edward III** (r. 1327–77), the maternal grandson of Philip the Fair of France, reckoned he had a good claim to the French throne – at least as valid as Philip's nephew, **Philip de Valois**, who became Philip VI.

The aristocracy of Flanders naturally sided with the French, so England responded with sanctions: all wool exports to Flanders ceased. Since English wool was the foundation stone of the Flemish textile trade, this had a rapid effect and the wealthy Flemish wool merchants were faced with ruin. In 1338 a brewer from Ghent called **Jacob van Artevelde** led a successful rebellion against the French, put the Count of Flanders to flight, and invited **Edward the Black Prince** (1330–76), son of Edward III, to become the new Count. Edward III arrived in Flanders with an army, and proclaimed himself king of France in Ghent in 1340. But Jacob van Artevelde became dictatorial, and was murdered by rioting Ghent citizens in 1345. **Louis de Male**, Count of Flanders (r. 1346–84), reasserted control, and even extended his domain by seizing Brabant.

Peace conferences between the English and the French were held in Bruges in 1374 and 1375. Meanwhile, Ghent and Bruges went to war over a canal. When the people of Ghent refused to pay for an extravagant tournament, Louis de Male enlisted the support of Bruges by the promise of a canal link to the sea. Work on the canal began, but was stopped at the intervention of troops despatched from Ghent deeply anxious about trade competition. From 1381 to 1382 **Philip van Artevelde** (son of Jacob) led an uprising in Ghent and defeated Bruges in battle. Count Louis was forced to flee.

14th Century

Bruges Matins statue, the 19th-century statue in the Markt marking the Flemish rebellion of 1301–2, p.72

Genuese Loge, trading house of the merchants of Genoa, dating from 1399, p.120

Poedertoren, the arsenal, built in 1398, p.91

Prinsenhof, site of the palace of the Dukes of Burgundy, p.117

Smedenpoort, earliest of the surviving city gates, built 1367, p.114

Stadhuis, the town hall built originally in 1376–1420, p.73

At this point Louis appealed for help from his son-in-law, **Philip the Bold** of Burgundy, who was married to his daughter Margaret. Assisted by a massive French army, Louis was able to crush the Flemish rebels at the **Battle of Westrosebeke** in 1382. **Charles VI** of France then reaped revenge for the Battle of the Golden Spurs by sacking Courtrai. In the shake-out Bruges was forced to hand over many of its privileges.

The 14th century was tumultuous, punctuated by civil strife, as well as by a famine due to crop failure from 1315 to 1317, and the plague that killed 24,000 in 1349. But paradoxically it was also a time of great prosperity for Bruges – perhaps its greatest. Its population stood at about 40,000 – comparable to London and Paris. In the next century it became the centrepiece of the splendid and lavish Burgundian empire, but it was already being eclipsed by trading rivals, and by growing competition in textile manufacture from England and Holland. Bruges retrenched by specializing in luxury products, such as tapestry, paintings and illuminated books, which found a ready market . But at the height of its glory, the writing was already on the wall.

1384–1494: The Burgundian Period

In 1384 Louis died, and **Philip the Bold**, Duke of Burgundy, became Count of Flanders. Bit by bit, through negotiation, marriage and conquest, the Burgundians took control of a vast territory, split into two distinct areas: the Burgundy region of central eastern France, and the area covering most of modern Belgium plus the Netherlands.

Philip the Bold was the brother of Charles V of France. As a member of this ruling Valois family, he and his heirs had a close stake in the throne of France. They also ruled over one of the wealthiest regions in Europe. Bruges prospered. It played host to merchants, bankers and moneylenders from 17 countries. The Venetians were the first to open a trading house of their own, in 1322, thus becoming the first foreign 'nation' in Bruges.

As the Hundred Years' War rumbled on, the aspirations of the Dukes of Burgundy became a cause for conflict within France. **Charles VI** (r. 1380–1422) succeeded his father to the French throne; known as Charles the Mad, he was of unsound mind, and control of France seemed up for grabs – a prize contested by the Dukes of Orleans and Burgundy.

Now events became really complicated. In 1407 the Duke of Burgundy, **John the Fearless**, had Louis Duke of Orleans murdered, plunging France into civil war. John then negotiated with the English, offering to support **Henry V**'s claim to the French throne. Henry thereupon opened up a new campaign with his famous victory over the French at **Agincourt** in 1415.

As the English laid siege to Paris, John the Fearless, Duke of Burgundy, got cold feet. He attempted to negotiate with the new Duke of Orleans, but was himself murdered. In revenge John the Fearless's son, **Philip the Good** (r. 1419–67), gave his open support to the English, and had soon forced Charles VI to sign the **Treaty of Troyes**, in which Henry V was named as Charles's successor to the French throne.

But it was not to be. Henry V died just two months before Charles, and the throne went to Charles's son, **Charles VII** (r. 1422–61). The French then launched a new campaign, inspired by **Joan of Arc** (1412–31), and eventually pushed the English out of their lands.

During Philip the Good's long reign Bruges enjoyed an era of unprecedented splendour. The Prinsenhof, an extensive palace in the city, became his main residence, and in 1429 Bruges became the capital of all the Burgundian domains, supplanting Dijon.

One of Bruges's great landmark events took place in 1430 when Philip the Good married **Isabella of Portugal**. Her arrival in Bruges and the celebration of her wedding was accompanied by one of the most stupendous beanfeasts of the medieval era. It was also marked by the foundation of the prestigious **Order of the Knights of the Golden Fleece**.

It was the greatest honour to be appointed a knight of the order, a title reserved for high-ranking nobility, even kings. The basic idea was to uphold Christianity and the ideals of chivalry, and to settle any disputes between this ruling elite at the semi-religious conventions, called 'chapters', which were held at various locations within the Duchy of Burgundy. Bruges hosted three chapters: in 1431 in the church of St Donatian, in 1468 in the Onze-Lieve-Vrouwekerk, and in 1478 in the Sint-Salvatorskathedraal.

Bruges was by now a truly international city. Philip the Good was the richest man in Europe and his court was the height of European fashion, attracting some of the greatest men of the times – including composers, writers and painters. This was a dazzling period for Flemish art: **Jan van Eyck**, **Hugo van der Goes** and **Hans Memling** were all working in Bruges.

Philip died in 1467 and was succeeded by his son, **Charles the Bold** (r. 1467–77). He married Margaret of York, sister of Edward IV of England. This marriage was the second great highlight of Bruges's Burgundian age, celebrated with processions and a lavish celebration at the Prinsenhof. Through this marriage, relationships with England could barely have been closer. But Charles was not a popular ruler: he raised taxes, rashly renewed aggression against France, now under **Louis XI** (r. 1461–83), and was killed at the **Battle of Nancy**. Louis XI then seized the French part of Burgundy for France.

Charles's only heir was his daughter, **Mary**, who was thus left with just the Burgundian lands of the Low Countries. Aged only 20, she faced opposition from the Flemish cities and, to pacify them, she was obliged to give them greater powers of autonomy. Her rule was also undermined by subversion orchestrated by agents of Louis XI, who had plans to coerce her into marriage with his own son. But Mary's mother, **Margaret of York**, had a scheme to thwart the French: in 1477 she arranged a marriage between Mary and the 19-year-old **Archduke Maximilian I** (1459–1519), a member of the ruling German-Austrian Habsburg family, and future Holy Roman Emperor – as the heirs to the eastern Frankish kingdom liked to call themselves, in the style of Charlemagne.

Maximilian and Mary had two children, **Philip the Handsome**, and **Margaret of Austria**. Then, in 1482, aged just 25, Mary died when she fell from her horse while hunting, and her broken ribs punctured her lungs. She was buried in a splendid tomb in Bruges's Onze-Lieve-Vrouwekerk. Maximilian now assumed regency over the Burgundian Low Countries. He made himself deeply unpopular in Bruges by attempting to reduce the privileges of the citizens, while also increasing taxes. This triggered a revolt in 1488, and he was placed under house arrest for 21 days in the Craenenburg, overlooking the Markt. To show they meant business, the rebels executed his treasurer, **Pieter Lanchals**, in the square below. Maximilian hastily agreed to the terms for his release, which included pledges to respect Flemish privileges. But this promise was ignored by his father, **Emperor Frederick III**, who marched on the Flemish cities and brutally crushed all signs of revolt.

It was a critical turning point. From now on Bruges began its slow decline. Maximilian moved his court from Bruges to Ghent, and insisted that all foreign merchants leave. Although they returned in 1492, the damage was done. More vitally, dredging on the Zwin was not vigorously pursued, and the rising silt made access to the city ever more difficult. Sluis, 10km beyond Damme, had now became the avant-port, but even here the Zwin was choking.

Bruges had to concentrate on more localized trade. Antwerp's star was rising, and Bruges's key trading 'nations' – Germany, Italy and England – as well as many of its old merchant families, relocated. The die was cast. Only the Spanish stayed on, maintaining a profitable trade in light textiles using Spanish wool. In the early decades of the 16th century some 5000 houses were standing empty in the city.

1494–1609: Emperor Charles V (r. 1506–55)

In 1494 Maximilian became Holy Roman Emperor and passed control of the Low Countries to his son, Philip the Handsome. Two years later, Philip married Joanna of Castile, and they ruled Castile together for just one year (1506) before Philip died. This was enough, however, to assure the

The First Printed Book in English

One of the guests at the marriage of Charles the Bold and Margaret of York was the governor of the English Merchant Adventurers, a resident of Bruges since 1442. His name was William Caxton. He became the personal secretary to Margaret of York, who despatched him to Cologne to learn about a new-fangled invention called printing. Back in Bruges, Caxton set up a press and produced the *Recuyell of the Historyes of Troye* in 1474 – the first printed book in English, dedicated to Margaret of York. Two years later Caxton returned to England, and set up his press in Westminster.

succession of their son, Charles V, to an unprecedentedly vast kingdom.

Charles V was by far the most powerful ruler of Europe in his day. Born in Ghent, he grew up in Mechelen and always regarded the Low Countries as his homeland. However, events and his restless energy took him much further afield, and for most of his reign the home countries were governed by his sister, **Mary of Hungary**.

In 1517 Charles took over the Spanish throne on the death of his grandfather. Then in 1520 he assumed the crown of Holy Roman Emperor after the death of Maximilian – taking with it Austria and Germany, Burgundy and the Low Countries, as well as the kingdoms of Naples and Sicily. He put down rebellions in Spain, defeated the Turks, and in Italy he fought the French under **François I** (r. 1515–47), his long-term rival, whom he succeeded in capturing at the **Battle of Pavia** (1525). As part of the settlement, under the Treaty of Cambrai of 1529, France was finally forced to give up control of Flanders, after 685 years.

Meanwhile **Hernán Cortés** conquered Mexico (1521) and **Francisco Pizarro** conquered Peru (1532) in the name of Spain, bringing in vast new territories and huge quantities of gold. The Age of Exploration was also an age of extravagance, fostering a get-rich-quick mentality in which huge sums were speculated on trading expeditions and the gains were spent lavishly on fancy buildings, paintings, banquets and feasting.

At home, land reclamation schemes began to push back the sea from the flat lands of the north, while the gardens of the Low Countries became the envy of Europe. Tapestry, pottery and glass were produced and exported, and the linen industry also took off. By the 1560s Antwerp's population had risen to 100,000, but Bruges's had dropped to 30,000. Its merchants did not take up the opportunities which the era offered.

Charles's reign coincided with the remarkable advances of Renaissance learning and art in northern Europe. The great humanist **Desiderius Erasmus** acted as adviser to Charles. At the same time Bruges emerged as an intellectual crossroads, a centre for humanism that brought together notable thinkers of the day such as Erasmus, **Thomas More**, and **Juan Luis Vivés**. The new thinking promoted by the Renaissance, however, smacked to some of subversion, and its most feared and controversial manifestation was **Protestantism**. **Martin Luther** posted his 95 theses to the church door of Wittenberg in 1517, and the course was set: the Reformation spread among the dissident German states and in the northern Netherlands. It was the one challenge that Charles was not equal to.

Bruges, with its open-house traditions and intellectual tolerance, welcomed the Reformation, but the potential for incandescent conflict quickly emerged. Condemnations for heresy were recorded as early as 1523, and the first execution took place in 1527 when a Protestant was burnt at the stake in the Burg. This became a regular activity in the city for the next 50 years. Meanwhile the people of the Low Countries were taxed heavily for the privilege of being part of Charles's mighty empire. It was, after all, expensive to run. When Ghent rebelled in 1540, Charles personally saw to a crushing suppression – a rude shock from their favourite son. Bruges escaped with less vengeful treatment when it was brought to heel in 1548. In 1555, exhausted by his struggles, Charles announced that he was abdicating: he gave his Spanish crown to his son Philip and the crown of the Holy Roman Empire to his brother Ferdinand.

The Low Countries did not take kindly to the fact that, shortly after the beginning of his reign, **Philip II** decided to rule at arm's length, from Spain. 'I would prefer to lose all my domains and die 100 times than rule over heretics,' Philip, a fanatical Catholic, is quoted as saying. He meant it, and the **Inquisition** was sent to the Low Countries in 1559 in order to apply its ruthless answer to Protestantism. All unconventional thinking came under the Inquisition's scrutiny, and Bruges stood in the firing line: many of its citizens had rejected the Roman Catholic faith in favour of Calvinism.

When heavy taxes were imposed to finance Philip's extravagant wars, resentment in the Low Countries boiled over into rebellion. Good citizens and Catholics were caught up in this mood, as well as the Protestants. The Low Countries had been placed under the governorship of **Margaret of Parma** (daughter of Charles V), who bore the brunt of increasingly vociferous criticism. The opposition found a champion in **William of Orange** ('the Silent'), whose forebear had been rewarded for his loyalty to Charles V with substantial estates in the Netherlands. William formed a **League of Nobility**, which appealed for moderation in the treatment of Protestants. Their petition, however, was roundly rejected by Margaret's advisers.

In 1566 the resentment of Calvinist Protestants turned to violence. Throughout the Low Countries they vented their pious wrath on the churches, vandalizing the interiors in an orgy of iconoclasm. More moderate forces recoiled in horror and swung back in favour of Margaret. William of Orange and the Governor of Flanders, Count Egmont, tried to find a compromise, but as events slipped out of control William withdrew to Germany.

Philip's answer was to send the **Duke of Alva** with 10,000 troops to restore order. He was assisted by the Inquisition, which set up the **'Council of Disorders'** (also known as the

'Council of Blood') and handed out 8000 death sentences; Count Egmont was among the victims. From 1568 William began a military campaign against Spanish rule. After several false starts, William gained the upper hand and took the towns of the Low Countries one by one. Facing mutinous troops and angry creditors, the Duke of Alva fled in 1573. William entered Brussels in triumph in 1576 and won Amsterdam in 1578. Protestants took over in Ghent in 1578, then invaded Bruges. The abbeys of Bruges were closed, the monks persecuted and expelled and by 1581 Protestants had taken over all the city's churches.

However, Protestantism had many fierce critics in the southern half of the Low Countries – essentially modern Belgium. Here the bulk of the population clung more steadfastly to Roman Catholicism, and did not believe it shared a destiny with the Protestant provinces of the north. Indeed, Catholics were now being persecuted in the north.

In 1578 Philip of Spain sent **Alexander Farnese, Duke of Parma**, into the south at the head of a large army, and he was rewarded by a series of capitulations in the

16th Century

Bust of Juan Luis Vivés, a modern portrait of the Spanish humanist, p.84

De Malvenda House, a late Gothic mansion, built c. 1500, p.77

Genthof No.7, one of the very few surviving wooden houses of old Bruges, p.123

Gruuthusemuseum, for a portrait bust of Charles V, p.86

Monument to Simon Stevin, a 19th-century statue to the Bruges-born Renaissance mathematician, p.111

Oude Griffie, Old Recorder's House, a Renaissance building on the Burg, built 1534–7, p.74

Renaissancezaal van het Brugse Vrije, a Renaissance meeting room, with the Charles V chimney piece, 1529–33, p.74

Schuttersgilde Sint-Sebastiaan, house of the Marksmen's Guild, dating from 1565, p.102

French-speaking provinces. Many of these then signed the Union of Arras in 1579, declaring their allegiance to Spain. In response, the Protestant northern provinces – called the United Provinces – declared their independence and appointed William of Orange as their *stadhouder* (governor). The Duke of Parma pressed on north, retaking Bruges after a long siege in 1584, and Antwerp and Brussels in 1585. Hundreds of citizens from Bruges fled to Holland, joining a flood of refugees from Flanders that would help fuel the Dutch Golden Age. Most of Flanders and the French-speaking provinces now became known as the Spanish Netherlands. By this time Bruges was in dire economic straits. A canal driven through to Sluis in 1562 had already been defeated by the silt, and much of the city lay in ruins.

Just before his death in 1598, Philip II handed the Spanish Netherlands over to his daughter, the **Infanta Isabella** (1566–1633), and her husband, **Albert, Archduke of Austria** (1559–1621). The news was received with great joy in Brussels, and Isabella entered the city amid celebrations, sumptuously dressed and riding on a saddle studded with diamonds and rubies. The Spanish, however, still aspired to regain the United Provinces – but they insisted that only Catholicism would be tolerated. In 1601 Isabella refused to change her shirt for the duration of her husband's siege of Ostende; the siege lasted three years. The Twelve Years' Truce of 1609 sealed independence for the United Provinces, at which point a further 100,000 Protestants from Flanders emigrated.

1609–1713: Europe's Battleground

For a while the Spanish Netherlands enjoyed a period of peace and prosperity. The mood is caught by the ebullient paintings of Rubens, who was court painter to Isabella and Albert. But Europe was overshadowed by the **Thirty Years' War** (1618–48), in which Protestants contested the power of the

Catholic Habsburgs. Isabella and Albert took the opportunity to take up the cudgels once more against the United Provinces, which drove them into an alliance with the French in 1633. The lasting result was that **Philip IV of Spain** (r. 1605–65), desperate to be able to turn all his military strength on France, signed the **Peace of Münster** in 1648, which gave formal recognition to the independence of the United Provinces. The terms of the treaty allowed the United Provinces to stop all traffic through the mouth of the River Scheldt, which ran through territory now controlled by them. Antwerp's and Ghent's access to the sea was sealed off and their fortunes doomed until Napoleon lifted the ban 150 years later.

For Bruges, there was some optimism during this turmoil. In 1613 a new canal was opened to connect the city with Ghent, which had direct access to the sea via a canal completed in 1547. Then in 1622 a canal was opened to Ostend. This proved fortuitous when the Scheldt was closed under the Peace of Münster. In 1665 a new mercantile dock, the Handelskom, was opened in the north of Bruges and the canal to Ostend was widened. Trade picked up, but Bruges was a mere shadow of its former self. Meanwhile, the old city walls were updated to current military thinking and converted into large earth ramparts.

Spain's conflict with France was a running sore throughout the 17th century, and inevitably the Spanish Netherlands were drawn into it. When **William III of Orange**, *stadhouder* of the United Provinces, became king of England in 1689 by virtue of his marriage to Mary, Protestant daughter of James II, the stage was set for a major big-power conflict.

The first phase was the **War of the Grand Alliance** (1690–7), designed to put an end to the expansionist exploits of **Louis XIV** of France. In the Spanish Netherlands the conflict was inconclusive, with a series of sieges by Louis' forces – including, temp-orarily, of Bruges. France came out the loser in the war, but Louis' antics were not over yet.

17th Century

Almshouses, in Noordstraat, Driekroezen-straat and Nieuwe Gentweg, p.91

Begijnhof, founded in 1244 but built mainly in the 17th and 18th centuries, p.89

Ezelpoort, the picturesque city gate, rebuilt in 1615, p.118

Gruuthusemuseum, for mementoes of Charles II of England, p.86

Onze-Lieve-Vrouw ter Potterie, a highly ornate Baroque church, p.96

Schuttersgilde Sint-Sebastiaan, with mementoes of Charles II of England, p.102

Sint-Annakerk, a parish church rebuilt in 1624, p.98

Sint-Walburgakerk, Bruges's finest Baroque church, p.98

In 1700 Charles II of Spain died – the last of the Spanish Habsburgs. Charles had no direct heir, so he passed the crown of Spain to **Philip, Duke of Anjou**, the grandson of Louis XIV. Louis leaned upon Philip to hand over the Spanish Netherlands to France, but such a solution was unacceptable to either England or the United Provinces of the Netherlands, who greatly feared the French domination of Europe.

The result was the **War of the Spanish Succession** (1701–13). England, the Netherlands, Austria and many German states formed an alliance against France, and the brilliant generalship of the **Duke of Marlborough** and Prince Eugene of Savoy drove the French out of the Spanish Netherlands, but not before the armies had raged across Flanders. Ghent and Bruges changed hands twice, while the allies won two victories on Belgian soil: at Ramillies (1706), and Oudenaarde (1708). At the end of the war France was left in tatters. In the **Treaty of Utrecht** it renounced its claims to the Spanish Netherlands, which passed into the hands of **Charles VI**, the Habsburg Emperor of Austria, and became the Austrian Netherlands. This high-handed reassignment of ownership was bitterly resented in some quarters.

1713–1815: The Austrian Netherlands

Charles VI of Austria had no male heir, so in 1713 he announced a 'pragmatic sanction' – eventually accepted by most of the European powers – that the succession would pass into the female line through his daughter **Maria Theresa**. However, when Charles died in 1740 the European powers disregarded this arrangement and Maria Theresa had to contend with the **War of the Austrian Succession** (1740–8), a complex conflict in which rivalries between France, Britain and the United Provinces of the Netherlands were played out across most of Europe, as well as in North America. Bruges was occupied by French troops from 1744 to 1748. Maria Theresa emerged from the war with her succession affirmed, and the Austrian Netherlands then enjoyed decades of prosperity.

In 1741 Maria Theresa put these provinces in the hands of her enlightened brother-in-law, **Charles of Lorraine** (1712–80), who set up a dazzling court in Brussels, famed for its generous and elegant hospitality and its ceaseless round of masked balls and merry-making. The sedate neoclassical style was adopted for ambitious building projects, and spread as far as Bruges, where the old medieval Waterhalle was pulled down and replaced by a stately neoclassical building in 1786.

Industry was transformed by investment; new roads connected the cities and linked Brussels to Vienna. But while the aristocracy partied, the poor faced crowded, insanitary conditions exacerbated by high levels of unemployment. In Bruges, this was the era when the greatest number of almshouses were created.

Charles of Lorraine died in 1780 and Maria Theresa died five months later, to be succeeded by her son, **Joseph II**. He was in many ways a child of the Enlightenment, and introduced various reforms – in education and administration, as well as freedom of worship – which allowed Protestants to build churches, to become full citizens, and to take up public office. He ordered the destruction of old city walls (emblems of the past) and monasteries that served no social purpose were also closed – an edict that hit Bruges particularly hard since it had accumulated a large religious community. For all Joseph's good intentions, his reforms were interpreted in Belgium as unwelcome. He simply went too far and too fast: he tried, for example, to streamline Austrian government by centralizing power in Vienna; and in 1784 announced that German was to be the official language of the empire. With the Age of Enlightenment came the rumblings of intellectual discontent.

A vociferous opposition arose, composed of two quite different tendencies: on the one hand there were the liberals who wanted to expel the Habsburgs in favour of a democratic, modern state; on the other there were the Catholic conservatives and aristocracy, who looked back nostalgically to the *ancien régime* of Maria Theresa. The latter were led by **Henri van der Noot**, who, following an insurrection in 1788, became the main voice of the opposition. This was in stark contrast to the fervently radical political atmosphere which carried the French Revolution the following year.

Nonetheless, the Revolution in France inspired an uprising in Belgium, and when this was crushed by the Austrians at Turnhout, the whole country rose to the call in what has become known as the **Brabançon Revolt**. In January 1790 the provinces agreed to form their own Congress, with Van der Noot as its prime minister, and they unilaterally proclaimed an independent United States of Belgium, which was readily recognized by England, Holland and Prussia.

But events were about to overtake this first attempt at Belgian nationhood. In February 1790 Joseph II died, to be replaced by **Leopold II** (r. 1790–2) who immediately despatched troops to crush the revolution and returned Belgium to the Austrian fold. However, in 1792 the French Revolutionary Armies went to war against Austria and quickly scored a success at Jemappes. They had enthusiastic supporters in Bruges, who greeted the victory by demolishing the statues of the Counts on the Stadhuis as the carillon in the Belfort rang out the *Marseillaise*. Austria expelled the French in 1793, but the following year the French Revolutionary Armies under **Marshal Jourdan** finally scored the decisive victory at Fleurus, thus ending Austrian rule in Belgium.

The French were welcomed by many Belgians as an army of liberation – one that heralded the advent of a modern state in which merit, not family connections and wealth, would be rewarded. Initially the French proceeded carefully, wisely respecting the power of the Church and Belgian autonomy. But to many of the more radical French revolutionaries, Belgian Catholicism was anachronistic and a hindrance to change.

In October 1795 Belgium was absorbed into France and religion was suppressed. The churches were closed: many were vandalized and appropriated as stables, warehouses and factories; others were auctioned off as state property. This was the fate of many churches and abbeys in Bruges, while its fine old church on the Burg, St Donatian's, was demolished in 1799. This, as well as the humiliation and hounding of the priesthood, caused deep resentment.

It was relieved to some extent in 1800 when, under the rule of the **Consulate**, priests were released from hard labour, returned from exile and began holding services in private houses. Meanwhile citizens held 'dry masses', without priests, in the ruins of the churches. The Concordat in 1801 between **Pope Pius VII** and **Napoleon** saw the beginnings of a slow return to normality.

Despite his charisma as leader of the young French state, Napoleon failed to win over the

18th Century

De Pelikaan, an almshouse founded in 1714, p.76
Landhuis van het Brugse Vrije, a neoclassical public building built in 1722–7, p.75
Sint-Janshuysmolen, a windmill built on the city ramparts in 1770, p.104

Belgians. In 1815, when he was finally defeated by the allies (Britain, Prussia, Austria and Russia) at **Waterloo**, just south of Brussels, the majority of Belgians celebrated his downfall too. They thought their hour had come.

1815–32: The United Kingdom of the Netherlands

It hadn't. The **Congress of Vienna** in 1815 decided instead to create the United Kingdom of the Netherlands, tacking Belgium on to the Netherlands and entrusting it to the care of **William of Orange**.

It was an insensitive decision: all the historic resentments about big-power carve-ups and about rule by a Protestant Netherlands, combined with the aspirations to Belgian nationhood, gave William I an impossible task. He was not exactly a master of diplomacy: he tried to impose Dutch as the national language of the whole country, and he failed to grant Belgium fair represen-tation in the States General (the Netherlands parliament). Above all, he was Protestant.

All the while, the economy of Belgium was beginning to stir with the **Industrial Revolution**. Ghent became the centre of a vibrant textile industry, but Bruges slum-bered. However, it was appointed the capital of the province of West Flanders, and main-tained a certain dignity in its repose, now witnessed by the new trail of tourists from Britain who passed through the city on the way to visit the battlefield of Waterloo.

In 1830 the July Revolution in France removed the revisionist **King Charles X** (r. 1824–30) and put the more egalitarian **Louis Philippe** (r. 1830–48) in his place. In Belgium, too, revolt was in the air. On 25 August a new opera called *La Muette de Portici* (*The Dumb Girl of Portici*) by the contemporary French composer Daniel-François-Esprit Auber was performed at the Théâtre de la Monnaie in Brussels. The story concerns a revolutionary called Masaniello

who led an uprising in Naples against the Spanish in 1647. Such sentiments as 'Far better to die than to live a wretched life in slavery and shame!' incited the audience to a ferment. They ran out to join a workers' demonstration already taking place in the Place de la Monnaie, stormed the Palais de Justice, drove out the Dutch garrison and raised the flag of Brabant over the Hôtel de Ville. William of Orange responded by sending in the troops, which defeated the rebels at Hasselt.

On 23 September the Dutch troops advanced on Brussels and four days of street fighting ensued. Gradually the Dutch were confined to what is now the Parc de Bruxelles, surrounded by revolutionaries. From there, during the night of 27 September, the Dutch simply melted away. Brussels was free. On 4 October the Provisional Government declared Belgium independent, but the fighting was not quite over yet. In the northeast of the country volunteers (dressed in their distinctive indigo-blue tunics) took on Dutch troops and battled to free Ghent and Antwerp, which finally fell to them in 1832, with the support of the French.

1832–1907: The New Nation Flourishes

Largely because Belgium's revolution was widely supported by the nobility and was not simply the work of an unruly rabble, inde-pendence was accepted by the international community at the London Conference of 1831. The European powers also insisted on Belgian neutrality.

Since constitutional monarchy was in vogue, the Belgians then looked for a king, and Prince Leopold of Saxe-Coburg, an uncle of Queen Victoria, agreed to take the throne as **King Leopold I** (r. 1831–65). In 1832 Leopold married Louise-Marie, daughter of King Louis Philippe of France, thus sealing the friend-ship between the two nations.

Belgium's 1830 constitution embodied many jealously guarded liberties, such as freedom of speech, of the press, and of association. As a result it became a refuge for numerous writers and intellectuals, such as **Karl Marx** and **Victor Hugo**, and something of a cultural and artistic melting pot. This also helped to fuel a constant fear of subversion on the part of the authorities: in the late 1840s Bruges came close to revolution as the city swelled with refugees from the crisis in farming, and as the price of linen – now one of its staple industries – collapsed. The poorer quarters of the city were crammed with inadequate one-room slums, where unemployment, alcoholism, typhoid and cholera were rife. In 1847 starving rioters attacked the bakeries in a desperate search for food. But Belgium weathered the European-wide spirit of revolt.

Leopold I was succeeded by his son **Leopold II** (r. 1865–1909), a man with great ambitions for his nation. During his reign Belgium was transformed into a modern industrial state, drawing on its great reserves of coal to fuel its new factories, producing iron and steel, textiles and pottery. Leopold II both presided over what in retrospect appears to be an age of rapid progress and modernization accompanied by a sense of national pride and dignity, and a growing empire. In Leopold's case this was the **Belgian Congo**, which he ruled with cruel tyranny as a personal fiefdom until 1908. But again Bruges missed the boat of economic development.

This was a period in which the French-speaking south prospered at the expense of the Flemish north. The Walloons tended to be the pit-owners, the industrialists, the magnates. French, formerly the language of the nobility and the educated, was the language of success; indeed Flemish was not recognized as an official language of equal value until 1898. For many of the Flemish, cast as the workforce of the nation, life was a Dickensian nightmare of drudgery and squalor. Women and children worked in the mines until the 1890s, half a century after this practice had been outlawed in Britain. This transparent inequality was expressed in

> ## 19th Century
> **Bisschoppelijk Seminarie**, the Episcopal seminary established after Bruges became a bishopric again in 1833, p.96
> **Gruuthusemuseum**, one of the first major neogothic restorations, p.86
> **Guido Gezellemuseum**, for the childhood house of, and exhibition on, Bruges's most famous poet, p.102
> **Museum voor Volkskunde**, a folk museum revealing daily Bruges life in the 19th century, p.98
> **Provinciaal Hof**, the neogothic provincial government building, built 1881–1921, p.71
> **Stadhuis**, the town hall, restored with neo-medieval murals in 1895, p.73
> **Stadsschouwburg**, a neoclassical municipal theatre built in 1863, p.120
> **Vismarkt**, the fishmarket, erected in 1826, p76

a growing Flemish movement, initially linguistic and literary, but later political.

Undisturbed by the industrial revolution, trapped in the past and gently mouldering, Bruges appealed to the Romantics like Sir Walter Scott and the French poet Charles Baudelaire. British neo-medievalists fell in love with the city too, and helped to initiate a programme of renovation and (sometimes heavy-handed) restoration. But just as this work was putting a fresh face on many of the delapidated vestiges of the medieval past, Bruges's reputation for decay was sealed by a novella called *Bruges-la-Morte* (*Bruges the Dead*) by the Belgian symbolist writer **Georges Rodenbach** (1855–98). The pronouncement of death was premature. In 1907 the Boudewijn Canal was built to link Bruges with a new port at Zeebrugge. Completed in 1907, it encouraged the beginnings of an industrial base.

1907–45: The Two World Wars

By the early 20th century the European nations were again jostling dangerously with each other for pre-eminence. In June 1914 the assassination in Sarajevo of the **Archduke Ferdinand**, heir to the Austro-Hungarian throne, triggered off a complicated system of alliances that dragged all the great powers of Europe into war. Germany invaded Belgium, breaching its neutrality, and came to a grinding halt close to the Belgian border with France. Three years of devastatingly costly trench warfare ensued. The beautiful medieval and Renaissance trading city of Ypres (Ieper) found itself at the heart of the conflict, and was flattened. The nearby region around **Passchendaele** was the scene of further carnage (1917–18), in which 245,000 British troops died.

The German occupying powers treated the Belgians harshly, brutally suppressing opposition. Meanwhile the King of Belgium, **Albert I** (r. 1909–34), nephew of Leopold II, led the Belgian army in a spirited defence from the polders around the River Yser in northwest Belgium, causing havoc to the Germans by opening the sluice gates to flood the land. His persistence and fortitude endeared this 'Soldier King' to his nation.

After the First World War Belgium was left to pick up the pieces. Like the rest of Europe it faced the huge task of reconstruction against the background of **the Depression**. Many of Bruges's canal and port facilities had been destroyed in the war, setting back its agenda of prospective development.

The 1930s was a bleak decade, economically and politically. Albert I died when rock-climbing near Namur in 1934. He was succeeded by his son, **Leopold III** (r. 1934–51).

Belgium had renounced its neutrality after the war, but in the early 1930s the rise of **Adolf Hitler** in Germany began to send shudders through the nation. Belgium reasserted its neutrality in 1936, but to little avail. On 10 May 1940 Germany invaded the Netherlands and Belgium, and Leopold III surrendered.

The Belgian government found exile in England, but Leopold III stayed on. The German army of occupation gradually turned the screws on the Belgian people, transporting workers to factories in Germany, rounding up the Jews (25,000

> ## 20th Century
> **Koningin Astridpark**, a memorial to Queen Astrid, wife of Leopold III, p.92
> **Muur der Doodgeschotenen**, scene of First World War executions by German occupying forces, p.105

Belgian Jews died in the war), meeting any activity of the Belgian Resistance movement with harsh reprisals. It was a time of immense bravery: Jews were concealed by non-Jewish families for years, and downed Allied pilots were spirited back across the Channel by clandestine Resistance networks at incalculable personal risk. Belgium also had its share of Nazi sympathizers and home-grown Fascists, particularly – but by no means exclusively – among the Flemish population, who were already disenchanted with Belgian nationhood and the traditional dominance of the French-speaking south. The Nazis were happy to exploit these tensions, and accorded Flanders a special status. There were even two Flemish units of the SS (the dreaded German security forces), which helped to run Belgium's own concentration camp at Breendonk.

Belgium was liberated in September 1944, but Allied progress very nearly came unstuck in December. As the nation settled down to enjoy its first Christmas in freedom for five years, German tank divisions under Field Marshal von Rundstedt launched a last-ditch counteroffensive across the Ardennes (the **Battle of the Bulge**), and bombed Antwerp and Liège. But eventually the Germans were pushed back. The offensive had cost them a total of 120,000 men and contributed to the rapid conclusion of the war.

1945 Onwards: Post-war

Belgium was free again, but immediately encountered a constitutional crisis about the controversial role of Leopold III during the war. Some argued that he had spared the nation a calamity by surrendering; and that he had suffered as an effective prisoner of the Germans, who had confined him to his palace at Laeken, then deported him to Germany in 1944. Many British military analysts argue that, by holding out against massive odds for 18 days, Leopold's 60,000 troops had permitted the Allied evacuation at Dunkirk. (Churchill had deliberately avoided informing Leopold of the evacuation, and sent a cable to Lord Gort, commander in chief of the British Expeditionary forces, saying: 'We are asking the Belgians to sacrifice themselves for us.' His vilification of Leopold after the war was considered quite shameful by many, including George VI.) In Belgium, however, Leopold's performance was compared unfavourably with that of his father, Albert I, in the First World War, and many hinted darkly at collaboration. His wartime marriage to a commoner, Mary Lilian Baels, in 1941 didn't help.

Leopold's brother Charles stood in as regent from 1944 to 1950, and during this period Socialists and Communists (mainly from Wallonia) campaigned actively to form a republic. While Leopold III remained in self-imposed exile in Switzerland, a referendum showed that 57 per cent of the nation favoured his return – but the fact that 58 per cent of Walloons voted against it was effectively a thumbs-down. He returned to Belgium nonetheless, but the mood soon turned ugly. Violent clashes resulted in three deaths, and Belgium seemed on the brink of civil war. In 1951, under pressure from Walloon socialists, Leopold III abdicated in favour of his son (by Queen Astrid), **Baudouin I** (r. 1951–93), hoping thereby to restore unity. These hopes were justified: Baudouin, although only 21 years old, demonstrated an exceptional ability to heal the rifts in the nation.

Since the war Belgium has once again found its historic form as a major industrial and trading nation. Like other European countries, it had to give up its colonial economy, and it granted independence to the **Congo** (later Zaire) in 1960 – although it was much criticized for its haste. It also had

Key Facts and Figures

Belgium is a small country. At 30,520 sq km, it's not much bigger than Sicily or Wales. You can drive from north to south in less than three hours. Its population numbers just over 10 million. There are cities in the world with more people but Belgium nevertheless has one of the highest average population densities, at 312 inhabitants per sq km. Brussels, the capital, accounts for one-tenth of them, with a population of about 950,000. Antwerp has 486,000, Ghent 231,000, Charleroi 207,000, and Liège 196,000. Bruges is a comparative tiddler with 118,000.

The northern part of Belgium is Flanders, inhabited by the Flemish, who speak Dutch. The southern part of the country is Wallonia, home to French-speaking Walloons. Brussels is primarily French-speaking, but is more or less surrounded by Flemish communities. There are also two German-speaking cantons on the German border.

There are five Flemish provinces, and Bruges is the capital of West Flanders (West-Vlaanderen). It is also one of a famous trio (with Ghent and Antwerp) of historic Flemish trading cities that in the past have relished a strong sense of autonomy. This heritage is still evident today. And if you detect a prosperous, buoyant mood in Bruges, this is not simply the product of its formidable income from tourism: in the last decade or so, Flanders has developed one of the most vibrant and successful economies of the entire European Union.

to go through the painful transition from heavy industry towards the light and service industries. This effectively removed the trump cards from the hands of the French-speaking south in favour of the Flemish north. Bruges took a part in this. Its link to the sea was restored during the 1950s, laying the foundations for a thriving industrial sector (set well away from the historic city) producing glass, electrical goods and chemicals.

The language divide, exploited successfully by politicians from both communities, has

21st Century

Concertgebouw Brugge, the new concert hall for Brugge 2002, p.112

Pavilion on the Burg, Toyo Ito's ultra-modern architectural work to celebrate Brugge 2002, p.75

resulted in an increasingly devolved, federal system of government, with an undercurrent of tension. Under the '**St-Michel Accords**' of 1993, Belgian federalization was further reinforced, with the result that Belgium is now effectively ruled by three regional governments (Wallonia, Flanders and Brussels), overseen by a national government.

In its post-war history, the **European Community/Union** has proved a godsend to Belgium in two ways. Belgium was a founder member of the EEC, and Brussels, geographically at the heart, became its headquarters in the 1960s, with all the attention, status and income that that entails. Bruges became the seat of **Europa College**, founded in 1949, a respected postgraduate centre for European studies, which maintains the city's long cosmopolitan tradition.

In addition, Belgium's view of itself within the political framework of Europe – a Europe seen as a confederation of nations – has allowed it to accommodate a confederation within its own boundaries. By defining itself in terms of Europe, there is less pressure to define itself as a nation. But this has still not been enough to dampen the ardour of many Flemish people who want nothing to do with their Walloon counterparts, and see the French-speaking south virtually as a foreign country.

Throughout so much of its history, Belgium has stood between competing nations, earning itself the sobriquet 'the cockpit of Europe'. History has taught it to be flexible and agile, and given it the ability to accept with grace what has become respectfully known as the 'Belgian Compromise'. It remains to be seen whether this essential characteristic of the nation is strong enough to prevent the country falling apart in the new millennium.

Bruges has always had an independent spirit, and traditionally regards itself as an autonomous entity rather than a bit part in the game of regional politics. It has had a golden opportunity to examine its true status in the new millennium when celebrating its appointment as **Cultural Capital of Europe in 2002**. As this also marks the 700th anniversary of the Battle of the Golden Spurs, it is a moment for Bruges to reflect on its unique heritage, as well as on the qualities that can ensure a vibrant future.

Art and Architecture

Belgium has an enviable artistic heritage. It can lay claim to a host of exceptional painters who have become household names: Bruegel, Rubens, Van Dyck, Magritte. But Bruges is celebrated above all for its set of supreme artists who emerged in the late Middle Ages, and – thriving on the rich patronage of this great trading city – showed what the new medium of oil painting could achieve. Jan van Eyck, Rogier van der Weyden and Hans Memling all lived and worked in these streets, and although their work now hangs in galleries around the world, Bruges has managed to hold on to a rich collection, seen above all in the Groeningemuseum.

But as the Groeningemuseum vividly demonstrates, Belgian art is a bigger story than the work of these so-called 'primitives', and so what follows is a canter through its entire history to the present day, with notes about the architecture that evolved in parallel.

700–1500: The Middle Ages

For over 700 years, until the Renaissance, the main inspiration for European art and architecture was the Church. When Charlemagne set up his court in Aachen in the late 8th century, it attracted some of the leading manuscript illustrators of the day; illuminated books remained one of the chief fields of artistic endeavour in the Low Countries for five centuries. One of the best-known series of illuminations, the *Très Riches Heures du Duc de Berry*, was produced by friars from the province of Limburg in around 1411.

The achievements of architecture during the Middle Ages were likewise principally ecclesiastical. The chief influences came from France, and for about 150 years after the 11th century the **Romanesque** style (called Norman in Britain) predominated. Romanesque churches were robust and solid, with massive supporting columns and semicircular arches. (They were

supposedly influenced by Roman architecture, hence the name.)

If you look at the cross section of two intersecting rounded arches, you will see a pointed arch. This became the leading motif of the next phase of architecture, which evolved in the mid-12th century and was later dubbed **Gothic** by Renaissance architects, who considered it a barbarian perversion of the classical ideal. Architects now attempted to create magical illusions of space and light, filling walls with huge, elongated windows held in place by delicate columns and supported by external buttresses.

Flanders developed its own distinctive form of **Scheldt** (or Scaldian) **Gothic**: robust and sturdy, clinging on to Romanesque solidity with the tendency to fill in corners with towers, or by the use of polygonal ground plans. Because of the scarcity of stone, brick was often used, seen most strikingly in the towering spire of the Onze-Lieve-Vrouwekerk in Bruges. However, in the 14th century an increasingly frothy and flamboyant Gothic style was adopted, applied not just to churches, but also to civic architecture. The Stadhuis of Bruges (1376–1420) was a pioneer in this trend, setting a standard in exuberant self-confidence that was soon mirrored in other Flemish city halls.

Manuscript illuminations were highly detailed, brightly coloured and demonstrated great technical skills in portraiture and the depiction of textiles and artefacts. These same talents were put to work when oil painting was developed in the 15th century. Previously, any large-scale paintings had had to be done on the walls, but although fresco painting might have been appropriate in Italy, where it had been used since Roman times, it was not a suitable technique for the damp conditions of northern Europe. Oil paints, however, provided the ideal solution: a broad range of rich colours could be manufactured and applied to wooden panels with great control to give the kind of detail and intense coloration that were achieved in illuminated manuscripts. Furthermore, the paintings were now easily portable, which helped to create a new kind of art market.

Jan van Eyck (1390–1441) was the first artist to demonstrate the full potential of oil painting, and he produced some of the most dazzling work of the late medieval period. *The Adoration of the Mystic Lamb* (1426–32; painted with his brother Hubert) in Ghent cathedral is one of the supreme masterpieces of European art, full of saintliness and sensuality and luminescent detail. His second greatest work is the most prized possession of the Groeningemuseum: the *Madonna with Canon van der Paele* (1436).

Born in Ghent, but based in Bruges after 1430, Jan van Eyck was official painter to Philip the Good, Duke of Burgundy, who presided over an economic boom in the Low Countries. He is one of the earliest Flemish painters known to us by name, as he signed his work. At that time painters worked in guilds, usually remaining anonymous, hence speculative titles such as the Master of the St Lucy Legend. But as van Eyck was in the duke's employ, he was not subject to the restrictions imposed by the painter's guild.

As in Florence, the painters' guild in Bruges went by the name of St Luke's, patron saint of painters. Almost all the leading artists were members of the guild, which negotiated terms of contracts, the payments, the dimensions of the work commissioned, use of colour and so on. They worked for wealthy patrons, such as the nobility, merchants and city officials, who by and large commissioned them to paint sacred subjects – often church altarpieces before which prayers could be said for their souls after death. But increasingly in this era painters were called upon to do straightforward portraits, thus freeing art from the constraints of sacred subject matter. Jan van Eyck's *Arnolfini Marriage* (1434; in the National Gallery, London) is one of the most remarkable examples of this. Giovanni Arnolfini was a wealthy merchant from Lucca who settled in Bruges in 1420, and married here in 1434. Like many paintings of this era – secular or religious – it offers a fascinating insight into the quality of life of the well-to-do of the time, from the sumptuous textiles and furs, to the upholstery and ornately carved furnishings.

Petrus Christus (c. 1420–72), who came to Bruges from Ghent in 1444, may have studied under van Eyck; certainly he was strongly influenced by him, and he evokes a similar mood of silent wonder and spirituality with the same infinitely patient attention to detail. The Groeningemuseum has a number of his works (all panels of larger works), including *Isabella of Portugal and St Elizabeth* (c. 1458), portraying the wife of Philip the Good in her embroidered finery.

Van Eyck's place at Philip the Good's court was later taken by his pupil, **Rogier van der Weyden** (c. 1400–64), whose religious paintings are emotionally charged and full of stress, as in his great triptych, *The Seven Sacraments* (in the Koninklijk Museum voor Schone Kunsten, Antwerp). He spent much of his career in Brussels, but a contemporary copy of his *Philip the Good* is in the Groeningemuseum.

Other major names of this late medieval period include **Dirk Bouts** (1415–75) and **Hugo van der Goes** (c.1435–82) who, although gifted artists in their own right, worked together on the painfully lurid *Triptych with the Martyrdom of St Hippolytus* (c. 1468) in the Groeningemuseum.

But in Bruges the only figure who really matches van Eyck in stature is **Hans Memling** (1435–94): the rich collection of his work commissioned by the Sint-Janshospitaal is still normally housed in its chapel over 500 years on. Born near Frankfurt in Germany, Memling came to Bruges in the 1460s, and soon became one of the most successful and wealthiest painters of the Burgundian era. His work is like an illuminated manuscript writ large, often filled with an exquisite tenderness, found in the gesture and portraiture. His most extraordinary piece is the *St Ursula Shrine*, an ornate casket with 14 jewel-like painted panels.

Gerard David (c. 1460–1523) carried these traditions into the 16th century, bringing a new richness and density of composition to works such as *The Judgement of Cambyses* (1498).

Finding Bruges's Architecture

The Middle Ages: Belfort, p.70; Genthof No.7, p.123; Heilig-Bloedbasiliek, St Basil's Chapel, p.73; Hof Bladelin, p.115; Huis Ter Beurze, p.121; Jeruzalemkerk, p.97; Kruispoort, p.104; De Malvenda House, p.77; Onze-Lieve-Vrouwekerk, p.85; Oud Tolhuis, p.122; Poortersloge, p.122; Sint-Gilliskerk, p.97; Sint-Janshospitaal, p.88; Sint-Salvatorskathedraal, p.110; Smedenpoort, p.114; Stadhuis, p.73

The Renaissance: Oude Griffie, p.74; Renaissancezaal van het Brugse Vrije, p.74

16th–18th-century Vernacular: Almshouses in Noordstraat, Driekroezenstraat and Nieuwe Gentweg, p.91; Begijnhof, founded 1244, but built mainly in the 17th and 18th centuries, p.89; Ezelpoort, p.118; De Pelikaan, p.76; Schuttersgilde Sint-Sebastiaan, p.102

Baroque: Engels Klooster, p.104; Onze-Lieve-Vrouw ter Potterie, p.96; Proostdij, Provost's House, p.76; Sint-Annakerk, p.98; Sint-Jakobskerk, p.115; Sint-Walburgakerk, p.98

Neoclassical: Arentshuis (Brangwyn-museum), p.83; Landshuis van het Brugse Vrije, p.75; Stadsschouwburg, p.120; Vismarkt, p.76

Neogothic: Gruuthusemuseum (restoration), p.86; Heilig-Bloedbasiliek, Chapel of the Holy Blood, p.73; Oud Tolhuis (restoration), p.122; Poortersloge (restoration), p.122; Provinciaal Hof, p.71; Sint-Magdalenakerk, p.92; Stadhuis (restoration), p.73

Art Nouveau: Onze-Lieve-Vrouwekerkhof Zuid Nos. 6–8, p.85

21st Century: Concertgebouw Brugge, p.112; Pavilion on the Burg, p.76

A distinctive mark of the work of these artists, however, was a limited understanding of space: perspective is either not rendered with complete confidence, or shows overmuch concern; landscapes are naïve, and groups of people are often packed slightly too closely together. These problems were addressed by the next great phase of painting in the Low Countries.

1500–1600: The Renaissance

The Renaissance was a watershed between the medieval and the modern world, a long and gradual phenomenon that began in Italy in the 13th century and lasted for some 300 years. It was triggered by the rediscovery of classical learning and literature, and the gradual realization that not only had the Greeks and Romans achieved rather more than the medieval world in terms of science, medicine, architecture and philosophy, but that they had done so without the assistance of Christianity. The Renaissance, therefore, effectively freed people from the straitjacket of purely Christian teaching and encouraged them to approach all questions with an open mind.

Italian art and architecture were the leaders of fashion during the Renaissance, and accomplished artists from northern Europe travelled to Italy to admire and learn from the likes of Leonardo da Vinci, Michelangelo, Titian and Tintoretto. The Italian Renaissance, however, was only partially assimilated in the Low Countries. Although architects were happy to borrow Renaissance motifs, such as classical columns and garlands of flowers, their application of these was mainly cosmetic: their Renaissance façades were essentially adaptations of the traditional step gable (which had been around since the 11th century) tacked on to traditional Flemish houses. Bruges proved particularly resistant: Renaissance influence can be seen, for example, in the façade of the Oude Griffie in the Burg, but this is more the exception than the rule; the Gothic style remained popular even into the 17th century.

The heyday of the **North European Renaissance** was the 16th century, but this coincided with the decline of Bruges as a trading centre – and the rise of Antwerp. Art followed the money, and Antwerp became the main artistic centre in the southern Low Countries, while Brussels became the centre of power.

Flemish painting now followed two main tendencies. One set of artists was directly influenced by Italian painting: **Quentin Metsys** (1466–1530) represents the link between the medieval world and the Renaissance; his *The Lineage of St Anne* (c. 1508; in the Musées Royaux des Beaux-Arts, Brussels) shows a real understanding of architectural perspective, and also uses the kind of hazy, distant blue landscape so beloved of Leonardo da Vinci. **Jan Provoost** (1465–1529) studied at Metsys' studio in Antwerp before coming to Bruges in 1494; his *Crucifixion* in the Groeningemuseum clearly shows the influence of the Italian Renaissance.

Bernard van Orley (c. 1499–1541) brought the Renaissance to Brussels, both in painting and in his designs for tapestry and stained glass. Other 'Romanists' include van Orley's pupil **Michiel Coxie** (1499–1592), who lived in Rome in the 1530s, and **Jan Gossaert of Mauberge** (1478–1532) (also known as Mabuse), who painted the first classically inspired nudes in Flemish art.

The most overtly classically inspired artist working in Bruges was **Lancelot Blondeel**

The Seven Wonders of Bruges

A poster hangs in the tourist office in the Burg showing a painting of about 1550, attributed to the Bruges artist Pieter Claeissens the Elder. It depicts, in a kind of collage form, the *Septem Admirationes Civitatis Brugensis*, the Seven Wonders of Bruges. It is a slightly odd selection (the Stadhuis is omitted, for instance), but shows what was most universally admired at the time:

Belfort, p.70
Huis de Zeven Torens (now a shell), p.75
Onze-Lieve-Vrouwekerk, p.84
Oosterlingenhuis (all but disappeared)
Poortersloge, p.122
Waterhalle (replaced by the Provinciaal Hof)
Waterhuis (the pumphouse, since demolished)

(1498–1531), the painter, sculptor and architect responsible for the triumphant monumental chimney piece in the Renaissancezaal van het Brugse Vrije (1528–31) in the Burg. He also had a line in highly individualistic religious paintings, in which elaborate and fantastical architectural decoration takes precedence over the main subjects.

Meanwhile, followers of the second tendency developed a more independent Flemish style of painting, reflecting the distinctive outlook and heritage of the Low Countries. Supreme among them was **Pieter Bruegel the Elder** (c. 1525–69), who trained in Antwerp and whose trip to Italy in about 1551 appears to have left him unmoved. His interest lay in the people and landscape of his homeland: even when painting a classical subject such as his famous *Fall of Icarus* (1567; in the Musées Royaux des Beaux-Arts, Brussels) his main focus is rural life, leaving poor Icarus' plight as virtually incidental. Bruegel was particularly successful in translating religious scenes into Flemish village life, breathing into them a new poignancy and relevance. Another line of work took him into the realms of fantasy associated with the Dutch painter Hieronymus Bosch (1450–1516) – as in *The Fall of Rebel Angels* (1562).

In 1563 Pieter Bruegel moved to Brussels and married. He had two sons late in life, both of whom became painters in their own right well after their father's death. **Pieter Bruegel the Younger** (1564–1638) painted numerous versions of his father's work, using a more polished style that somehow lacks the naïve spontaneity of his father's paintings (of which only some 40 examples have survived). His younger brother **Jan 'Velvet' Bruegel** (1568–1625) is celebrated for his landscapes and his delicate flower paintings.

Bruges and the rest of the Low Countries went through a traumatic period of religious strife at the end of the 16th century, during which many of the churches were destroyed by Protestant iconoclasts. In addition, Bruges was now in terminal commercial decline. This sombre period is reflected in the work of the last notable Bruges artist of the early era,

Pieter Pourbus (c. 1523–84), who is celebrated more for his portraits than for his rather heavy-handed religious works, influenced by the Italian mannerists. He married Lancelot Blondeel's daughter and founded a dynasty of distinguished painters (Frans the Older and Frans the Younger).

1600–1700: Antwerp's Golden Age

A measure of stability returned during the 17th century, and now the Counter-Reformation brought its own flourish in both art and architecture.

Antwerp remained a cultural centre in the Low Countries during the 17th century largely because of one remarkable genius: **Pieter Paul Rubens** (1577–1640). In his twenties, he lived and worked in Italy for eight years, where he was strongly influenced by the work of Michelangelo, Titian and his contemporary Caravaggio, returning to Antwerp in 1608 with a glittering reputation; the following year he became court painter to Archduke Albert and the Infanta Isabella. His *Raising of the Cross* (1610) and *Descent from the Cross* (1612) for Antwerp Cathedral caused a sensation.

Rubens' ability to handle vast paintings on dramatic subjects was unsurpassed. His compositions carry the eye through the paintings with a unique vigour, assisted by his deft, virtuoso touch, often applied in thin, almost sketchy layers of paint. Throughout almost all his work there is a lusty, life-enhancing quality, very Flemish in nature.

After his first wife died in 1625, Rubens entered the diplomatic service. He travelled to Spain and England in an effort to broker peace, and he was rewarded for his services in England by a knighthood. He also won several major commissions in both countries (including the ceilings of the Banqueting House in Whitehall, London). He maintained a flow of work right up to the end of his life, bringing his total *oeuvre* to over 2000 major paintings.

The other two great Antwerp painters of this era were both closely associated with Rubens. **Antoon (Anthony) van Dyck** (1599–1641) was celebrated for his sedate portraits, which capture the solemnity and dignity of the affluent – notably after he became court artist to Charles I of England in 1632. **Jacob Jordaens** (1593–1678) painted in a vigorous, expressive style in the manner of Rubens, and specialized in joyous, bacchanalian scenes.

During this period Flemish 'genre' painting also thrived – portraits of ordinary rural and town life in inns, markets and kitchens, often spiced with gentle humour. Two of the leading genre painters of the period were **David Teniers the Younger** (1610–90) and **Adriaen Brouwer** (1605–38).

The fecund, flowing style of Rubens and his followers is typical of the **Baroque** period, which can be most readily identified in architecture. Baroque architecture was essentially a lavish, curvaceous interpretation of the classical style: pediments became broken pediments, columns became barley-sugar twists, façades became embellished with *oeil-de-boeuf* windows. Baroque can become overbearing, but with the right balance it is joyous and delicate, elegant and swanky, befitting the ostentatious lifestyles of the wealthy merchant classes of the 17th century.

It is a measure of the decline of Bruges that it partook in these developments only at second-hand. It has no artists who came anywhere near the calibre of Rubens, Van Dyck and Jordaens, although **Jacob van Oost the Elder** (1601–71) produced memorable and highly competent pictures of 17th-century society, which – without the Antwerp swagger – probably better reflected the mood in Bruges. His pupil **Jan Baptist van Meuninckxhove** (c. 1620–1703) was a gifted landscape artist whose work included beautifully observed views of Bruges.

As elsewhere, the damage wrought by the iconoclasts in Bruges was usually repaired with Baroque flourishes. The Sint-Walburgakerk (1619–41), however, is pure Baroque, and delicately judged by its Bruges-born architect, **Pieter Huyssens** (1577–1637). This was also the era of fantastically elaborate wooden

Finding Bruges's Art

The Middle Ages and Renaissance

Groeningemuseum, for a supreme collection, including work by Jan van Eyck, Petrus Christus, Rogier van der Weyden, Dirk Bouts, Hans Memling, Hieronymus Bosch, p.82

Memlingmuseum, an unrivalled collection of works by Hans Memling, p.88

Onze-Lieve-Vrouwekerk, with late medieval tombs of Charles the Bold and Mary of Burgundy; Michelangelo's *Madonna and Child*; paintings by Bernard van Orley and Pieter Pourbus, p.85

Sint-Jakobskerk, with a collection of paintings of the 15th to 17th centuries, p.115

The Age of Rubens

Groeningemuseum, with mainly Bruges artists, such as Jacob van Oost the Elder, p.82

Sint-Walburgakerk, for an elaborate pulpit by Artus Quellinus the Younger, p.98

18th Century

Groeningemuseum, for artists such as Jan Antoon Garemijn, p.82

Heilig-Bloedbasiliek, the Chapel of the Holy Blood, with a pulpit by Hendrik Pulinx, p.73

19th Century and Symbolism

Groeningemuseum, for paintings by Pre-Raphaelitesque Edmond van Hove, post-Impressionist Emile Claus, and Symbolists Fernand Khnopff, Léon Frédéric and Jean Delville, p.82

Public statues, such as Paul de Vigne's *Bruges Matins*, p.72, and Henry Pickery's *Jan van Eyck*, p.122

Stadhuis, with neo-medieval murals, p.73

20th Century

Arentshuis (Brangwynmuseum), an impressive collection of work by British-born artist Frank Brangwyn, p.83

Groeningemuseum, for Sint-Martens-Latem School painters Gustave de Smet, Constant Permeke and Gustave van de Woestijne; also works by Edgar Tytgat, Rik Wouters and Magritte, p.82

Sculptures in 't Zand, for the most ambitious of the public sculptures by Stefaan Depuydt and Livia Canestraro, p.112

pulpits: **Artus Quellinus the Younger** (1625–1700), from an Antwerp family of sculptors, excelled in this specialist art, and supplied the pulpit in the Sint-Walburgakerk. Bruges produced its own home-grown pulpit-maker in the next century, **Hendrik Pulinx** (1698–1781).

1700–1830: Classical Revival

During the 18th century fashions imitated the French once more, and in particular the styles associated with Louis XV. During this period architects reassessed the lessons of classical architecture and pressed for more stringent, sober adherence to these models, with emphasis on well-modulated proportions and symmetry. Both churches and mansions took on the outward appearance of Greek temples: in Bruges the greatest example of this was built on the Markt in the 1790s, to replace the medieval Waterhalle, but it survived only a century. Bruges also acquired its own Academy of Art, founded in 1717 and housed in the medieval Poortersloge. One of its directors was the prolific Rococo artist **Jan Garemijn** (1712–99), who painted the Bruges social set with a kind of Hogarthian crudeness.

The end of the 18th century was marked by the turbulence of the Brabançon Revolt and the French occupation. The prevailing style was again neoclassical. The French neoclassical painter Jacques-Louis David (1748–1825) spent the last years of his life in Brussels and had a number of disciples in Belgium but, with one or two possible exceptions, they lacked David's ability to inject a sense of noble drama into their classical scenes. A glance at work by **Frans J. Kinsoen** (1771–1838) and **Jozef Odevaere** (1775–1830) in the Groeningemuseum will show just how difficult it was to achieve this aggrandizing effect without drifting into the absurd.

1830–80:
Truly Belgian Art

Belgian independence in 1830 gave fresh impetus to artists, sculptors and architects. The new nation needed to make its own statements about its role in the world and to glamorize its heritage. Sculptors were called in to evoke the Belgian past through historical sculptures, often to rather leaden effect; **Paul de Vigne** (1843–1901) of Ghent and **Henry Pickery** (1828–94) of Bruges contributed such statues to Bruges's public places. In painting, a wave of **Romanticism** – passionate, vigorous and poetic – swept neoclassicism before it.

Then, after the 1850s, a **realist** school evolved in the fashion of the French painter Gustave Courbet (1819–77), in which ordinary scenes such as peasants at work and cow byres were depicted with the Romantics' eye, but unprettified and (in principle) devoid of interpretation; in Belgium **Hippolyte Boulenger** (1837–74), **Jan Stobbaerts** (1838–1914) and **Henri de Braekeleer** (1840–88) are the best-known exponents of this trend. The social implications of Realism were taken up with greater vigour by the painter and sculptor **Constantin Meunier** (1831–1905), who focused on both the misery and the dignity of industrial labour.

In the latter part of the century, architecture took on all shapes and forms, ranging from the neogothic to the neoclassical, which were seen as complementary rather than contradictory. In Bruges, however, neogothic was considered the only appropriate style. Promoted vigorously by a British contingent of antiquarians, collectors and restorers such as John Steinmetz, William Brangwyn, James Weale and Robert Chantrell, it was adopted enthusiastically by a number of artists and architects.

Notable among them was Bruges's municipal architect **Louis Delacenserie** (1838–1909), who restored the Gruuthuse mansion, the Tolhuis, the Poortersloge, the Heilig-Bloedbasiliek, and designed the new Provinciaal Hof in the Markt.

Belgium was also noted as a liberal country, a refuge for artists from more repressive regimes, particularly France, and this fuelled a taste for the avant-garde. In Brussels various societies were formed to discuss and promote contemporary work. One of these was **Le Cercle des Vingt** (Les XX), founded by Octave Maus in 1883, which held controversial exhibitions of invited artists, many of whom were unknown at the time. Paul Cézanne, for example – later dubbed the 'father of modern art' – was exhibited by Les XX long before he was recognized in his own country.

1880–1900:
Post-Impressionism and Symbolism

Despite the influence of innovative groups such as these, Belgian art essentially followed the patterns of French painting during the late 19th century. Artists such as **Théo van Rysselberghe** (1862–1926) adopted a form of pointillist Impressionism; **Emile Claus** (1849–1924) created a kind of late Impressionism that he called 'Luminism', depicting rural scenes with famously fetching charm; there is a fine example, *River Lys at Astene* (1885), in the Groeningemuseum.

Belgium also produced more individualistic talents, notably the decidedly bizarre **James Ensor** (1860–1949). He began his painting career with well-made Post-Impressionist paintings of interiors and portraits; however in the mid-1880s his palette suddenly became charged with intense, clashing colours, which he applied with aggressive vigour to increasingly oddball subject matter, such as dead fish, animated skeletons and Punch-and-Judy-like caricatures. His great masterpiece is the carnival-like *Entry of Christ into Brussels* (1888).

At the same time a very loosely defined group of painters called the **Symbolists** began to explore the world of suggestion, mystery and dreams. Many of their works are fascinating for their sheer idiosyncrasy, such as the visionary fantasy world of **Jean**

Delville (1867–1953). By contrast **Léon Frédéric** (1856–1940) painted large triptychs of social realism infused with the kind of saintly clarity found in the works of the medieval Flemish masters.

But perhaps the most haunting Symbolist of them all is **Fernand Khnopff** (1858–1921), who used a soft, polished style to bring a dreamlike quality to his work. He spent six years of his childhood in Bruges, and created two memorable works set in the city: *Secret-Reflet* (1902; in the Groeningemuseum) and *La Ville Abandonnée* (1904).

Another highly individual painter associated with Symbolism is **Léon Spilliaert** (1881–1946), a self-taught artist who brought a strong sense of design to his stylized interiors and unmistakable landscapes – often brooding silhouettes set against empty twilight coastlines around his native Ostend, filled with the abstract shapes of cloud and reflected patches of water.

Yet another kind of Symbolism can be seen in the work of artists influenced by the Pre-Raphaelite Brotherhood in England, such as **Théophile M. F. Lybaert** (1848–1927) of Ghent, and **Edmond Van Hove** (1853–1913) of Bruges. Their mystical, highly polished and detailed work reflected the paintings of the 'primitives' and fitted the neogothic mood in turn-of-the-century Bruges.

Les XX were superseded by **La Libre Esthétique** (1894–1914) as Brussels' leading artistic circle. This group encouraged cooperation between artists, architects and craftsmen, creating an atmosphere that fostered the emerging decorative style, 2, a style that chimed well with Symbolism. Belgium was at the forefront of Art Nouveau, with leading figures such as **Victor Horta** (1861–1947), and **Henry van de Velde** (1863–1957), who became director of the Art and Crafts School in Weimar in 1901, which in 1919 evolved into the Bauhaus. Art Nouveau remained fashionable until the First World War in most major cities in Belgium, but is seen in Bruges only in a few isolated places.

1900 Onwards

Out of Impressionism and Post-Impressionism grew **Fauvism**, whose name was based on a term of abuse meaning 'wild beast', applied by a critic, and reflecting their unbridled use of colour. Belgium's most successful exponent was **Rik Wouters** (1882–1916) – also a gifted sculptor – who used bright but carefully modulated colours to produce work of great charm and subtlety, usually featuring his wife Nel.

Meanwhile, a school of painters developed in the village of Sint-Martens-Latem, near Ghent. The first wave, founded in around 1904, included mystic, Symbolist-style painters such as **Valerius de Saedeleer** (1867–1941) and **Albert Servaes** (1883–1966). The second wave developed in around 1909, and in the post-war period was centred upon **Constant Permeke** (1886–1952), who painted emotionally charged, blocky portraits with thick dingy colours, a unique combination of social realism, Cubism and Expressionism.

Two of Belgium's best-known 20th-century painters are **Surrealists**. Surrealism developed in Paris in the 1920s as an effort to unveil a reality in the subconscious through spontaneous, automatic behaviour and events, usually of a highly unconventional nature. By extension, the term was applied to the dreamworld evoked by painters such as Salvador Dali. **René Magritte** (1898–1967) lived in Paris in the 1920s then returned to Belgium to begin producing his inimitable small-scale paintings of witty absurdities and visual puns, such as floating men in bowler hats, paintings within paintings, trains emerging from fireplaces and nude female torsos which become faces.

Meanwhile, **Paul Delvaux** (1897–1994) painted countless versions of his primary obsessions over his long lifetime: trams and stations by night, peopled by sleepwalkers, skeletons and reclining nudes, all suffused with a haunting, dreamlike quality and latent eroticism.

During most of the 20th century, Belgian art has tended to reflect movements elsewhere in the world. In the immediate post-war years, a group called **La Jeune Peinture Belge** (1945–48) attempted to gather together the various strains of contemporary art. Its members produced primarily abstract work, influenced particularly by the mechanistic abstractions of **Victor Sevranckx** (1897–1965). **Anne Bonnet** (1908–60), **Louis van Lint** (1909–89) and **Gaston Bertrand** (b. 1910) are probably the best known of these today.

In 1948 an international group called **Cobra** (an acronym from Copenhagen, Brussels, Amsterdam) formed around a common interest in children's painting and primitive art, free of the encumbrance of Western painting traditions; Belgium's most famous participant is **Pierre Alechinsky** (b. 1927), whose poetic, semi-figurative works (particularly in inks) have reached the international stage.

Now, with growing prosperity and self-confidence, as well as new, pace-setting collections of contemporary art in both Antwerp and Ghent, Flanders is once again generating its own artistic impetus. Could it possibly be on the threshold of a new Golden Age?

Travel

GETTING THERE

Bruges (Brugge in Dutch) is in the north of Belgium, about 100km northwest of the capital, Brussels, and 14km south of Zeebrugge on the coast.

By Air

Brussels, 'the capital of Europe', is well served by the world's airlines, jostling to harness the ceaseless ebb and flow of Eurocrats, multinational business travellers and a large population of expatriates – as well as tourists. There are many flights from all points of the globe, and they tend to be packed; if you are on a tight schedule, book early. International flights arrive at Belgium's main airport at Zaventem, just 14km from the centre of Brussels (for onward connections to Bruges see 'Arrival').

From the UK and Ireland

The main carriers to Brussels offer up to seven flights daily from London Heathrow, and there are also daily flights from London Gatwick, Bristol, Manchester, Birmingham, Leeds, Newcastle, Glasgow, Edinburgh and Dublin. The full London–Brussels fare for unrestricted economy travel is around £330 return. However, if your journey includes a Saturday night, prices for APEX fares drop to about £120–150. The flight from London to Brussels takes about 60 minutes. An airport tax of £18 is payable when you purchase your ticket.

Scheduled Flights to Brussels

Aer Lingus, *t (01) 866 8888*, *w www.aerlingus.ie*. Up to five flights a day direct from Dublin. Ticket prices vary enormously. For under-25s, a fully flexible unrestricted ticket is available for £152 (when bought within seven days of departure). Apex prices start at £110 if your stay includes a Saturday night. Add IR£10 to all fares to cover airport tax.

British Airways, *reservations t 0845 77 333 77*, *w www.britishairways.com*. Look out for their occasional 'World Offers': return tickets

Flights on the Internet

The best place to start looking for flights to Brussels is the Web – just about everyone has a site where you can compare prices (see the airlines listed), and booking online usually confers a 10–20% discount.

In the UK and Ireland
w www.airtickets.co.uk
w www.cheapflights.com
w www.flightcentre.co.uk
w www.lastminute.com
w www.skydeals.co.uk
w www.sky-tours.co.uk
w www.thomascook.co.uk
w www.trailfinders.com
w www.travelocity.com
w www.travelselect.com

In the USA
w www.air-fare.com
w www.airhitch.org
w www.expedia.com
w www.flights.com
w www.orbitz.com
w www.priceline.com
w www.travellersweb.ws
w www.travelocity.com
w www.smarterliving.com

In Canada
w www.flightcentre.ca
w www.lastminuteclub.com
w www.newfrontiers.com

for as little as £56 (plus tax), which must be booked at least a month in advance. Tickets available at BA Travelshops, *t 0845 606 0747*, located throughout the country (*open daily 6am–6pm*).

British Midland (bmi), *t 0870 607 0555*, *w www.flybmi.com*. From Heathrow, East Midlands, Edinburgh, Leeds and Manchester.

Low-cost Flights to Brussels

The cheap no-frills low-cost carriers can offer astonishingly low prices if you book well in advance. You can book directly over the Internet and a discount is usually offered if you do. Prices go up the closer you get to your leaving date; fares booked last minute are often not much cheaper than those of the major carriers. Each ticket has various conditions attached, for example whether you can get a refund or whether the date of the flight can be changed.

Ryanair, *t 08701 569569*, *w www.ryanair. com*. Operates three flights daily from London Stansted and Dublin and one flight a day from Glasgow Prestwick to Charleroi, two hours' drive from Brussels. Flights can be supercheap.

Virgin Express, *t (020) 7744 0004*, *w www. virgin.express.com*. There are nine flights daily from London Heathrow. Tickets are non-transferable and cost from £82.

From the USA and Canada
Scheduled Flights to Brussels

There are direct flights to Brussels from just about all the major gateway cities of the USA. Prices vary enormously; the round-trip price quoted by airlines for New York–Brussels is around US$350–500 in the low season (winter), and rises to at least US$800 in the high season (summer). All fares are sub-ject to additional airport taxes, which amount to about $40. Canadians are rather less well served: travellers have to take a two-stage journey, changing in the USA or in Europe.

Air Canada, *t 888 247 2262*, *w www. aircanada.com*. Flies via London from Montreal, Toronto, Vancouver, Calgary, Winnipeg and Halifax.

British Airways, *t 800 403 0882*, *w www. britishairways.com*. Flights through Heathrow and Gatwick from a host of US cities.

Airline Offices in Brussels

Aer Lingus, *98 Rue du Trône*, *t (02) 548 9848*.
Air France, *149 Av Louise*, *t (02) 541 4251*.
American Airlines, *98 Rue du Trône*, *t (02) 714 4916*.
British Airways, *Centre International Rogier*, *t (02) 548 2111*.
British Midland (bmi), *15 Av de Pléiades*, *t (02) 771 7766*.
Delta Air Lines, *Brussels National Airport*, *1930 Zaventem*, *t (02) 723 8260*.
Lufthansa, *1 Bvd Anspach*, *t (02) 212 0922*.

Continental Airlines, *t 800 231 0856*, *w www.continental.com*. From New York JFK, Boston, Los Angeles and many other major US and Canadian cities.

Delta Air Lines, *t 800 241 4141*, *t 800 221 1212 (in Montreal dial 337 5520)*, *w www.delta.com*. From New York JFK and Atlanta, with con-nections from many US cities.

Charter Flights to Brussels

Numerous agencies offer competitive prices through charter flights or consolidated fares on scheduled flights; look in the travel pages of your newspaper. Check the Sunday *New York Times* listings or try:

Council Travel, *205 East 42nd St, New York, NY 10017*, *t 800 2COUNCIL*, *w www.council travel.com*.

TFI, *34 West 32nd St, New York, NY 10001*, *t 800 745 8000*, *t (212) 736 1140*.

By Sea (from the UK)

The ferry can be a good option if you're travelling by car or with young children (under 4s free; under 14s reduced rates). For people in Scotland and the north of England wishing to travel to Bruges, the ferry may still be the most convenient option. Calais is 100km from Bruges, Ostend is 35km, Zeebrugge is 14km.

Dover to Ostend

Hoverspeed, *t 0845 674 6006*, *w www. hoverspeed.com*. Operates a fast-ferry 'SeaCat' service. In summer there should be three crossings a day at 7am, 3pm and 8pm. For the early morning ferry, you'll pay £150 for a 5-day return for a car and two passengers. Peak mid-afternoon rates for a similar ticket are closer to £200. Apex fares are around £110 and foot passengers pay £28 on all crossings. The journey takes about 2hrs and Ostend is about half an hour's drive from Bruges. Unfortunately, this service is often liable to delay or cancellation in poor weather.

Dover to Calais

Thanks to improved road links on the conti-nent following completion of the Channel

Tunnel, it is well worth considering this route. The E40/A16 is now open all the way from Calais to the Bruges turn off (on the E40/A10); the drive should take no more than 1½ hours. A standard return should set you back something in the region of £150, whilst a day return can be bought for as little as £10.

P&O Stena Line, t *0870 600 0600,* **w** *www.posl.com.*

Sea France, t *08705 711711,* **w** *www.seafrance. com.* Up to 15 departures a day.

Hull to Zeebrugge

P&O North Sea Ferries, t *08701 296002,* **w** *www.mycruiseferries.com*, runs the overnight service. Standard foot passenger fares range from £44–310 depending on accommodation. For those with a car, a five-night return, which must include a Saturday night, can be bought in summer for £86 (with passenger fares on top of this). Bruges is just 14km away on the N31 dual-carriageway.

By Train

From the UK

The Channel Tunnel, one of the great marvels of modern engineering, has transformed Britain's links to mainland Europe. To reach Bruges by train via the Channel Tunnel, you first have to go to Brussels. The total journey time from London to Bruges is about four hours.

The rail company operating the Channel Tunnel passenger service is **Eurostar**. Trains depart from Waterloo Station in London, and take 2 hours 40 minutes to reach Brussels, arriving at the Gare du Midi/Zuid Station. There are usually eleven departures a day. Be sure to check in at least 20 minutes before departure, or you simply will not be allowed on board.

Prices are on a par with Eurostar's direct competitor – air travel – and vary between £70 and £300, depending on how far in advance you book, and whether or not your stay includes a Saturday night. However, it's well worth asking about special deals.

Eurostar, UK t *0870 160 6600,* **USA t** *800 EUROSTAR,* **w** *www.eurostar.com.*

Rail Europe, *179 Piccadilly, London W1,* **t** *08705 848848,* **w** *www.raileurope.co.uk; in North America, US,* **t** *877 456 RAIL, Canada* **t** *800 361 RAIL,* **w** *www.raileurope.com.* For rail tickets to Belgium from England, or vice versa.

From Brussels

There is a direct train link between Brussels and Bruges, leaving from both the Gare du Midi/Zuid Station and the Gare Centrale/Centraal Station (which are on the same line). There are two trains an hour, running from about 5am to 11pm. The journey takes an hour – provided that you take the intercity train, and not one of the slow ones. It costs around €10 each way.

There are reductions of 40 per cent for return/round-trip fares at the weekend (Friday after 7pm to Sunday night).

Children under 6 travel free at all times; children aged 6 to 11 travel free at weekends, and on weekdays if departing after 9am.

If you intend to cycle in Bruges, you can purchase a rail ticket that includes cycle hire from Bruges Station under the 'Trein + Fiets' scheme (*see* 'By Bicycle', p.55).

Belgian Railways (NMBS in Dutch, SNCB in French), t *+32 (0)2 555 25 55,* **w** *www.nmbs.be.*

Bruges station/train information, t *(050) 38 23 82.*

Other Railway Options

Some Eurostar trains also stop at Lille (called Rijsel in Dutch), in northeastern France, 60km from Bruges. Local trains connect to Bruges, and take 1hr 15mins. There is also a connecting bus service between Lille and Bruges, operated by Eltebe of Bruges, **t** *(050) 32 01 11.*

Trains from Charing Cross Station in London link up with the Hoverspeed SeaCat service from Dover to Ostend, and from there with trains on to Bruges. This route is a bit slow, requiring a courtesy bus to the port at Dover, but it is economical, with prices starting at £29 return for a three-day excursion, or £46 return for five days. Since the Hoverspeed departure from Calais is at 11am and the return from Ostend departs at 5pm, there is not enough time for a day trip.

Tickets are available at major UK railway stations or contact Hoverspeed (*see* p.49).

From elsewhere in Europe – Paris, Amsterdam, Schiphol (Amsterdam's airport), Rotterdam, Düsseldorf, Cologne – you can reach Brussels on one of the super-fast 'Thalys' TGV (*train à grande vitesse*) services. Twice a day the Thalys service runs directly from Paris Nord to Bruges via Brussels, a journey of 2hr 25mins (departures at 7.55am and 5.55pm). More details are available at **w** *www.thalys.com*. There is also a direct train service between Antwerp and Bruges, one per hour, taking 1hr 15mins.

By Coach (from the UK)

The Eurolines service between Bruges and London (via Calais) takes six and a half hours, but operates only at weekends (departing and returning on Fridays and Sundays), although more frequent crossings are made in the summer months. Coaches depart from Victoria Coach Station in central London at 10.30am and arrive in Bruges at 5pm. A standard return ticket to Bruges for an adult costs £46 but a Europapex fare is available for £33 if booked more than seven days in advance.

There are also daily coaches from Scotland and Liverpool/Manchester to connect up with the overnight ferry from Hull to Zeebrugge, with an onward bus to Bruges.

Eurolines, t *08705 143 219,* **w** *www. eurolines.co.uk.*

By Car

Many visitors from the European continent will arrive by car, but it is worth noting here that Bruges is a very small city. If you intend to visit the city alone, a car is of little practical value. In fact it is more of an encumbrance.

Eurotunnel (formerly known as Le Shuttle) transports cars on purpose-built railway carriers between Folkestone and Calais. The UK terminal is situated off junction 11a on the M20. The journey time is a mere 35 minutes platform to platform; once in France you can reach Bruges in about an hour on the newly completed E40/A16 autoroute.

The standard economy fare between 6am and 10pm rises to £299 in the summer months. There are cheaper rates for travelling between 10pm and 6am, and special rates for 5-day breaks (£180 in August). Day-trip return crossings can cost as little as £49 (non-refundable), though the standard fare is £170. The fare is for car space only regardless of the number of passengers. It is advisable to reserve space in advance although it is possible just to turn up and wait.

Eurotunnel, t *0870 535 3535,* **w** *www. eurotunnel.com.*

Driving in Belgium

To drive a car in Belgium, you'll need a valid EU driving licence – or your own national licence, or an international driving licence – plus valid insurance and your vehicle registration documents. It is advisable to take out an additional insurance policy to cover your car against the cost of breakdown and rescue while abroad. You are required by law to carry a warning triangle and a fire extinguisher, and are expected to have a first-aid kit. Your headlights should be adjusted for driving on the right-hand side of the road, but they do not need to be yellow. Seatbelts are obligatory in both the front and rear seat, and children under 12 must be seated in the rear, if space is available.

The roads in Belgium are well maintained, and the motorway network is free of charge. The speed limits are 120km/hr (75mph) on the motorway, 90km/hr (55mph) on major country roads and 50km/hr (30mph) in built-up areas. Drinking and driving is against the law (you'll be over the limit after more than one drink) and liable to severe penalties.

By law, vehicles must give way to pedestrians wanting to cross at a marked pedestrian crossing, but the concept is fairly new to the Belgians.

TOUR OPERATORS

Short breaks are part and parcel of Bruges's tourist industry, and a number of companies provide packages that combine transport and accommodation. These may offer significant reductions in overall cost compared with booking the separate elements yourself – particularly if you take advantage of such features as 'fourth night free' or 'kids go free' (free accommodation for children, if sharing with parents). But even if it's not all that much cheaper, buying a package allows you to hand over to one single company all the bother of the booking, ticketing and scheduling.

In the UK

Ace Study Tours, *Babraham, Cambridge CB2 4AP, t (01223) 835055, f 837394, w www. study-tours.org.* Cultural and garden tours.

Belgian Travel Service, *Bridge House, 55–59 High Rd, Broxbourne, Herts EN10 7DT, t 0870 727 5858, e belgian@bridge-travel. co.uk, w www.belgiantravel.co.uk.*

British Museum Traveller, *46 Bloomsbury St, London WC1B 3QQ, t (020) 7323 8895, f 7580 8677, w www.britishmuseumtraveller.co.uk.* Guest lectures, art and architecture tours.

City Breaks Online, *t 0800 542 2282, w www.citybreaks-online.com.*

City Holidays, *14 City Business Centre, Basin Rd, Chichester, West Sussex PO19 2DU, t (01243) 775770, w www.city-holidays.co.uk.*

Compass Agencies, *669 Honeypot Lane, Stanmore, Middx HA7 1JE, t (020) 8952 1532, f 8930 2283, w www.compassagencies.com.*

Cox and Kings, *4th Floor, Gordon House, 10 Greencoat Place, London SW1P 1PH, t (020) 7873 5027, f 7630 6038, w www.coxand kings.co.uk.* Short breaks, gourmet and escorted cultural tours with guest lecturers.

Cresta Holidays, *Tabley Court, Victoria St, Altrincham, Cheshire WA14 1EZ, t 0870 161 0909, w www.crestaholidays.co.uk.*

Crystal Holidays, *King's Place, Wood St, Kingston, Surrey KT1 1JY, t 0870 848 7015, f 0870 848 7031, w www.crystalholidays. co.uk.*

Driveline, *Greenleaf House, Darkes Lane, Potters Bar, Herts EN6 1AE, t 0870 757 7575, w www.driveline.co.uk.*

Eurobreak, *Inghams Travel, Gemini House, 10–18 Putney Hill, London SW15 6AX, t (020) 8780 7700, f 8780 7705, w www.euro break.com.*

Eurotours, *St George's House, 34–36 St George's Rd, Brighton, East Sussex BN2 1ED, t (01273) 883838, f 383123, w www.eurotours.co.uk.*

Great Escapes, *t 0800 731 2929, w www. greatescapes.co.uk.*

Holts Battlefield Tours, *The Old Plough, High Street, Eastry, Kent CT13 0HF, t (01304) 612248, f 614930, w www.battletours.co.uk.*

Kirker Holidays, *3 New Concordia Wharf, Mill St, London SE1 2BB, t (020) 7231 3333, w www.kirkerholidays.com.* Specializes in tailor-made holidays.

Leisure Direction, *Image House, Station Rd, London N17 9LR, t 0870 442 8945, w www.leisuredirection.co.uk.*

Lupus Travel, *Triumph House, 189 Regent St, London W1B 4JS, t (020) 7306 3000, f 7287 2142.*

Martin Randall Travel, *10 Barley Mow Passage, Chiswick, London W4 4PH, t (020) 8742 3355, f 8742 7766, w www.martinrandall. com.* Cultural tours accompanied by a lecturer.

Off 4 the Weekend, *t (01892) 559811, w www.off4theweekend.com.*

Page & Moy, *135–140 London Rd, Leicester LE2 1EN, t 08700 106212, w www.pagemoy.com.*

Prospect Music and Art Tours Ltd, *36 Manchester St, London W1U 7LH, t (020) 7486 5704, f 7486 5868.* Cultural breaks of various sorts.

Shortbreaks Ltd UK, *t (020) 8402 0007, w www.short-breaks.com.* All-inclusive Eurostar breaks.

Sovereign, *Groundstar House, London Rd, Crawley, West Sussex RH10 2TB, t 08705 768373, f (01293) 457760, w www.sovereign.com.*

Travelscene, *11–15 St Ann's Rd, Harrow, Middlesex HA1 1LQ, t 0870 777 4445, f (020) 8861 4154, w www.travelscene.co.uk.*

Voyages Jules Verne, *21 Dorset Sq, London NW1 6QG, t (020) 7616 1010, f 7723 8629, w www. vjv.co.uk.* Speciality tours including food and drink, art and history and the single traveller.

Where 2 Break, *Cresta Holidays Ltd, Tabley Court, Victoria St, Altrincham, Cheshire WA14 1EZ, t 0870 169 0708, w www.where2break.com.*

In Ireland

Go Holidays, *28 North Great George's St, Dublin 1, t (01) 874 4126, f 872 7958.*

United Travel, *Stillorgan Bowl, Stillorgan, Co. Dublin, t (01) 283 2555, f 283 1527, w www. unitedtravel.ie.*

In the USA

Contiki Travels, *300 East Katella Av, 450 Anaheim, CA 92806, t (888) CONTIKI, f (714) 935 2556, w www.contiki.com.* Bus tours for 18–35-year-olds.

Europe Through the Back Door, *109 4th Av N, Box C-20009, Edmonds, WA 98020, t (425) 771 8303, f 771 0833, w www.ricksteves.com.* Fully guided and more independent bus tours.

Jet Vacations, *880 Apollo St, Suite 243, El Segundo, CA 90245, t 800 JET 0999, f (310) 640 1700, w www.jetvacations.com.* Independent travel packages and customized group packages.

Kesher Tours, *347 Fifth Av, Ste 706, New York, NY 10016, t (212) 481 3721, f 481 4212, w www. keshertours.com.* Fully escorted kosher tours.

Worldwide Classroom, *PO Box 1166, Milwaukee, WI 53201, t (414) 251 6311, f 800 276 8712, w www.worldwide.edu.* Database listing worldwide educational organizations.

ENTRY FORMALITIES

Passports and Visas

Citizens of the UK and other EU countries just need a valid passport (with at least three months' validity after your planned return) for stays of up to 90 days. Americans, Canadians, Australians and New Zealanders also just need valid passports, and no visa. Strictly speaking you are supposed to be able to produce your passport or identity card at any time, so keep it with you.

Customs

Since July 1999, duty-free goods have been unavailable on journeys within the European Union, but this does not necessarily mean that prices have gone up, as shops at ports, airports and the Channel Tunnel do not always choose to pass on the cost of the duty. It does mean that there is no limit on how much you can buy, as long as it is for your own use. Guidelines are issued (e.g. 10 litres of spirits, 800 cigarettes, 90 litres of wine, 110 litres of beer) and, if they are exceeded, you may be asked to prove that it is all for your own use.

Non-EU citizens flying from an EU country to a non-EU country (e.g. flying home from Belgium) can still buy duty-free. Americans can take home 1 litre of alcohol, 200 cigarettes and 100 cigars, etc. Canadians can take home 200 cigarettes and 1.5 litres of wine or 1.14 litres of spirits or 8.5 litres of beer.

ARRIVAL

Zaventem Airport

Most visitors travelling by air will arrive at Belgium's main international airport, Brussels Zaventem. Zaventem Airport is 14km from Brussels' city centre. From the airport, visitors can travel on to Bruges by train, bus, hire-car or taxi.

The airport is divided into five levels, with shops, bars, restaurants and a viewing gallery on level 4; departures on level 3; arrivals on level 2; buses and taxis on level 0; and trains on level –1. You can pick up a detailed plan of the airport at the main information point beside the escalators on level 2 (arrivals). Also in the arrivals hall is a bureau de change, a bank, a post office (*open Mon–Fri 8am–7pm and Sat 8.30am–1.30pm*) and a tourist information point. Flight information and transport details are listed on the airport Web site, **w** *www.brusselsairport.be.*

Transport to and from Brussels Airport

Trains for Bruges leave from Brussels Gare Centrale/Centraal Station and Gare du Midi/Zuid Station in the city centre.

Taxis from Zaventem Airport to Brussels city centre cost around €25, but taxis with an orange and white aeroplane sticker in the top right-hand corner of their windscreens offer special reduced rates, usually 25% off.

It's far cheaper to travel by train. Special train services (**t** *(02) 753 4221*) leave the airport three times an hour from around 4.45am to 11.40pm, and connect with the Gare Centrale/Centraal Station. The journey takes 20 minutes. A second class ticket costs €2.25.

Arriving by Sea

Ostend is about 20 minutes' drive from Bruges. For foot passengers there are also local rail services to Bruges from Ostend Station, which is located close to the Hoverspeed terminal; it is a 13-minute journey to Bruges, with three trains per hour, costing €2.85 single. For passengers arriving at Zeebrugge from Hull with P&O North Sea Ferries there is a connecting service by coach to Bruges's main railway station (*see* below), costing £2 (UK) each way.

Arriving by Train

Trains arrive in Bruges at Stationsplein (B–C9), about 1.5km from the city centre. There are connecting buses to the centre of town (€1), plus a taxi rank. The ticket offices are usually open from 5am to 10.50pm, and the station offers a left-luggage office, buffet and restaurant, and a tourist information office (*open Mon–Sat 10am–6pm*). For arrival by Eurostar (via Brussels), *see* p.50.

GETTING AROUND

Maps

The maps in this book will provide all the detail that you need for this small and compact city. Other single-sheet maps are available free in hotels, or found in the tourist office brochures; the Bruges tourist office has also posted one on its internet site (*see* p.66). For a wider view, the Michelin road maps are reliable and fairly comprehensive. No.409 covers the whole of Belgium; No.213 covers northern Belgium in more detail.

On Foot

Almost everything in Bruges takes place within the oval ring of canals that traces the path of the old city walls. This is no more than 3km across, so it takes no longer than 40 minutes or so to cross the entire city on foot. Walking is the best way to get around, and because of the low volume of traffic it's pleasant and pretty safe.

Two words of warning, though. You will find pedestrian crossings painted across the road, but do not assume drivers will stop at them, though they are obliged to by law. Given enough distance, they will probably reluctantly give way once you are on the crossing. Also: bicycles are permitted to go up one-way streets the wrong way.

Many of the city streets are paved in cobbles – nice to look at, but hard on the feet after a while. Bring a stout pair of walking shoes, with thick soles.

By Bus

Bruges has its own public bus service, called De Lijn, which links the centre with outlying districts. The main bus stops are at the railway station (B–C9), and in the centre at the Markt (D5), Wollestraat (D5–E6) and the Biekorf (City Library; D5) on Kuipersstraat. Information about the services is available from the kiosk outside the railway station, and from the Tourist Information Office (*see* p.65; E5). Tickets cost around €1, and a one-day pass (for unlimited travel on city buses) is available for €2.85. Alternatively, for €5.70 you can buy a *Stadskaart*, valid for 10 journeys.

By Taxi

Taxis are available from stands at the railway station (*t (050) 38 46 60*; B–C9) and at the Markt (*t (050) 33 44 44*; D5). These are ordinary saloon cars with 'Taxi' written on the top. They cannot be hailed from the street. Fares are expensive: about €1 per kilometre within the city, twice this outside the city limits, plus add-ons – but you can be fairly sure the price quoted is honest. It is normal to add 10–15 per cent as a tip, or round up to the nearest €1.

By Car

Bruges is a small city, and highly conscious of its limited capacity for traffic. The authorities have therefore acted to restrict traffic within the city limits. It makes sense: this is a very walkable city, and few people actually need a car to get around within it. Parking in the centre is therefore at a premium. If you are planning to stay in a hotel near the centre, ask whether the hotel has its own parking, or what parking arrangements it can offer.

There are a few small public car parks near the centre. These are well signposted from outside the city (*vrij* means spaces available), but they can be awkward to reach because of the one-way system, tend to fill up early in the day (especially in summer), and are pricey (about €15 per day). Alternatively, there are several very large car parks to the south and west of the city which are less expensive. The nearest to the centre is the underground car park at 't Zand (around €9 per day); there is another at the railway station (€0.50 per hour, €2.50 per day), and another near Katelijnepoort. If you are on a day visit, the best advice is to head straight for one of these outlying car parks, and walk into the centre (no more than 20 minutes). To

encourage you more, the car park at the railway station offers a free use of the public (De Lijn) bus service into town.

Parking meters (for example, on Steenstraat) are for limited duration of up to three hours only. There are also 'Blue Zones', where drivers can park for free for the duration indicated, if they display a parking disc (obtainable from service stations). Both these parking facilities can be used free and for unlimited hours overnight (*7pm to 9am*) and on Sundays.

By Bicycle

Because of Bruges's restrictive traffic policies it is a pleasant place to cycle around. Bruges's railway station (baggage hall) offers bicycles for hire under the 'Trein + Fiets' scheme (*t (050) 30 23 29*), and there are other bike-hire shops in the centre, such as 't Koffieboontje (*4 Hallestraat, beside the Belfort tower, t (050) 33 80 27*; D5); and Eric Popelier (*26 Mariastraat, south of Sint-Salvatorskathedraal, t (050) 34 32 62*; D7). Prices range from about €4 to €8.50 per day, or €1.80 per hour. Some hotels even provide bicycles. You will be provided with a bicycle lock. Use it! Bicycles tend to walk in Bruges.

Note that bicycles are permitted to travel in both directions on one-way streets, but you are not allowed to ride through pedestrianized areas. The tourist office (*see* p.65) publishes a useful leaflet (with route map) called '5 x by bike around Bruges' (i.e. five times around Bruges by bike).

Quasimodo (*7 Leenhofweg, 8310 Brugge 3, t (050) 37 04 70, f 37 49 60, w www.quasimodo.be, e info@quasimodo.be*), a sympathetic local tour company run by Lode and Sandi Notredame, offers a daily bicycle tour with English commentary called 'Bruges by Bike', covering 8km and some of Bruges's less-visited backwaters. Tours depart from the Burg (D–E5; *mid Mar–Sept 10am, be there by 9.50am; €16.20 per adult, €12.40 for anyone under 26*). The price includes cycles and wet-weather gear. Helmets and baby-seats also available. Reservation essential.

Boat

...he canals offers a picturesque introduction to Bruges – but is madly popular and attracts long queues in summer. The tours, with commentaries in English and a handful of other languages, tend to follow the same circuit of the central canals. All the starting points are along the canal to the south of the Burg, mainly close to Blinde Ezelstraat and the Vismarkt (E5). Trips last approximately 30 minutes (*March–15 Nov daily 10am–6pm, 15 Nov–Dec and Feb weekends, school and public hols only; €5.20 for adults, €2.60 for children 4–11*).

On damp days take an umbrella, even if it is not actually raining: the bridges drip copiously. Also, take some small change to tip the boatman as you get off. For canal trips to Damme, *see p.126.*

By Horse-drawn Carriage

Trundling over the cobbles in a horse-drawn carriage seems an appropriate way to view this pre-automobile city. The carriages leave from the Markt (D5; *March–Nov 10am–6pm; €27.50 per carriage for 30 minutes, €13.50 per 15 minutes extra*). They carry up to four passengers and tend to ply a short circuit between the Markt and the Begijnhof in the south of the city.

There is also a folksy 'horse tram' (*peerdentram*), which makes a 45-minute journey across the southwest of the city, from its starting point on 't Zand square (B6) to the Minnewater lake (D8) (*all year from 10am; €5 for adults, €2.50 for children 4–11*).

Guided Tours

In July and August the tourist office (*see p.65*) organizes daily guided tours, leaving from their headquarters in the Burg (E5) at 3pm (*€3.75 per head, children under 14 free*); reserve your place in advance. The tour lasts about two hours.

English-speaking guides can also be hired through the tourist office, for individuals and groups (*maximum 25 people; €40 per guide for two hours, €20 for each extra hour*). You can also apply direct:

Gidsenbond, *t (050) 33 22 33, f 33 50 00, e info@bruges-guides.com, w www.bruges-guides.com.*

Gidsenkring, *t (050) 34 65 45, f 34 53 95, e info@gidsenkringbrugge.com, w www.gidsenkringbrugge.com.*

Thematic tours offered by these guides include Hanseatic Bruges, the ramparts, the almshouses, literary Bruges and a 'women's walk'.

The **Sightseeing Line** runs a 50-minute 'CityTour' by minibus, passing the main sights, with a well-prepared recorded commentary through headphones in a choice of seven languages. The buses run throughout the year, leaving from the Markt (D5; *on the hour from 10am; last bus Dec–Feb at 4pm, March–June and Oct–Nov 6pm, July–Sept 7pm; €9.50 for adults, €6.25 for children 6–12*). The tours are professional and user-friendly, and not a bad option if your time is limited, or the weather is inclement, or you just can't face walking any further.

Sightseeing tours are also offered by **Quasimodo** (*7 Leenhofweg, 8310 Brugge 3, t (050) 37 04 70, f 37 49 60, e info@quasimodo.be, w www.quasimodo.be*), including organized bicycle trips to Damme, and informative and relaxed mini-bus day-trips beyond Bruges. One called 'Triple Treat' takes chocolates, waffles and beer as its main themes and visits medieval castles and Damme. The other, the 'Battlefields Tour', visits the First World War trenches around Ypres: sympathetically done and highly recommended. Price €37.50, under-26s €30; includes picnic lunch.

Practical A–Z

02

Climate

Belgium has a similar weather pattern to the UK – that is to say there are glorious summers of endless sunshine, and there are summers when it never ceases to rain. The average temperature in Brussels is 16°C in summer and 3°C in winter. In winter, however, temperatures can be noticeably colder than in Britain, sometimes dropping to –20°C if the wind is blowing from the Baltic; and the entire north of the country can be shrouded in an eerie cold fog for days.

The best weather occurs between April and October, with midsummer temperatures sometimes in the 30s. The warmer the season, the busier and more crowded Bruges becomes, especially during school holidays. But all the seasons have their merits – even winter – and, as any Belgian knows, in filthy weather, you can always retreat to a restaurant and eat well. Clear, ice-cold winter days can be invigorating; the low-pitched sunlight gilds the old stonework, while lakes and canals may be thronged with skaters and sprawling children, like a scene from Bruegel. In December Bruges's central square, the Markt, hosts a merry Christmas market serving hot spiced wine around an improvised outdoor skating rink. In spring daffodils carpet the open spaces in the Begijnhof, a famously beautiful sight.

Average daily temperatures (°C)

Jan	April	July	Oct
1	11	19	12

Average rainfall (mm)

Jan	April	July	Oct
66	60	95	83

Crime and the Police

Central Police Station: *7 Hauwerstraat (B7), t (050) 44 88 44.*

You are unlikely to encounter crime in Bruges. This is the kind of city where you can walk safely day and night. But there are always the exceptions – pickpockets, opportunists, vandals, drunks, tourists. Don't drop your guard.

If you are the victim of crime, go straight to the police (*politie*). Most officers speak English, and you can expect a sympathetic hearing. Remember that you have to report theft to the police within 24 hours of discovery in order to claim insurance. Note also that you are obliged to carry your passport or another form of identity at all times, and this is the first thing the police will ask to see. (They can check it, but they are not allowed to take it away from you.) If you are arrested for any reason, you have the right to insist that your consul is informed (*see* 'Embassies and Consulates'). Proper legal representation can then be arranged.

Disabled Travellers

Bruges is never going to be an easy city for the disabled – all those cobbled streets, steps and staircases, and narrow pavements. But the tourist office (*see* p.65) is making significant efforts to accommodate people of restricted mobility where it can; it also supplies a special guide for the disabled that all the Flemish provinces are obliged to publish. Furthermore, the Belgians generally show greater respect, sympathy and patience towards the disabled than many of their European counterparts, and their welcome, and offers of assistance where required, may help to compensate for the absence of lifts and ramps in museums, restaurants and public offices.

In our **museum** entries throughout this book, we use the term 'wheelchair accessible' for those places that are officially accessible for disabled travellers. Note that most museums are only partially accessible: bathrooms and cafeterias are often located in inconvenient spots, so calling ahead is the safest bet. In our 'Eating Out' chapter we list those **restaurants** with wheelchair access and/or equipped with a wheelchair-accessible toilet, though they are few and far between. In the 'Where to Stay' and

'Entertainment' chapters, whenever possible we also list those hotels, cinemas, theatres, etc., that are wholly or partly accessible – but, as before, call ahead.

For the Brugge 2002 celebrations, the city has published an *Accessibility Guide* (*Toegankelijkheidsgids Brugge 2002*), price €5, listing public buildings, hotels, restaurants and shops that are accessible to the disabled, with a mini-edition in English (and also in Dutch, French, German and Spanish), price €2. These should be available from the Bruges tourist office. The mini-editions are also available on the internet at **w** *www.accessiblebruges.be*.

Organizations in Belgium

Croix Rouge de Belgique (Belgian Red Cross), *98 Chaussée de Vleurgat (l12)*, **t** *(02) 645 4411*. General advice about facilities, loan of wheelchairs and other equipment. For emergencies call **t** 105.

International Organizations

Accessible Europe, *Promotur-Mondo Possibile, Piazza Pitagora 9, 10137 Turin*, **t** + *39 (0) 11 309 6363*, **f** *309 1201*, **w** *www.accessible europe.com*. Network of specialist European travel agencies, providing detailed information on major sights and transport, as well as organizing assistance for disabled travellers.

Mobility International, **w** *www.mobility-international.org*. This organization produces country guides that cover access and facilities for transport, accommodation, tourist attractions and sights, as well as information on personal assistance schemes and key travel contacts.

Organizations in the UK and Ireland

Holiday Care Service, *2nd Floor, Imperial Buildings, Victoria Rd, Horley, Surrey RH6 9HW*, **t** *(01293) 774535*, **f** *771500*, **w** *www. holidaycare.org.uk*. Up-to-date information on destinations, transport and suitable tour operators.

Web Sites for Disabled Travellers

w *www.accesstourism.com*: information on hotels and specialist tour operators.

w *www.sasquatch.com/able-info*: travel tips for disabled travellers.

w *www.emerginghorizons.com*: travel newsletter for disabled people.

w *www.geocities.com*: network with information and links on travel guides for disabled travellers.

Irish Wheelchair Association, *Blackheath Drive, Clontarf, Dublin 3*, **t** *(01) 833 8241*, **w** *www.iwa.ie*. They publish a range of guides with advice for disabled holiday-makers.

RADAR (Royal Association for Disability and Rehabilitation), *Unit 12, City Forum, 250 City Rd, London EC1V 8AF*, **t** *(020) 7250 3222*, **f** *7250 0212*, **w** *www.radar.org.uk*. Publishes several books with information on everything travellers with disabilities need to know.

Royal National Institute for the Blind, *105 Judd St, London WC1H 9NE*, **t** *(020) 7388 1266*. Its mobility unit offers a 'Plane Easy' audio cassette which advises blind people on travelling by plane. They also advise on accommodation.

Tripscope, *Alexandra House, Albany Rd, Brentford, Middx TW8 0NE*, **t** *08457 585641*, **f** *(020) 8580 7022*, **w** *www.justmobility.co.uk/ tripscope*. Practical advice and information on travel and transport for elderly and disabled travellers. Information can be provided by letter or tape.

Organizations in the USA

American Foundation for the Blind, *15 West 16th St, New York, NY 10011*, **t** *(212) 620 2000*, **toll free t** *800 232 5463*. The best source for information in the USA for visually impaired travellers.

Federation of the Handicapped, *211 West 14th Street, New York, NY 10011*, **t** *(212) 747 4262*. Organizes summer tours for members; there is a nominal annual fee.

Mobility International USA, *PO Box 3551, Eugene, OR 97403, t (503) 343 1248*. Offers a service similar to that of its sister organization in the UK.

SATH (Society for the Advancement of Travel for the Handicapped), *Suite 610, 347 5th Ave, New York, NY 10016, t (212) 447 7284, w www.sath.org.*

Travel Information Center, *Moss Rehab. Hospital, 1200 West Tabor Rd, Philadelphia, PA 19141, t (215) 456 9600.*

Electricity, Weights and Measures

The **current** is 220 volts, 50 hertz. Standard British equipment requiring 240 volts will operate satisfactorily on this current. **Plugs** are the standard European two-pin type. Adaptors are available locally, but it is easier to buy a multi-purpose travelling adaptor before you leave home. Visitors from the US will need a voltage converter in order to use their electrical appliances.

Belgium uses the **metric** system and continental clothing sizes. Below are some conversion factors for the most common metric units. For clothing and shoe sizes it is best simply to ask in the shop and get an assistant to measure you.

1 centimetre (cm)	= 0.39 inches (in)
1 metre (m)	= 3.25 feet (ft)
1 kilometre (km)	= 0.621 miles
1 hectare (ha)	= 2.47 acres
1 litre (l)	= 1.76 UK pints or 2.11 US pints
100 grams (g)	= 3.20 ounces (oz)
1 kilogram (kg)	= 2.2 pounds (lb)
1in	= 2.54cm
1ft	= 30.5cm
1 mile	= 1.61km
1 acre	= 0.4ha
1 UK pint	= 0.57 litre
1 UK gallon	= 4.55 litre
1 US pint	= 0.47 litre
1 US gallon	= 3.78 litre
1oz	= 28.3g
1lb	= 0.45kg

Embassies and Consulates

In Brussels

Canada: *2 Av de Tervuren, 1040, t (02) 741 0611.*
Ireland: *89 Rue Froissart, 1040, t (02) 230 5337.*
UK: *85 Rue Arlon, 1040, t (02) 287 6211.*
USA: *27 Bvd du Régent, 1000, t (02) 508 2111.*

Belgian Embassies Abroad

Canada: *4th Floor, 80 Elgin St, Ottawa, Ontario K1P 1B7, t (613) 236 7267.*
Ireland: *2 Shrewsbury Rd, Ballsbridge, Dublin 4, t (01) 269 2082.*
UK: *103–105 Eaton Sq, London SW1W 9AB, t (020) 7470 3700.*
USA: *330 Garfield St, Washington DC 20008, t (202) 333 6900.*

Health, Emergencies and Insurance

Emergencies

Ambulance/fire/rescue: *t 100.*
Police: *t 101.*
Red Cross Ambulance: *t (050) 32 07 27.*
Anti-poisoning centre: *t (070) 245 245.*
There should always be at least one English-speaking operator on duty for emergency calls.

Doctors on night call during the week: *t (050) 51 63 76.*
Doctors on call at weekends (Fri 8pm–Mon 8am): *t (050) 81 38 99.*

Hospitals

AZ Sint-Jan, *10 Rudderhove, t (050) 45 21 11.*
AZ Sint-Lucas, *29 Sint-Lucaslaan, t (050) 36 91 11.*
Sint-Franciscus Xavieruiskliniek, *t (050) 47 04 70.*

Health

Belgium has an excellent **medical service**, with first-class modern hospitals and well-trained staff. Under the Reciprocal Health Arrangements, visitors from EU countries are entitled to the same standard of treatment in an emergency as Belgian nationals. To qualify, you should travel with the E111 form; application forms are available from post offices in the UK. With an E111 you can claim back about 75 per cent of the cost at the local Belgian sickness office; it is advisable, therefore, to take out personal health insurance as well, which permits you to claim the entire cost on your policy. Note that you will be expected to pay for all medicine and treatment in the first instance, the cost of which can be claimed back later, provided that you have the correct documentation; ensure that you have a receipt (*Getuigschrift voor verstrekte hulp*).

Hotels have a list of **doctors** and **dentists** to whom their guests can apply, but a trip to a pharmacy may be sufficient for minor complaints. Pharmacists have a good knowledge of basic medicine and are able to diagnose: if in doubt, they will recommend that you visit a doctor, and can provide you with details. A list of 24-hour duty **pharmacies** is posted on every pharmacy door, together with a list of doctors on call.

Insurance

All travellers are strongly advised to take out insurance as soon as they book their tickets. Insurance packages for European travel are not expensive compared with the total cost of a holiday, or the cost of replacing stolen goods or paying any medical bills yourself. Standard packages include insurance to cover all unrefundable costs should you have to cancel, compensation for travel delays, lost baggage, theft, third-party liabilities and medical cover.

Internet

There are two main cybercafés in Bruges, both fairly central, and good.

The Coffee Link, *Oud Sint-Jan Congress Centre, Mariastraat 38 (D7)*, **t** *(050) 34 99 73*, **w** *www.thecoffeelink.com*. **Open** *10am–9.30pm daily.* Located in the same complex as the Memlingmuseum, this is a very stylish

Useful Web Sites

These official and unofficial tourist sites provide a good starting point for your holiday research:

w *www.brugge.be (official tourist office Web site)*

w *www.brugge.com (unofficial site)*

w *www.brugge2002.be (Web site covering the Bruges 2002 celebrations)*

w *www.brusselstourism.com (Brussels Web site)*

w *www.bruxelles.irisnet.be (Brussels tourist-board Web site)*

w *www.cybercafes.com (for listings around the world)*

w *www.flandersholidaystore.com (for online hotel and travel reservations)*

w *www.frites.be (French-language Webzine for everything Belgian, particularly chips!)*

w *www.opt.be (Wallonie/Brussel tourist-board site)*

w *www.visitantwerpen.be (Antwerp tourist-board site)*

w *www.visitbelgium.com (for Belgian Web links of all kinds)*

w *www.visitflanders.com (Flanders tourist-board site)*

w *www.webwatch.be (for links with a wide variety of Belgian sites)*

cybercafé, mixing old and new to stunning effect. The café prides itself on its coffee, plus 18 computers and print facilities. Initial access charge of €1.24 for 15 mins, thereafter €0.07 per minute.

Bauhaus DNA Cybercafé, *Langestraat 145 (G4)*, **w** *www.bauhaus.be*, **t** *(050) 34 10 93*. **Open** *Mon–Fri and Sun 9am–noon and 5–9pm, Sat 9am–9pm.* Part of the Bauhaus youth hostel complex, a modern white room with 15 screens and printing facilities. Flat rate of €0.07 per minute; 10 per cent reduction for youth hostel card holders.

Media

The main Dutch-language newspapers in Belgium are *Het Laatste Nieuws*, *De Standaard* and *De Morgen*. But since you are reading this guidebook, the chances are you will not be a Dutch speaker. Rest assured: Bruges is well supplied with **English-language newspapers**, such as the British broadsheets and the *International Herald Tribune*, sold at newsstands.

The local free 'what's on' paper is called *Exit* (available in the tourist offices and in many hotels and restaurants). It's in Dutch but, even if you know no Dutch, it doesn't require too much lateral thinking to get the gist of it. The tourist office also publishes its own free events calendar called **w** *events@brugge*.

Most hotels have **cable television** with a full range of channels piped in from the UK and the USA. In fact, you might find a rather depressing familiarity in the fare on offer.

Almost all **films** shown in cinemas in Flanders are in the original language, with subtitles, and not dubbed.

Money, Banks and Taxes

On 1 January 1999, the euro (€) became the official currency of Belgium (at the rate of 40.34 BF to the euro) and Belgian franc notes and centimes became obsolete on 28 February 2002, although they will be exchangeable at banks for several years.

The **euro** is now the currency of 12 countries in the European Union: Austria, Belgium, Finland, France, Germany, Greece, Italy, Luxembourg, Netherlands, Portugal, Republic of Ireland and Spain. The euro is divided into 100 cents. Coins are produced in the following denominations: 1, 2, 5, 10, 20 and 50 cents, 1 and two euros. Banknotes are issued as 5, 10, 20, 50, 100, 200 and 500 euros. The banknotes are uniform in design across the eurozone, but participating countries have been allowed to mint coins with their own national designs on one side; these are, however, valid throughout the eurozone.

Changing Money

You will find no shortage of banks offering exchange facilities in the city centre. **Banking hours** are not absolutely rigid but are usually Mon–Fri 9.30am–noon and 2–4pm, although some larger branches do not close over lunch. The Bank Brussel Lambert, at Markt 18, is also open Sat 9am–noon. **Exchange bureaux** (labelled *Wissel*) have extended opening hours, including weekends; their rates of exchange and commission charges vary, but may compare favourably with banks for traveller's cheques and currency notes.

The tourist office in the Burg (E5; *see* p.65) also has an exchange desk, open 9.30am–6.30pm, which advertises itself as 'the best exchange office in town', and probably is under some obligation to maintain this claim.

Traveller's Cheques

Traveller's cheques, especially in euros, are widely accepted not only for exchange, but also in lieu of cash.

Credit Cards

Visa, MasterCard/Eurocard, Cirrus and Switch cards can be used to draw cash from banks, but usually only through automatic cash dispensers, which means you must come armed with your PIN code. Visa, MasterCard/Eurocard, Diners Club, American Express and a handful of other leading cards are all widely accepted in shops, restaurants, hotels and petrol stations, but you should always check this first: you are sure to find the occasional surprising exceptions.

Taxes

All shop prices include **Value Added Tax** (TVA/BWT) where applicable. At the time of writing this stands at 21 per cent. Non-EU visitors may claim a refund on purchases in excess of €175 made in any one shop. This is a fairly complex procedure, most effectively

---

Lost or Stolen Credit Cards

Amex, *100 Vorstin, Brussels,* **t** *(02) 676 2121 (lost cards:* **t** *(02) 676 2323 or* **t** *(02) 676 2121).*

Diners Club, *1 Bvd du Roi Albert II, Brussels,* **t** *(02) 206 9511 (lost cards:* **t** *(02) 206 9800).*

Mastercard/Eurocard/Visa, *159 Bvd Emile Jacqmain, Brussels,* **t** *(02) 205 8585 (lost cards:* **t** *(070) 34 4344).*

dealt with if you are departing from Brussels international airport (Zaventem).

When making your purchase, ask the shop for a form called a 'Tax-free Shopping Chèque'. At the airport, have it stamped by Customs (who may wish to inspect the goods), then take it to the refund office in the departure hall.

Refunds are also available at the Interchange offices in central Brussels (88 Rue du Marché aux Herbes) and in Antwerp (36 Suikerrui). If you prefer, you can apply for a refund by post through Interchange. Further information is available at any major shop or tourist office, or from Global Refund (*Bvd Emile Bockstaellaan 93A, B-1020 Brussels*, *t* (02) 479 94 61, *f* (02) 478 36 64, *w* www.globalrefund.com).

Opening Hours

The standard opening hours for **shops** are 9am–6pm, but many bakeries, small shops and tobacconists open at 7.30am. Shops that close for lunch usually remain open until 7 or 8pm. On Sundays, supermarkets and high-street shops are closed but pâtisseries and other specialist food shops open in the morning to cater for the tradition of Sunday lunchtime indulgence. In the summer many tourist-oriented shops in Bruges are open on Sunday. For bank opening hours see 'Money, Banks and Taxes' above; for post offices see 'Post and Fax' below.

The public **museums and galleries** are open over the weekend; watch out for Tuesdays in winter (1 Oct–31 March), which is the day of closure for several museums and churches, including the Groeningemuseum. The churches have frustratingly idiosyncratic opening hours, particularly in winter.

Packing

In winter, keep warm by wearing several layers, which can be judiciously removed according to conditions – in winter, Belgian homes, hotels and restaurants can be heated to hothouse temperatures.

Public Holidays

Belgium has a generous number of public holidays. On these days all banks and post offices are closed, as are many shops, bars and cafés. When a public holiday falls on a Sunday, the following Monday is often taken as a public holiday in lieu.

1 Jan	New Year's Day (*Nieuwjaar*)
Mar/Apr	Easter Monday (*Pasen*)
1 May	Labour Day (*Feest van de Arbeid*)
6th Thurs after Easter	Ascension Day (*Hemelvaart*)
7th Mon after Easter	Whit Monday (*Pinksteren*)
21 July	Independence Day (*Nationale Feestdag*)
15 Aug	Assumption (*Maria Hemelvaart*)
1 Nov	All Saints' Day (*Allerheiligen*)
11 Nov	Armistice Day (*Wapenstilstand*)
25 Dec	Christmas Day (*Kerstmis*)

Public offices and institutions are also closed on 15 November (Dynasty Day) and 26 December (Boxing Day), and on 11 July, the Festival of the Flemish Community, called Gulden Sporenslag (recalling the Battle of the Golden Spurs, *see* p.23).

Three further tips: remember to pack some sturdy, sensible and stout-soled shoes for walking. Take a small umbrella to fend off uncertain weather (although cheap umbrellas are widely available, e.g. in the shops in Steenstraat). Lastly, more surprisingly perhaps, take some mosquito repellent if you are staying in Bruges in the summer months (May onwards): the canals provide a favourable habitat for mosquitoes.

The dress code in Belgium is fairly relaxed. Generally people dress casually, but with attention to detail. Belgians appreciate elegance, but take a dim view of pretension or impracticality.

Photography

Camera film of all kinds is widely available in Bruges – even newsagents sell it. There are a number of places where you can get film professionally developed, at a reasonable price and in less than 24 hours. There is a one-hour printing service at:

Print Point, *Philipstockstraat 4 (D5)*, *t (050) 33 42 30*. **Open** *Mon–Sat 9am–6pm.*

Photography is permitted in most of the museums – even the Groeningemuseum – provided that you do not use flash or a tripod. Exceptions include the Arentshuis, Onze-Lieve-Vrouw ter Potterie, and the Bruges Diamond Museum. Professional photographers requiring special access should consult the museum administration.

City Museum Direction, *Dijver 12 (D6)*, *8000 Brugge*, *t (050) 44 87 11*, *f 44 87 78*, *e musea@brugge.be.*

Post and Fax

The **main post office** is on the western side of the Markt, close to the Belfort (*5 Markt, t (050) 33 14 11; open 9am–5pm; D5*). It is possible to pick up **poste restante** here, and this post office has **fax** facilities. Otherwise, for faxes, it is best to use your hotel, or ask your hotel reception for the nearest bureau.

Stamps are also available from tobacconists and shops selling postcards; however, for reliable information about the cost of postage, it is best to ask at a post office.

Smoking

In Belgium, smoking is not permitted in confined public places, such as on public transport and in municipal buildings. But generally smoking is widely tolerated, and cigarettes are not heavily taxed, so comparatively cheap (about €3.70 a packet). In fact, it is the non-smokers who are more likely to complain: smokers feel at liberty to light up cigarettes, cigars and pipes in restaurants and cafés, often to the discomfort of fellow customers nearby. Only a few restaurants have non-smoking sections.

Students

Bruges has one university-level institution, the Europa College, but this is a specialist school for high-flying post-graduates – not your average campus. Students in search of fellow travellers would be best advised to visit the youth hostels/hotels (*see* p.168) and their restaurants, notably the Bauhaus (G4; *see* p.177) and Charlie Rockets (E5; *see* p.181).

Telephones

Telephoning in Belgium presents few problems. If you are staying in a hotel, the switchboard can connect your call, but this is usually far more expensive than using a public telephone. These take coins, but if you intend to make a lot of calls a '**Telecard**' is a good investment. Telecards are available from tobacconists, newsagents, post offices and public transport ticket offices and cost either €5 for 20 units or €25 for 105 units. They can be used in any public telephone bearing the Telecard sign; telephone boxes showing a row of foreign flags on the window can be used for international calls. The illustrated instructions in telephone boxes are easy enough to follow, and a liquid-crystal display tells you how many units you have left on your card.

In Belgium, **area codes** are now an integral part of every telephone number, so for Bruges numbers you need to dial the whole number (including 050) as listed in this guide, even within Bruges itself. From abroad, the **country code** for Belgium is 32, and if you are calling Bruges you should then dial 50 instead of 050.

To make **international calls** from Belgium dial 00, then the country code, then the area code without the initial 0, then the number. The country code for the UK is 44, for Ireland 353, for the USA and Canada 1, for Australia 61 and for New Zealand 64.

Mobile phone users need to check with their own network about access and pricing.

All telephone enquiries: *t* 1207.
National directory enquiries: *t* 1307.
European directory enquiries: *t* 1304.
International directory enquiries: *t* 1324.
Reverse-charge (collect) calls: *t* 1324.

Time

Belgium is on Central European Time and is one hour ahead of Britain throughout the year. For Belgian Summer Time (two hours ahead of Greenwich Mean Time), clocks go forward one hour on the last Sunday of March, and back one hour on the last Sunday of October. This means that in midsummer, evenings are very long. In the summer Belgium is seven hours ahead of US Eastern Standard Time, ten hours ahead of California and eight hours behind Sydney.

Tipping

On the question of tipping, relax. Except in the few circumstances mentioned here, it is not generally expected. In restaurants a 16% service charge is usually included in the bill, along with 21% TVA (Value Added Tax), and so additional tipping is not expected – but if service has been noticeably good a further 5% or so would be appreciated. If you have had table service at a bar or café, it is usual to leave any small change, but this is not essential.

Service is included in hotels, so there is no need to tip porters or staff providing room service. In taxis it is usual to round up the total by 10–15%, but note that in metered taxis the tip is included in the fare. Attendants in public lavatories will expect €0.30 or so; minimum charges are posted at the entrance, and the attendant herself will usually be there to enforce it.

Toilets

Public toilets (*heren* for men, *dames* for women) are usually kept scrupulously clean by dedicated middle-aged women with their own brand of hearty chat; for this service you are obliged to pay around €0.30. In central Bruges there are toilets in the same courtyard as the tourist office in the Burg, and more in the courtyard of the Halle, beneath the Belfort (belfry) in the Markt. Most Belgians will freely make use of facilities

Useful Numbers
Ambulance/fire/rescue: *t 100*
Police: *t 101*
Police Station: *t (050) 44 88 44*
Railway station: *t (050) 38 24 06*
Telephone enquiries: *t 1207*
Tourist office: *t (050) 44 86 86*

offered by bars and cafés, but it is considered polite to act as a legitimate customer by buying a drink in passing.

Tourist Offices

In Bruges

Toerisme Brugge, *11 Burg (E5), B-8000 Bruges,* **t** *(050) 44 86 86,* **f** *44 86 00,* **e** *toerisme@brugge.be.* **Open** *April–Sept Mon–Fri 9.30am–6.30pm, Sat–Sun and holidays 10am–noon and 2–6.30pm; Oct–March Mon–Fri 9.30am–5pm, Sat–Sun 9.30am–1pm and 2–5.30pm.* The main tourist office is in an imposing building in the Burg, the centrepiece of historic Bruges. The staff can offer all kinds of advice about what to see and when, and about special activities and guided tours; they will also make hotel reservations for you. They publish a useful illustrated brochure about Bruges (complete with a simple but adequate map). But be warned: in the high season, this office becomes very busy.

Railway station *(C9),* **t** *(050) 38 80 83.* **Open** *Mon–Sat 10am–6pm.* This smaller tourist office can be handy for hotel reservations.

Ask at the tourist office about **museum passes**, which can offer useful discounts if you intend visiting all the major sites. The scope of these passes varies from year to year. Currently a *combinatieticket* (combination ticket) is available for five museums of your choosing for €15.

Abroad

Canada: *Belgian Tourist Office, PO Box 760, NDG Montréal, Quebec H4A 3S2,* **t** *(514) 484 35 94,* **f** *489 89 65,* **e** *infobelgium@video tran.ca.*

UK: *Tourism Flanders–Brussels, 31 Pepper St, London E14 9RW.* **Open** *Mon–Fri 9am–5pm. Automated telephone service,* **t** *09001 887 799 (calls cost 60p per minute),* **f** *(020) 7458 0045,* **e** *office@flanders-tourism.org.*

USA: *Belgian Tourist Office, 780 Third Av, Suite 1501, New York 10017,* **t** *(212) 758 8130,* **f** *355 7675,* **e** *info@visitbelgium.com.*

Alternatively, visit the Bruges Web site, which contains virtually the same information as the tourist office brochure: **w** *www.brugge.be*. Further information on Flanders generally can be found at the Tourism Flanders–Brussels Web site at **w** *www.toervl.be* and **w** *www.visit belgium.com.*

Central Bruges

Central Bruges

Central Bruges is perfect for a gentle wander: the streets are virtually traffic-free, while the bridges and canalside paths afford classic and ever-changing views of the spires, gables and bridges reflected in the waterways.

The centre of Bruges is the true historical heart of the city. This is where Bruges began: the Burg is the site of the original 9th-century castle, bounded by canals. Today, the city's multi-layered history can be traced from the foundation stones of its first church to the splendid neogothic renovations of the Stadhuis. The Markt, the old commercial centre, was once served by canals that brought goods directly to the doors of the city's great trading halls. The dizzying landmark of this area is the Belfort, which provides the visitor prepared to make the climb with a spectacular panorama that clearly reveals how the medieval streetplan of Bruges spreads out logically from this centre point.

1 Lunch

De Visscherie, *Vismarkt 8*, **t** *(050) 33 02 12*. **Open** *Wed–Mon noon–2pm and 7–10pm*. **Expensive**. Treat yourself at Bruges's premier fish restaurant.

2 Tea and Cakes

Het Dagelijks Brood, *Philipstockstraat 21*, **t** *(050) 33 60 50*. **Open** *Mon and Wed–Sat 7am–6pm, Sun 8am–6pm*. Delicious, rustic-style bakery for cakes and sandwiches.

3 Drinks

Bierbistro Erasmus, *Wollestraat 35*, **t** *(050) 33 57 81; wheelchair accessible*. **Open** *Tues–Sun 11am–midnight*. Small friendly bistro and bar serving countless types of Belgian beer.

Highlights

Couples' City: A horse-drawn carriage tour of the city centre, p.56

Beer: A beer at De Garre, an atmospheric old pub off Breidelstraat, p.181

Venice of the North: A walk along the quayside and picturesque bridges of the Groenerei canal, p.76

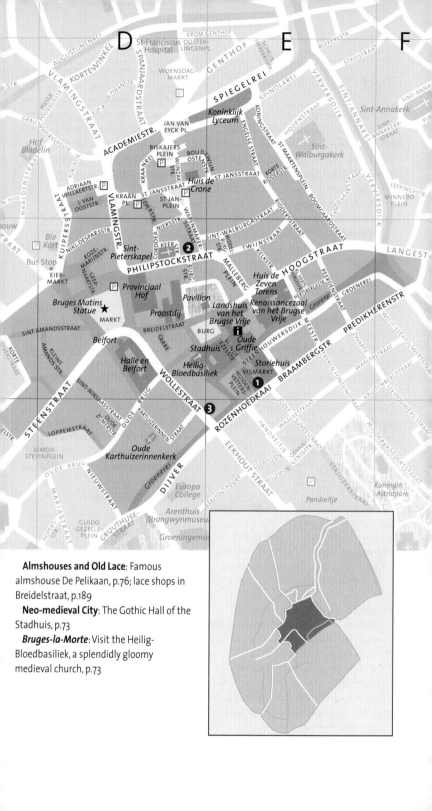

Almshouses and Old Lace: Famous
almshouse De Pelikaan, p.76; lace shops in
Breidelstraat, p.189

Neo-medieval City: The Gothic Hall of the
Stadhuis, p.73

Bruges-la-Morte: Visit the Heilig-
Bloedbasiliek, a splendidly gloomy
medieval church, p.73

THE MARKT

The old marketplace is at the very centre of the city. This was the scene of great trade fairs, of grand medieval jousts and public executions. Given this pedigree, it is architecturally somewhat disappointing and workaday, especially if compared with the gilded brilliance of some of the central squares of other Belgian towns, such as Antwerp and Brussels. The 17th-century gabled houses on its north and western flanks have been much altered, and now house banks, souvenir shops and the kinds of restaurants that offer menus in four languages. Yet, the Markt has an invigorating sense of space, underlined by the soaring tower of the Belfort.

It is still a working market square. For a thousand years it was the scene of a regular Saturday market, a tradition interrupted in 1993 when the market was shifted to 't Zand (*see* pp.111–2) in the west of the city. This was soon regretted, and the market was reinstated, but now takes place on Wednesdays (8am–1pm).

The Belfort D5

*Markt 7. **Open** April–Sept daily 9.30am–5pm (last admission 4.15pm); Oct–March daily 9.30am–12.30pm and 1.30–5pm; **adm** €5. Only 70 people are allowed at a time, so come early.*

The Belfort is by far the most impressive feature of the Markt, a gawky but endearing giant dominating the square's southern flank. It is also one the city's most prominent and striking landmarks, and provides one of its most exhilarating attractions – if you have the stamina to mount its 366 stairs.

The belfry has always been at the very heart of civic life. Over seven centuries it has served as a watchtower, a clocktower and as the symbol of Bruges's independent spirit. The city aldermen used to meet in the building below the belfry, and important announcements were proclaimed to the public from its balcony.

The tower is a remarkable hybrid building, with three main tiers rising to 83m through a series of architectural styles. The lower part dates from 1282–96, the four corner towers from 1396, and the octagonal belltower from 1482–87. There used to be an additional tiered, knobbly spire which somehow made architectural sense of what lay beneath it, but this was destroyed by lightning in 1741 and was never replaced. The result is that the tower now looks strangely top-heavy and architecturally unresolved. (The English author and wit G. K. Chesterton compared it to a giraffe.)

You have to be fit to climb the steep and narrow staircase to the top. A strongroom called the **Schatkamer** (Treasury) near the base (after 55 steps) is where the burghers of Bruges kept, under numerous locks and keys, the precious documents guaranteeing the privileges granted to them by the Counts of Flanders. Look out also for the **iron fire-trumpet**, which was used up to the 19th century as the city fire alarm.

Two-thirds of the way up the tower is the lonely looking '**Victory Bell**', with a diameter of over 2m. It was brought here from the Onze-Lieve-Vrouwekerk in 1680, and is rung only on special occasions.

The Clock Carillon

Close to the top is the splendid automatic clock carillon, installed in 1748, which rings 47 bronze bells on the quarter-hour like a giant musical box, and the room where the *beiaardier* (carillon player) has his keyboard to play the carillon bells directly.

From the summit of the tower there are unrivalled views over the waterways and rooftops of the city to the port and flat surrounding countryside. The noise from the wondrous Heath Robinson configuration of bells (weighing a total of 27 tons), wires and pulleys is all enveloping; having made it all the way to the top, it is definitely worth waiting to hear it chime at least the quarter-hour.

Bruges's *stadsbeiaardier* (town *carillon-neur*), Aimé Lombaert, follows in a long line

Carillons

The happy jingle of carillon bells has been a familiar feature of the Low Countries since the 1500s. They have won many admirers, from Peter the Great of Russia to John D. Rockefeller; they have also exerted a fascination on writers. The American poet, Henry Wadsworth Longfellow, an admirer of Bruges, wrote of the carillon in his poem *The Belfry of Bruges* (1845). Georges Rodenbach's sequel to *Bruges-la-Morte* was called *Le Carillonneur* (1897).

At their simplest, carillons consist of a set of bells, usually mounted in the town's clock tower, which play a ditty to alert the public that the hour is about to strike. The mechanism, attached to the clock, is like a giant musical box. Metal pegs, fixed to a revolving drum in a carefully planned order, trigger keys that pull wires attached to the clappers in the bells to sound out a tune. The one at the top of Bruges's Belfort is a particularly fine specimen, dating from 1748 and operating 47 bells.

Like many of the great carillons, this one can also be played manually, from a keyboard. This operates rather like a piano, but instead of triggering hammers to hit strings, the carillon keyboard pulls wires attached to the bells. It is not easy to play: a *carillonneur* (*beiaardier* in Dutch), has to undergo years of training, such as the six-year diploma course at the famous Royal Carillon School at Mechelen. It's also hard work: playing a carillon keyboard and controlling up to 40 tons of bells requires real physical strength.

Carillon-playing nearly became an extinct art in the 19th century, when it was dismissed as unsophisticated and folksy, but it was saved by the work of various practitioners who improved the responsiveness of the keyboard to provide a more controlled and expressive sound.

of respected predecessors, and has a treasured role in the community. His keyboard is in a cramped office at the top of the Belfort (prompting the quip that he is Bruges's 'highest paid official'). From here his music rings forth across the city in regular concerts throughout the year, performed to a published schedule, with increased frequency during the summer (*usually winter Sun, Wed and Sat 2.15–3pm; summer Mon, Wed and Sat 9–10pm, Sun 2.15–3pm*).

The Halle en Belfort

The Belfort rises up from a massive complex of buildings set around an austere courtyard. This is the Halle, an old covered market originally built in 1239, but added to over the next three centuries. In the 14th century this was a bustling marketplace for cloth, carpets, gloves, wooden clogs, saddles, clerical hats, exotic fruits and spices traded through Venice. There is a set of arches (1561–6) at the rear, spanning the pavement of the Oude Burg, where money-changers used to set out their stalls.

Provinciaal Hof D5

*Markt. **Closed** to the public.*

In the centre of the eastern side of the Markt is the provincial government building (Bruges is the capital of the province of West Flanders). It was built in neogothic style between 1881 and 1921 – dainty with its crocheted spires and finials, tracery balustrades, dormer windows and arches; but its neat and unweathered finish betrays it as a johnny-come-lately.

The Provinciaal Hof stands on the site of the remarkable old Waterhalle, built between 1285 and 1294, which was a central feature of Bruges's trading life. Vast and handsome with Gothic detail, it ranked as one of the 'Seven Marvels of Bruges' in the 16th century. As its name suggests, it was a covered hall over the Kraanrei canal, where cargoes of trade goods were unloaded from flat-bottomed barges.

The Kraanrei, a canalized section of the River Reie, used to run down this side of the Markt, connecting the Spiegelrei to the present set of canals to the south. By the late

18th century the crumbling Waterhalle was deemed to have outlived its function. It was pulled down between 1787 and 1789, the canal was filled in, and a large neoclassical building rose in its place – elegant, but out of keeping with medieval Bruges.

When this was destroyed by arson in 1878, the ardent neo-medievalists insisted on a new building reflecting Bruges's Gothic heritage. The Bruges-born municipal architect Louis Delacenserie (1838–1909) came up with this scheme, reflecting his own neogothic passions which he brought to bear in many restorations and rebuildings throughout the city. He is best known for the magnificent Renaissance-style railway station that he designed for Antwerp 20 years later.

Bruges Matins Statue D5

In the centre of the Markt is a statue (1887) by Paul de Vigne of the weaver Pieter de Coninck (c. 1250–1333) and the butcher Jan Breydel (c. 1264–c. 1331), leading figures of the 1301–2 Flemish rebellion against the French (*see* p.23). They helped organize the massacre of the French at the notorious Bruges Matins in 1302, which was followed by the resounding victory of the Flemish over the French at the Battle of the Golden Spurs later that year – from which time Coninck and Breydel became potent symbols of Flemish independence and pride.

Over 500 years later, these same tensions resurfaced with the débâcle surrounding the inauguration of the statue in 1887. The local Breydel Committee celebrated the completion of the statue on the anniversary of the battle, 11 July, but the city authorities had arranged for the official unveiling by King Leopold II to take place on 15 August, which happened to be the anniversary of the Battle of Pevelenberg (1304) – the battle that dealt the first serious blow to the Flemish revolt. Furthermore, Leopold and the Bruges burgomaster made their speeches entirely in French, inflaming Flemish sensitivities.

Markt Façades D5

To the west of the Markt, on the corner of Sint-Amandstraat, is the step-gabled **Craenenburg** (Markt 16), now a café (*see* p.173), with a neogothic façade dating from 1955. This was once a grand private house where Archduke Maximilian of Austria, the governor of Flanders, was held prisoner for three weeks in 1488 (*see* p.26).

The oldest genuine façade in the Markt is the **Huis Bouchotte** (opposite the Craenenburg). It dates from the late 15th century, and was restored in the 1850s. The mighty Charles V (1500–58) is said to have stayed here during his infrequent visits to the city. The dial on the façade is not a clock; marked NOZW (*noord, oost, zuid* and *west*), it is part of a weathervane erected in 1682. With its needle connected to a weathervane on the roof, it indicated the wind direction to traders – critical information in the days of the sail.

The plot on the northwest flank of the Markt used to be occupied by a church – the medieval church of St Christopher, seen in topographical prints as a prominent feature of the Markt – but it fell into disrepair, and was destroyed in 1786 as part of the Austrian programme of modernization. Many of the buildings lining the Markt to either side of this were once guild houses, the headquarters of the powerful organizations that controlled the trades: **No.28**, with the conical basket on its step-gable, was the guild house of the Tilers (1622); **No.33** was the guild house of the Free Fishmongers (1621).

THE BURG

This small square is the historic heart of the city, and was once the site of the castle around which Bruges grew. The Burg contains Bruges's most impressive and beautiful concentration of public buildings.

Heilig-Bloedbasiliek D5

Burg 10, t (050) 44 81 11. Open April–Sept daily 9.30am–noon and 2–6pm, Oct–March Thurs–Tues 10am–noon and 2–4pm, Wed 10am–noon; adm €1.25.

The atmospheric grey-stone Basilica of the Holy Blood with its ornate ogive arches is a curious double act, with two quite distinct parts, one on top of the other. It is squeezed rather awkwardly into a corner of the Burg and surmounted by a strange trio of turrets, like fancy headdresses improvized from the Venetian doge's mitre.

St Basil's Chapel

The gloomy lower church is known as St Basil's Chapel after the relic (four vertebrae) of St Basil the Great that was brought back from Caesarea in the Holy Land in 1099. The chapel (entrance through the brown door to the left of the archway, marked Basiliek, beneath the array of neo-medieval gilded statues) is effectively a kind of undercroft, a robust piece of 12th-century architecture with massive pillars of raw, rough-hewn stone rising to Romanesque arches. The tone is bleak and thoroughly medieval: you could imagine crusaders clanking around here, haunted by distant memories of Jerusalem. To the right of the choir is a wooden polychrome statue of the Virgin and Child (dating from 1300), and there is a primitive stone sculpture depicting the baptism of Christ over the arch leading back from the side aisle to the nave.

Chapel of the Holy Blood

Upstairs, reached by a splendid, broad staircase, is the Chapel of the Holy Blood, a 15th–16th-century addition, destroyed by the French in the 1790s but rebuilt, and richly decorated by the neo-medievalists in the 19th century. The relic of the Holy Blood – apparently blood washed from the body of Christ by Joseph of Arimathea – was, according to tradition, given by Baldwin III of Anjou, King of Jerusalem, to Derick of Alsace, Count of Flanders, in 1148, for his heroic deeds during the Second Crusade. In fact, it is rather more likely that the relic was acquired by Baldwin IX, Count of Flanders, when during the rapacious Fourth Crusade he was elected First Latin Emperor of Constantinople.

According to the legend, when it arrived in Bruges in 1150 the blood in its rock-crystal phial appeared to be dry, but it miraculously suddenly became liquid again, and would repeat this phenomenon every Friday. The relic of the Holy Blood became the focus of fervent devotion, and miraculous healings took place among the worshippers who assembled before it on Fridays.

This tradition is still maintained: the relic is displayed for veneration in the chapel on Fridays – but it hasn't turned liquid since 1325. The chapel is appealing in its own bespangled, multicoloured way, enhanced by the ingenious pulpit in the form of a complete globe, designed by Hendrik Pulinx and carved from a single piece of oak in around 1728.

The Schatkamer

Open as Heilig-Bloedbasiliek; adm €1.

Next to the chapel entrance upstairs is a tiny museum called the Schatkamer, or Treasure Chamber, the focus of which is an elaborate gold reliquary made by Jan Crabbe in 1617. This is used in the Heilig-Bloedprocessie, when the Holy Blood relic is paraded around the city on Ascension Day (*see* p.198). Among the precious stones decorating it is a large diamond said to have belonged to Mary Stuart. There are also two fine paintings by Pieter Pourbus (1524–84), actually the wings of a triptych, dated 1556, portraying the very sanctimonious-looking Members of the Brotherhood of the Precious Blood.

Stadhuis D–E5

Burg 12, t (050) 44 81 11; wheelchair accessible. Open daily 9.30am–5pm; adm free.

Bruges's splendid town hall dates originally from 1376–1420, making it the oldest in Belgium. It is also one of the finest, with its tall Gothic windows and pepperpot ornamental towers. The town hall was the centre of the city's administration and a symbol of Bruges's prestige, setting a new standard for flamboyant civic architecture. It was later emulated (and exceeded) by Leuven's celebrated town hall, built between 1448 and 1478.

The Stadhuis has been heavily restored over the centuries, with the result that it is part medieval, part 19th-century medieval fantasy, part modern renovation. The statues of the counts and countess of Flanders in the niches between the windows were originally medieval, but were pulled down by French Revolutionaries in 1792 and later replaced.

The Gothic Hall

Open as Stadhuis; *adm* €2.50 *(ticket also valid for the Renaissancezaal van het Brugse Vrije).*

The Gothic Hall on the upper floor still has its original vaulted wooden ceiling, dating from 1385. It has been beautifully restored, so that the decorated vault keys (illustrating scenes from the New Testament) and consoles next to the walls (illustrating the twelve months of the year and the four elements) can be seen in their full splendour. The walls have been decorated with rich and well-executed neogothic murals depicting scenes from Bruges's history, painted in 1895 by Albert and Julien Devriendt – a visually stunning monument to neo-medievalism. A neighbouring room contains a selection of prints relating to Bruges's canal system.

Oude Griffie E5

*Burg 11. **Closed** to the public.*

The Oude Griffie (Old Recorder's House) is next to the Stadhuis. It is pierced by the arched entrance to an alleyway, and surmounted by a statue of blind Justice. An ornate Renaissance building dating from 1534–7, it acted as an annexe to the law courts next door between 1883 and 1984.

Renaissancezaal van het Brugse Vrije E5

*Burg 11A. **Open** daily 9.30am–5pm; **adm** €2.50 (ticket also valid for the Gothic Hall).*

Throughout much of the medieval period, the city of Bruges was virtually an autonomous state, administered from the Stadhuis. The region surrounding it, and stretching as far west as Dunkirk, was run separately, under another authority called the *Brugse Vrije* (Bruges Liberty). Ruled by four burgomasters and 24 aldermen, it had control of its own administrative, legal and financial affairs, but was finally abolished by the French in 1795.

The aldermen of the *Brugse Vrije* used to meet in the 'Renaissance Hall', in part of the old palace of the Brugse Vrije, which now also houses the Bruges archives (there is a display of ancient manuscripts and books in the main hall).

The Charles V Chimneypiece

The hall has just one principal exhibit: its huge oak and black marble chimneypiece (1529–33), a robust and sensuous installation designed by Lancelot Blondeel (1496–c.1561) and sculpted by Guyot de Beaugrant (d. 1551). This is effectively a monument to the ruler of the day, Charles V, whose oak statue appears in the centre, flanked by his two pairs of grandparents, Maximilian of Austria and Mary of Burgundy (left; parents of his father, Philip the Handsome), and Ferdinand of Aragon and Isabella of Castile (right; parents of his mother, Joanna of Navarre).

Charles V played a critical role in the history of Flanders by defeating the French king, Francis I, at the Battle of Pavia (1526), and forcing the French to give up their feudal power over Flanders in the Treaty of Cambrai (1529). Charles's prominent codpiece in this sculpture makes it plain enough that this is a work about fertility and lineage, but most remarkable is the pristine condition of the whole chimneypiece after more than 450 years.

Note also the brass handles beneath the upper rim of the fireplace, designed so that the aldermen could lean safely over the fire to keep themselves warm on cold days. The fire basket on wheels could also be filled with embers and drawn into the room.

Landshuis van het Brugse Vrije E5

Burg 11.

The Brugse Vrije's old palace, built in 1525, occupied the entire eastern flank of the Burg. But only the original façade overlooking the canal has survived; the rest was replaced in 1722–7 by the present stolid, neoclassical building around a courtyard. After the Brugse Vrije was abolished by the French in 1795, the building became the Gerechtshof (law courts), where justice was dispensed until 1984. It now contains city administrative offices, as well as the main **tourist information office**.

Huis de Zeven Torens E5

*Hoogstraat 6. **Closed** to the public.*

It's hard to credit now, but this grimy brick frontage (next to the Landhuis van het Brugse Vrije) was once part of one of the city's most spectacular medieval residences, the House of the Seven Towers. With its seven towers rising like jousters' lances from a huge Gothic hall, four storeys high, it ranked among the 'Seven Marvels of Bruges' in the 16th century, and is now semi-derelict.

It was built in about 1300, and known as the Domus Malleana, after its owners, the powerful de Male family. (Louis de Male was the last Count of Flanders (r. 1346–84), handing over power to the Dukes of Burgundy.) The future Charles II of England stayed here during his exile (1656–8). However, the towers were demolished in 1717, and the building slid into a long decline.

North Side of the Burg

The north side of the Burg is a leafy open space. This was not part of the original plan. On this site, squaring off the Burg, was the city's central church, a mighty Romanesque hulk with a squat lantern tower, built on the site of a 9th-century chapel dedicated to the 4th-century Roman bishop of Reims, Saint Donatian. The **Sint-Donaaskerk** was a major landmark, filled with numerous treasures. Jan van Eyck was buried here in 1441, and here Charles the Good, Count of Flanders, was murdered at prayer by a nephew of the provost in 1127, the victim of bitter clan warfare. This was the trigger for a bout of vicious slaughter, after which the streets of the Burg are said to have run with blood.

It became the city's cathedral in 1559, but this heritage meant nothing to the zealous French administrators charged with running Belgium after 1795, and anxious to rid it of the symbols of the *ancien régime*. The Sint-Donaaskathedraal was duly closed, then in 1799 they sent in a team of demolition experts, well experienced in flattening redundant church property. For years this site was piled high with rubble; now all that remains of the church fabric are some foundations that were excavated during building work on the adjacent Holiday Inn Hotel (where you can still ask to see them). There is also a small stone model of the church, as it may have looked in AD 900, in the square.

Pavilion on the Burg D–E5

Adm free.

As part of Brugge 2002, the celebration of Bruges as European City of Culture, a remarkable, ultra-modern pavilion was built under the trees in this open space attached to the Burg. It was designed by the leading Japanese architect Toyo Ito (b.1941) to serve as a meeting point, shelter and resting place. The concept is admirably simple: made of glass and aluminium mesh (to permit views of the surrounding buildings), it takes the form of an open-ended, rectangular box – like a giant version of a set of staples, before

The Bourse

Bruges proudly boasts that it produced the first stock exchange in Europe. From the 12th century, merchants would buy and sell shares and credit notes in and around an inn on Vlamingstraat (on the corner of Grauwwerkersstraat; *see* p.120). The inn was owned by a family called Van Ter Beurze, hence the origin of the term by which many European stock exchanges are known: *beurs* (Dutch), *bourse* (French), *borsa* (Italian), *börse* (German), *bolsa* (Spanish). There is another theory, also plausible: the merchants called the square where they met and did business by the medieval Latin term *bursa*, meaning a purse. The innkeeper then adopted the name Van Ter Beurze, referring to the location. One of the few languages that did not adopt the term *beurs* was English. 'Exchange' was preferred, and the London Royal Exchange was first established in 1566 by Sir Thomas Gresham – who had been Queen Elizabeth's ambassador in Flanders.

being loaded into a stapler – and forms a bridge over a circular pool of water. At the time of writing, it was unclear whether the Pavilion will be preserved as a permanent feature of the Burg.

Proostdij D5

*Burg 3. **Closed** to the public.*

The Provost's House is a finely orchestrated Flemish-Baroque building dating from 1662, and crowned by blind Justice. It used to belong to the provost of the Sint-Donaaskerk. The 18th-century neoclassical building tucked away behind it served as the bishop's residence until the French occupation. It has had a curious guest list since, including Napoleon and Empress Marie Louise on a state visit in 1810; King Leopold III agonizing over the capitulation of Belgium in 1940; and the German Field Marshal Erwin Rommel, the 'Desert Fox', sent to shore up North Sea defences, prior to his enforced suicide over the bomb plot that failed to kill Hitler in July 1944.

Blinde Ezelstraat E5

The vaulted passage between the Stadhuis and the Oude Griffie is called Blind Donkey Street. There is great speculation as to how it got its name. One theory is that donkeys had to be blindfolded to negotiate the narrow alley when fully loaded; however, it is probably a reference to a nearby tavern, perhaps so-called because it sold the cheapest beer in town, with the result that its clients became as drunk as 'blind donkeys'. The street leads on to Steenhouwersdijk, one of the most picturesque parts of Bruges.

VISMARKT AND AROUND

Vismarkt E5

*Steenhouwersdijk. **Open** Tues–Sat 8am–1pm.*

At the Fishmarket, fish is still sold from stone slabs set out beneath covered colonnades. Erected in 1826, this elegant neoclassical construction and its monumental water pump are among the very few architectural mementoes from the era when Belgium was ruled by the Netherlands.

Groenerei E5

Groenerei (green canal) offers some of the most famous views of the Burg, the Belfort, and the fetchingly crooked houses that overlook the canal. The bridges here, Meebrug and Peerdenbrug, are among the oldest and prettiest in the city.

De Pelikaan E5

*Groenerei 8–12. **Closed** to the public.*

This old almshouse, called De Pelikaan, is dated 1714. The pelican is a symbol of Christian charity because females were thought to peck at their own breasts to draw blood to feed their chicks.

Huidenvettersplein E5

This charming square is named after the tanners (*huidenvetters*), whose guild house (1630) was located here at **No.10**. The **statue** in the middle of the square (1925) depicts two lions, the emblems of the guild.

Rozenhoedkaai E5–6

This quay offers one of the classic viewpoints of Bruges, with the Belfort in one direction and the Onze-Lieve-Vrouwekerk in the other. Rozenhoedkaai means 'rosary quay'. Bruges's craftsmen were famed for their deft skills in the Middle Ages, and among their best-known products were rosaries – those made from amber (from the Baltic region) and ivory (from Africa) were a speciality. This picturesque quay has caught the imagination of a number of writers and poets, including the German Rainer Maria Rilke (1875–1965), who wrote a poem called 'Quai du Rosaire'. More prosaically, until the 16th century the quay was called Zoutdijk (salt embankment), because this was where traders brought shipments of salt, mainly from Germany and France. In medieval times salt was a valuable commodity, essential for preserving meat and fish.

Nepomucenusbrug E6

The bridge at the west end of Rozenhoedkaai, leading to Wollestraat (Wool Street), bears a **statue of St John Nepomuk** (1767, erected 1811) by the Bruges-born sculptor Pieter Pepers (1730–85). St John was confessor to the queen of Bohemia and, when in 1393 he refused to pass on the contents of her confessions, King Wenceslas IV had him thrown to his death in the River Moldau from a bridge in Prague, hence his role as patron saint of bridges.

De Malvenda House D–E6

Wollestraat 53.

The ornate De Malvenda house, built in late-Gothic style in around 1500, was the house of Juan Perez Malvenda, a Spanish magistrate, who hid the relic of the Holy Blood here during the period of Protestant iconoclasm (1578–84). This is now a public building and in 2002 was appointed to serve as key centre for Brugge 2002 activities.

Hof van Watervliet D6

*Oude Burg 27. **Closed** to the public.*

This old patrician's mansion was formerly called the Hof van Sint-Joris and was owned by Jan de Baenst, a leading figure in Burgundian Bruges under Philip the Good and Charles the Bold. It then became the home of the ill-fated treasurer of Maximilian I, Pieter Lanchals, who was executed in 1488.

The Almshouses of Bruges

Almshouses (*Godshuizen*) have been an integral part of the Bruges landscape since late medieval times. They were set up and endowed by the guilds for former members and their widows, and by wealthy merchants as sheltered accommodation for the deserving poor and aged. Many still bear the name of their original sponsors. *Godshuizen* usually consist of clusters of about six similar houses, perhaps sharing a communal garden and a chapel, where residents could pray for the founder's salvation. After Bruges went into decline in the 16th century, the need became even greater, and more and more almshouses were built. By the 18th century there were some 300 almshouses in the city; 42 of them still survive.

Since the French occupation from 1795 to 1814 they have been owned and operated by the municipality, and most are still used as homes for the elderly. Their charm lies in their small scale and their cottage-like intimacy, their whitewashed walls, trim gardens and windowboxes. Being house-proud is, of course, a deeply ingrained tradition among the Belgians, but the *Godshuizen* also manage to exude a timeless air of piety, charity and gratitude.

The house later belonged to the humanist Mark Laurin, Lord of Watervliet and dean of the church of St Donatian. His home was a gathering place for some of the leading humanists of the day, including Erasmus and Thomas More, who were drawn to Bruges on special occasions, such as the State Entry (Joyeuse Entrée/Blijde Intreden) for Charles V in 1515. It's now a centre for the social and health services.

Southern Bruges

Southern Bruges

This section of the city includes a rich cluster of Bruges's greatest museums, which lie just a stone's throw away from the city centre. Greatest of all is the Groeninge-museum, with its outstanding collection of medieval art, but the Memlingmuseum, housed in a medieval hospital, runs a close second. Then the Gruuthusemuseum provides a fascinating insight into the kinds of furnishings and domestic wares that the wealthy merchants of Bruges wanted to spend their hard-earned profits on. The Arentshuis has a fine collection of antique lace, as well as a powerful exhibition of the work of the British artist Frank Brangwyn. After this dose of high culture, the beauty and calm of the Begijnhof and the Minnewater will provide a welcome change of pace, as the southern edge of the city softens gently into lawns, leafy paths and expanses of still water.

1 Lunch

Marieke van Brugghe, *Mariastraat 17, t (050) 34 33 66. Open daily 10am–10pm. Moderate.* Fun, highly professional bistro-style restaurant, serving a good selection of traditional Bruges dishes.

2 Tea and Cakes

De Proeverie, *Katelijnestraat 6, t (050) 33 08 87. Open daily 9am–6pm.* Tearoom with a fantastic range of chocolate goodies.

3 Drinks

L'Estaminet, *Gevangenisstraat 5, t (050) 33 45 91. Open Tues–Sat from 11.30am.* Pleasant, traditional old pub near the Koningin Astridpark, dating back to 1900.

Highlights

Couples' City: A walk around the Minnewater, often called the 'Lake of Love', p.90

Beer: Visit the pub and brewery De Halve Mann, where the beer called Straffe Hendrik is made, p.91

Venice of the North: The riches of the old trading city in the Groeningemuseum, p.82, and Memlingmuseum, p.88

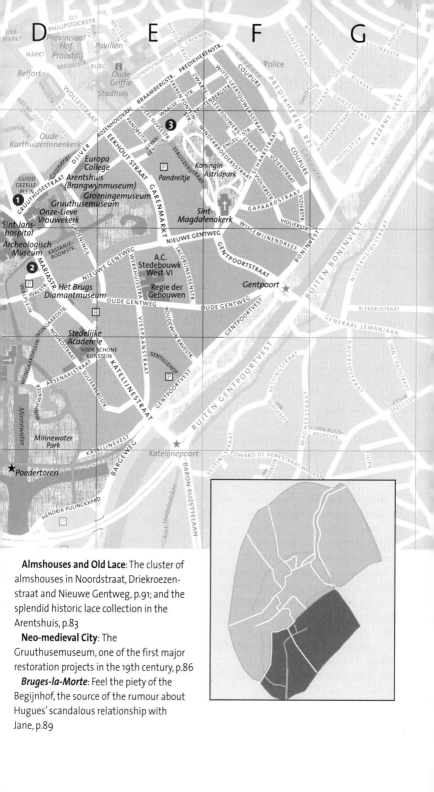

Almshouses and Old Lace: The cluster of almshouses in Noordstraat, Driekroezen-straat and Nieuwe Gentweg, p.91; and the splendid historic lace collection in the Arentshuis, p.83

Neo-medieval City: The Gruuthusemuseum, one of the first major restoration projects in the 19th century, p.86

Bruges-la-Morte: Feel the piety of the Begijnhof, the source of the rumour about Hugues' scandalous relationship with Jane, p.89

THE GROENINGE-MUSEUM AND AROUND

Groeningemuseum D–E6

*Dijver 12, t (050) 44 87 11; wheelchair accessible. **Open** Tues–Sun 9.30am–5pm; **adm** €7. (Until March 2003, the permanent collection will not be on display but will be replaced by the special Brugge 2002 exhibition called 'Jan van Eyck, Early Netherlandish Painting and Southern Europe'.)*

The treasures within the Groeningemuseum – one of Europe's most dazzling collections of medieval art – provide the best evidence of how magnificent the city was in its heyday. In fact, Bruges itself features in many of the pictures.

The museum occupies part of the extensive grounds of Eekhout Abbey, once one of Bruges's great religious institutions, until it became another victim of the French occupation – razed to the ground in 1795. The name of the museum comes from the street that flanks it to the west: Groeninge has a special significance in Flemish history as the plain near Kortrijk (Courtrai) where the Battle of the Golden Spurs was fought. Entered through an archway and a series of courtyards from Dijver, the low-rise modern building now housing this municipal museum comes as something of a surprise. The museum is actually too small to exhibit its entire collection at one time, so paintings are shown in rotation. Almost everything in it is of outstanding quality. It's a delight – provided that you can stomach the subject matter of so many of the exhibits: gruesome martyrdoms painted with loving attention to every horrific detail.

Jan van Eyck

The great star of the collection is Jan van Eyck's *Madonna with Canon van der Paele* (1436), a large work filled with stunning detail. The Madonna sits enthroned with Christ on her knee, while Canon van der Paele (who commissioned the work) kneels to her left, spectacles in hand. Behind him is St George, his patron saint, kitted out in a full set of ceremonial armour, and opposite him is St Donatian dressed in sumptuous vestments. (St Donatian was a Roman who in 390 became Bishop of Reims; his relics were brought to Bruges during the 9th century.) This is not simply a religious work, but a portrait of living people, surrounded by the kind of luxurious setting that existed in Burgundian Bruges. Note the oriental carpet, and the African parrot held by Christ – evidence of the scope of Bruges's trade. In terms of technique, and of the sophistication of detail, this painting outstrips anything that was produced in Italy by at least three decades.

Rogier van der Weyden

St Luke Drawing a Portrait of Our Lady, by van Eyck's pupil Rogier van der Weyden, is another snapshot of contemporary life, in which the Virgin gives her breast to a rather starved-looking baby Jesus, surrounded by Renaissance textiles and architecture.

Dirk Bouts

Dirk Bouts is represented by a triptych featuring the martyrdom of St Hippolytus, in which the saint is being pulled asunder by four horses, with ropes attached to each limb.

Gerard David

The Judgement of Cambyses (1498) was painted by Gerard David (c. 1460–1523), who lived and died in Bruges and was the last great artist of the Bruges school. It depicts the corrupt judge Sisamnes being flayed alive with surgical precision by knaves in boots and cloaks; Cambyses, king of Persia in the 6th century BC, and other surrounding figures – including a mangy dog – are painted in great detail and look entirely unconcerned. The painting was commissioned for the Stadhuis by the contrite magistrates of Bruges following the disastrous events of 1488, when the Bruges authorities ill-advisedly put the unpopular governor of the Low Countries, Maximilian, under house arrest and executed his treasurer Pieter Lanchals in the Markt.

Master of the *Legends of St Ursula*

A series of panels depicting the legends of St Ursula, by the Master of the Legends of St Ursula and dated to before 1482, tells the story of the saint and the fate of her 11,000 virgins. According to the legend, St Ursula, the daughter of a king of Britain, escaped to Rome to avoid being married against her will, accompanied by a retinue of virgins. They then went to Cologne in Germany, where they were murdered simply because they were Christian. All this is based on a small inscription in Cologne, but it clearly caught the imagination of the medieval mind and snowballed into a legend in which an original contingent of 11 virgins became 11,000, plus a few bishops thrown in for good measure.

Hans Memling

The subject of St Ursula was taken up more famously by Hans Memling (1435–94) in his *St Ursula Shrine* (in the Memlingmuseum; *see* p.88). The Groeningemuseum is guardian of his large and impressive *Moreel Triptych* (1484), named after the donor Willem Moreel, burgomaster of Bruges who is depicted in the left-hand panel, with his wife in the right-hand panel. The saints in the central one are Christopher, Maurus and Giles. The painting shows the greater confidence in figure work, and in the use of perspective and scale, that Memling brought to Bruges painting.

Other Highlights

These include a nightmarish *Last Judgement* by Hieronymus Bosch; the *Allegory of the Peace of the Netherlands* (1577) by Pieter Claeissens the Younger, one of a distinguished family of Bruges painters; and the startling portraits of Archduke Albert and Isabella the Infanta by Frans Pourbus the Younger (1569–1622).

The collection peters out somewhat in the period between the 17th and late 19th century, but it is worth looking out for a few

of the notable Bruges artists of this era. There are fine, evocative pieces by Jacob van Oost the Elder (1601–71), portraying the world of the well-to-do around the time when Charles II of England and his desperate band of supporters loitered around Bruges. They reflect a sombre, dignified and self-effacing society, very different from the self-confidence and bravura of Bruges at its medieval zenith. Especially good is his *Portrait of a Bruges Family* (1645). *Afternoon Tea* (1778), by Jan Antoon Garemijn (1712–99), in French Rococo style, shows a very different social atmosphere a century later.

The collection picks up again in the late 19th century. There are some finely detailed pieces by Edmond van Hove (1853–1913), in Pre-Raphaelite Brotherhood style, echoing the work of the neo-medievalists in Bruges at the time; his self portrait, aged 26, is particularly strong. Other names to seek out are the Post-Impressionist and Luminist Emile Claus, the Symbolists Fernand Khnopff, Léon Frédéric and Jean Delville; the Sint-Martens-Latem School of painters Gustave de Smet, Constant Permeke and Gustave van de Woestijne; and one-offs such as Edgard Tytgat, Rik Wouters and Magritte.

If you are intrigued by the *Bruges-la-Morte* myth, look out for Khnopff's *Secret-Reflet* (1902), which includes a drawing of the back of the Sint-Janshospitaal – a classic of dreamy Symbolist reverie.

Arentshuis (Brangwynmuseum) D6

Dijver 16, t (050) 44 87 63. Open Tues–Sun 9.30am–5pm; adm €2.50.

This rewarding little museum, housed in an 18th-century neoclassical mansion, contains a stunning collection of European lace, much of it assembled by the historian Baron Jean-Amédée Liedts, and illustrated by paintings showing lace being worn (abundantly). A splendid array of historic carriages and sleighs is on view behind the glass in the building opposite the museum.

Upstairs is an extensive collection of paintings, prints, drawings, furniture and carpets donated to Bruges in 1936 by Frank Brangwyn (1867–1956). This British artist was born in Bruges where his father, William Curtis Brangwyn, worked as a neogothic architect and muralist (he was involved in the remodelling of the Heilig-Bloedbasiliek). Frank Brangwyn left Bruges aged eight, but always held a deep affection for the city of his birth.

Brangwyn later trained in William Morris' workshop and was associated with Siegfried Bing in Paris at the outset of the Art Nouveau movement, a connection clearly visible in, for example, his carpet called *The Vine* (1896–7). His furniture shows how his later work evolved towards Art Deco. His large and curious *British Empire Panel* (1925–30) was commissioned for the House of Lords in London, but its rich, almost psychedelic collage effect was clearly too racy for their Lordships. He was a powerful, expressionistic draughtsman, with a deft touch in all that he turned his hand to. It is remarkable that he is not better known.

Europa College D6

Dijver 9. Closed to the public.

Along the pretty tree-lined Dijver is the headquarters of the Europa College, or College of Europe, a respected centre for postgraduate European studies, founded in 1949, which each year invites a European head of state to inaugurate its academic year. The British prime minister Margaret Thatcher came to Bruges on 20 September 1988 and made a famous speech in which she pronounced her deep reservations about European integration. 'Working more closely together does not require power to be centralized in Brussels,' she declared. 'Europe will be stronger precisely because it has France as France, Spain as Spain, Britain as Britain, each with its own customs, traditions and identity.' This inspired the foundation of the Conservative Euro-sceptic 'Bruges Group'

– not a tag that Bruges is particularly grateful for.

ONZE-LIEVE-VROUWEKERK AND AROUND

Bonifaciusbrug D6

This little footbridge that leads over the River Reie towards the huge church spire of the Onze-Lieve-Vrouwekerk is one of Bruges's most charming spots; but despite its weathered features, the bridge dates only from 1910. It was named after St Boniface of Crediton (c. 675–755), a much-loved Anglo-Saxon missionary sent to evangelize the Germans, who later became Bishop of Mainz. To help in his work he engaged a number of English missionaries from Wessex, including St Walburga (*see* p.100). Aged 70, St Boniface set off to convert the pagans of Friesland in the northern Netherlands, and met his death at their hands. Relics of the martyred saint later found their way to the Onze-Lieve-Vrouwekerk.

Close to the bridge is a modern bust of **Juan Luis Vivés** (1492–1540), a Spanish humanist of Jewish origin who fled the Inquisition in Spain aged 17, and later settled in Bruges. He studied in Paris and then taught at Leuven, before joining the court of Henry VIII of England. He refused to accept Henry's divorce from Catherine of Aragon in 1527 and, after a spell in prison, returned to the Low Countries. Resident in Bruges, he was visited by both Erasmus, his former teacher, and Thomas More. Vivés is best remembered for his radical proposals for education, which included using the vernacular instead of Latin, studying nature, broadening the education of women, and opening schools for the poor. This last idea was put into practice by the pioneering Bogaarden schools for poor children.

Onze-Lieve-Vrouwekerk D6

*Mariastraat. **Open** Mon–Fri 10am–noon and 2–5pm (closes 4.30pm Oct–March), Sat 10am–noon and 2–4pm, Sun 2–4pm; **adm** €2.*

The Church of Our Lady is Bruges's most imposing and endearing church. Built over some 200 years from 1220, it has a stark, medieval feel to it. Its soaring, pinnacle-like tower, completed in 1350, rises to 122m and is one of the highest in Belgium. The cream-painted interior has a bold simplicity, with hefty columns and black and white flagstones spread across three parallel aisles. This austerity is offset by outbursts of massive Baroque ornament in the side chapels, and in the exuberant pulpit (1743) designed by Jan Garemijn, decked with cherubs and a depiction of Wisdom sitting on a globe.

The *Madonna and Child*

Bruges has a historic affection for the Virgin Mary, as witnessed by the 300 or so Madonnas that appear on street corners and niches throughout the city. It is appropriate, therefore, that its greatest church should be dedicated to her. At the head of the southern aisle, protected by a glass screen, is one of Bruges's outstanding treasures: the *Madonna and Child* (1504–5) by Michelangelo, one of the very few Michelangelo sculptures outside Italy, and the only one to leave Italy during his lifetime. Originally intended for the cathedral of Siena, it was acquired by Jan van Moscroen, a wealthy merchant and municipal treasurer, who donated it to the Onze-Lieve-Vrouwekerk in 1514. In this deeply and delicately sculpted work, Michelangelo has succeeded in turning stone into an image of great tenderness: it puts to shame virtually every other sculpture in Belgium. It has twice been carried off as war booty, once during the Napoleonic Wars, and then by the Nazis.

Art Nouveau in Bruges

Opposite the Onze-Lieve-Vrouwekerk, note the rare intrusion of Art Nouveau in the façades of Nos. 6–8 Onze-Lieve-Vrouwekerkhof Zuid. Art Nouveau (here called Jugendstil) first emerged as an architectural style in Brussels in 1893, and rapidly became all the rage for new buildings in Brussels, Antwerp, Ghent and across Europe. Bruges, by contrast, remained unmoved, and Art Nouveau appears only in one or two isolated places, such as these houses, completed in 1904.

The Paradijsportaal

On the north side of the tower is the Paradijsportaal (Paradise gate), a baptistry originally built in 1465 to provide a grand entrance to the church away from the busy main road that abutted the western façade, but which was later closed off and converted into a chapel.

The Museum

The main altar sits oddly in the middle of the church, and the choir behind it is fenced off as a museum. The main exhibits are the elaborate tombs of Charles the Bold and his daughter, Mary of Burgundy, who married Maximilian of Austria, but died after a fall from a horse in 1482 at the age of 25. Her fine tomb was constructed between 1495 and 1502, surmounted by a gilt-brass effigy of her in contemporary costume; her feet rest on a pair of dogs, the symbol of fidelity. Her father, Charles the Bold, was the son of Philip the Good, Duke of Burgundy, whom he succeeded in 1467. He reigned for 10 years before waging a disastrous war against France, and was killed at the Battle of Nancy in 1477, where his body was buried after, apparently, being half eaten by wolves. It was Charles V who ordered that the body should be brought to Bruges in 1550, a move fiercely resisted by the people of Nancy, who may have substituted the body of a knight instead. It eventually reached Bruges and was placed in a tomb similar to that of his daughter, made between 1559 and 1562; his feet rest on a lion, the symbol of strength.

The Crypt

In the crypt, visible through glass panels, you can see simple mural paintings of crucifixions dating from the 13th and 14th centuries, as well as the coffins of three canons. Crouch down, and beyond these you can see the coffin of Mary of Burgundy (it's not in her tomb), and sitting on top of it an urn containing the heart of her son, Philip the Handsome (father of Charles V), who died in 1506.

The Choir

The choir stalls bear the coats-of-arms of the Knights of the Golden Fleece, mementoes of the chapter meeting called here by Charles the Bold in 1468, the year of his marriage to Margaret of York. The choir also contains a fine **altarpiece** by Bernard van Orley (1499–1541), and there are several paintings by Pieter Pourbus, including a *Last Supper* (1562), and the wings of a triptych (1573). Pieter Lanchals, the treasurer executed in 1488, is commemorated in a **chapel** off the south ambulatory, which also contains medieval coffins excavated from the crypt.

The Swans of Bruges

The coat-of-arms of Pieter Lanchals included a swan – a play on words on his name, from the Dutch *lang* (long) and *hals* (neck). Archduke Maximilian bitterly resented the execution of Lanchals, his treasurer, by the Bruges rebels in 1488. The story goes that he made the citizens of Bruges pay penance by commanding them to keep swans on their canals in perpetuity, as a constant reminder of their misdeed. Even today the municipality keeps a controlled flock of swans, identified by a Gothic 'b' inscribed on the side of the beak. It is clearly a myth that Maximilian was responsible for their introduction to the canals: they were here well before his time. But the myth carries with it the haunting memory of a historical truth.

Note the swan in Lanchals' coats of arms, which gave rise to the legend of Bruges's swans.

In the wall of the north ambulatory of the choir is a wooden **gallery**, which overlooks the altar. Built in 1472, it belonged to the Lords of Gruuthuse, whose mansion was next door (*see* the Gruuthusemuseum, below).

Gruuthusemuseum D6

Dijver 17, t (050) 44 87 11. **Open** *daily 9.30am–5pm (closed Tues Oct–March);* **adm** *€5.*

This grand 15th-century mansion owes its name to a herbal flavouring for beer called *gruut*, an alternative to hops. A tax on *gruut*, and later on beer, was the perk of an honorific title, 'Lord of Gruuthuse'.

The old Gruuthuse mansion, much restored, now contains a splendid collection of all the kinds of things that enriched the lives of the merchant classes of Bruges. This celebration of bourgeois home comforts offers an excellent way to get a feel for how the well-to-do used to live in Bruges. Most of the objects are solid and utilitarian, but beautifully crafted and often charmingly decorated. Follow the room numbers to pursue a serpentine course through the museum past antique furniture, weapons, kitchen implements, Delftware, musical instruments, linenfold cupboards, leather trunks, clocks, scales, spinets and hurdy-gurdies, textiles and lace – and criminals' shackles, and a guillotine with a genuine French Revolutionary pedigree. One of the most treasured possessions is a polychrome terracotta and wood bust portraying Emperor Charles V aged about 20, carved in about 1520 and attributed to the celebrated German sculptor Konrad Meit (c. 1480–1551). Note the chain and emblem of the Order of the Golden Fleece around his neck.

There are a number of mementoes of Charles II of England, who stayed in Bruges during his exile from 1656 to 1658. They

The Lords of Gruuthuse

The Lords of Gruuthuse were powerful figures in Bruges, and none more so than Lodewijk van Gruuthuse (or Louis of Bruges, c. 1427–92), son of Jan IV van Gruuthuse, who originally built the house now occupied by the Gruuthusemuseum in 1425. In 1449 Lodewijk was appointed cupbearer to Philip the Good, Duke of Burgundy – a great honour conferred by feudal lords only to their most trusted associates. He became governor of Bruges in 1452, and was made a Knight of the Golden Fleece in 1461.

This high office continued with Philip's successor, Charles the Bold, under whom Lodewijk became commander-in-chief of the army and navy. Charles was married to Margaret of York, whose brother, Edward IV of England, fled to Bruges (1470–1) with 800 followers. Lodewijk was appointed to act as his host, and Edward IV stayed for six months at this house along with his brother, the notorious Richard 'Crookback', the future Richard III. Edward so appreciated the services and financial assistance of Lodewijk van Gruuthuse that, on his restoration, he made him Earl of Winchester.

When Charles the Bold died in battle in 1477, leaving his 20-year-old daughter Mary to inherit the Duchy, Lodewijk assisted her mother in finding a husband for her, to ward off the predations of the French king. They selected Maximilian of Austria but, after Mary's early and tragic death, Lodewijk – like most of Bruges – fell from favour. He was even imprisoned for three years after 1485, being released only to help negotiate the release of Maximilian, who was under house arrest in the Markt. Lodewijk died at the Gruuthuse in 1492. Part of his legacy was a massive collection of illuminated manuscripts, but his son took these with him as he transferred his allegiance and relocated to France, and they ended up in the Bibliothèque Nationale de Paris.

The Gruuthuse mansion lay redundant and increasingly derelict for a century, until in 1628 it was taken over by the Berg van Barmhartigheid, a charitable bank founded by Archduchess Isabella and based on the Italian institution Mons Pietas. It lent money at low or no interest to those who had fallen on hard times: in the 17th century, as Bruges suffered bouts of economic depression, this bank came to the rescue of many who would otherwise have had to resort to exorbitant loans from the commercial banks.

In the late 19th century the house caught the attention of the new breed of antiquarians and enthusiasts, William Brangwyn among them. The architect Louis Delacenserie (he of the Provinciaal Hof in the Markt) restored it as a museum to house their collections, but the work, carried out from 1873 to 1900, involved almost as much neogothic fantasy as careful restoration, thus stripping it of much of its authenticity. It became a municipal museum in 1894.

include an impressive memorial bust in black and white marble (1660–1) by François Dieussart, a copy of the one in the Schuttersgilde Sint-Sebastiaan, and made for the fellow archers, the Schuttersgilde Sint-Joris.

A most unusual feature of the building is the little **wooden gallery**, erected in 1472, that leads across a bridge to the balcony-like oratory overlooking the interior of the Onze-Lieve-Vrouwekerk.

Guido Gezelleplein D6

In front of the Gruuthusemuseum, the north side of the street opens up as the Guido Gezelleplein, dedicated to Guido Gezelle (1830–99), Bruges's best-loved poet. The **statue** of the poet, by Jules Lagae (1862–1931), was inaugurated in 1930 by King Albert I and Queen Elisabeth to mark the centenary of his birth.

MEMLING-MUSEUM AND AROUND

Memlingmuseum D7

Mariastraat 38, t (050) 44 87 70; wheelchair accessible. Open Tues–Sun 9.30am–5pm; adm €7 (for Sint-Janshospitaal and Memlingmuseum).

The Memlingmuseum is a cultural jewel, a collection of exquisite paintings exhibited in the chapel of the very institution – the Sint-Janshospitaal, or Hospital of St John (*see* below) – which commissioned them in the late 15th century. The museum gives a rare opportunity to see medieval religious paintings in their proper context, and surrounded by a complex that still breathes piety and charity.

St Ursula Shrine

The most celebrated work in the collection is the *St Ursula Shrine*. Just one metre long, made of gilt wood, it contains a dozen or so small painted panels that tell in vivid and beautifully rendered detail the story of St Ursula and her 11,000 virgins (*see* p.83).

The Mystic Marriage of St Catherine

This painting (1479) demonstrates Memling's sparkling attention to detail, and shows baby Jesus sliding a ring on to the finger of St Catherine (with the broken wheel on which the Romans attempted to martyr her), while St Barbara reads a book beside her. St Catherine is believed to symbolize Mary of Burgundy (daughter of Charles the Bold), and St Barbara her mother, Margaret of York. This polyptych was commissioned for this chapel, and the wings show the two St Johns (patrons of the hospital), with John the Baptist spurting blood after decapitation, and John the Divine (the Evangelist) on the island of Patmos, to which he was exiled. John the Divine can also be seen being boiled

---

Hans Memling

According to tradition, the German-born painter Hans Memling (1435–94) came to the hospital as a wounded and dangerously sick mercenary in 1477, after the Battle of Nancy in which Charles the Bold, Duke of Burgundy, was defeated and killed. Memling was nursed back to health, and undertook to paint a series of works at low cost to express his gratitude (1479–80). It's an attractive theory, but a myth: Memling was already an established figure in Bruges 12 years before this.

Memling was probably a pupil of Rogier van der Weyden in Brussels before he settled in Bruges during the last years of the reign of Philip the Good, one of Bruges's most splendid periods. He became a leading figure in the city, and one of its wealthiest citizens. Celebrated particularly in the 19th century as one of the masters of Flemish art, Memling's prodigious output is now scattered around many of the world's great galleries.

---

in a vat in Rome, which he is supposed to have survived – but the story is apocryphal.

Other Works

Other exceptional works are the *Adoration of the Magi* (1479), a *Pietà* (1480) and a striking portrait of a patron, *Maarten van Nieuwenhove* (1487). The museum also has a large number of polychrome wooden statues, mainly of religious subjects dating from the 14th to the 19th centuries.

Sint-Janshospitaal D6–7

Mariastraat 38; wheelchair accessible. Open Tues–Sun 9.30am–5pm; adm €7 (for Sint-Janshospitaal and Memlingmuseum).

The Sint-Janshospitaal is a monument to the traditions of civilized, humanitarian behaviour, which have run like a thread through Bruges's history from early medieval times. The venerable old hospital was founded in about 1150, with three large parallel wards which can be visited; the earliest one was built in the early 13th century, and the others were added to the north and south about 100 years later. The adjacent convent buildings were built in the 16th century. The total area covers 4 hectares, making this one of the most extensive institutions in the city – a measure of the civic pride and orderliness of Bruges in its heyday.

Operated by the city council and run for most of its history by nuns, the Sint-Janshospitaal maintained a long and devoted tradition of caring for the sick, wounded, homeless, deranged and indigent – following the old definitions of a hospital's role. It only ceased to be an operational (medical) hospital in 1976, when it moved to modern premises in the parish of Sint-Pieters. Since then it has become a museum where it is possible to glimpse what it was like through the centuries. Adjoined to the enclave is a 15th-century Apotheek (pharmacy), complete with glass jars, ceramic pots and box-drawers. It remained in use until 1971.

Archeologisch Museum c7

Mariastraat 36a; wheelchair accessible. **Open** *Tues, Thurs, Sat and Sun 9.30am–12.30pm and 1.30–5pm;* **adm** *€2.*

This small museum is well presented, if a bit specialist, and also occupies part of the old Sint-Janshospitaal. It houses a collection of Roman glass, medieval pottery shards and painted tombs. The exhibits of eating habits, WCs and garbage through the ages are fascinating. Labels are in Dutch, but English cards give broader explanations.

Mariabrug d7

The view from the bridge, Mariabrug – where the Sint-Janshospitaal lines the canal – is the view that Fernand Khnopff used in his evocative pastel *Secret-Reflet*, in the Groeningemuseum (*see* p.83).

> ### Fanny Trollope and the Sint-Janshospitaal
>
> In the 1830s the English traveller and writer Fanny Trollope was invited to visit the Sint-Janshospitaal, where she witnessed the work of the Sœurs de la Charité, the unpaid nuns who ran the hospital and were its nurses:
>
> *The rest of the party declined from joining us, from a fear of encountering disagreeable objects; but they were wrong. The pain, which the sight, or even the idea of human suffering must ever occasion, was a thousand times overbalanced by the pleasure of witnessing the tender care, the sedulous attention, the effective usefulness of those heavenly-minded beings, Les Sœurs de la Charité.*

THE BEGIJNHOF AND MINNEWATER

Begijnhof d8

Wijngaardstraat, **t** *(050) 36 01 40; wheelchair accessible.* **Open** *in daylight hours; gate closes at sunset;* **adm** *free to the grounds.*

The delightful Begijnhof (in French *béguinage*) is one of Bruges's prettiest and most beguiling sights, celebrated for the infectious tranquillity of its spirit of place. *Béguinages* were founded originally as refuges for the large numbers of single women at the time of the Crusades. The *béguines* lived pious lives, doing charity work, but they were not nuns, and could leave the community to marry.

Bruges's *béguinage* has occupied this same site since 1244, since its foundation by Margaret of Constantinople, Countess of Flanders. Its full name is the Prinselijk Begijnhof ten Wijngaarden (Princely Béguinage of the Vineyard), because Philip the Fair, King of France, placed it under royal protection in 1299 (although no one can explain the vineyard bit).

Today it appears like an island, accessed by a bridge and a gatehouse (dated 1776). Within this charmed and restful enclave, low,

The History of Béguinages

Béguinages were communities of single women which developed during the 13th century, mainly in response to the imbalance caused by the Crusades: for several centuries there just weren't enough men to go round. Rather than living in isolation or with married relatives, many unmarried women preferred to join a *béguinage* until a suitable partner turned up. Widows (themselves often young) could also stay in a *béguinage*. By and large the women came from fairly well-off families as they had to pay an entry fee and maintenance.

These were pious communities, usually closely connected to a church, but the *béguines* were not nuns. They made simple vows of chastity and obedience to their elected superiors, applicable for the duration of their stay, and they led modest but comfortable lives, assisted by servants and estate workers, spending their time in prayer, in making lace, biscuits and sweets, in looking after the sick in their infirmary, and in distributing gifts to the poor.

The origin of the word *béguinage/begijnhof* remains obscure. One legend refers to St Begga, a 7th-century noblewoman who founded a convent and seven churches near Namur after her son found a hen shielding seven chicks from his hounds. A more plausible derivation recalls a priest from Liège, Lambert le Bègue ('the Stutterer'), who in about 1189 encouraged crusaders' widows to form communities, an idea that was revived by Margaret and Joanna of Constantinople, themselves orphaned by the Crusades. Their father was Baldwin IX, Count of Flanders, a leader of the infamous Fourth Crusade, who was captured by the Bulgarians and died in captivity in 1205.

Margaret and Joanna founded many of Belgium's most famous *béguinages*, at Antwerp, Ghent, Leuven and Bruges. The idea quickly spread throughout the Netherlands, and *béguinages* remained a widespread feature of society – the larger ones had over a 1000 members – until the 18th century. Even when deserted, they have a unique atmosphere of care and tranquillity.

white-painted gabled houses (mostly dating from the 17th and 18th centuries) are set around cobbled walkways shaded by tall trees and a spacious patch of grass which is awash with daffodils in spring. The last of the *béguines* died in 1928; the nuns seen in the Begijnhof today are Benedictine sisters, whose order took over the site in 1930; they have, however, adopted the habits once worn by the *béguines*.

Begijnhof Church

Open daily 7am–12.15pm and 3–6pm.

The church was built in 1602 to replace an earlier one that was burnt down; it has a simple wood-panelled interior and a contrasting Baroque altarpiece.

Beguinhuisje

Open April–Sept daily 10am–noon and 1.45–5.30pm (Sun until 6pm), March and Oct–Nov 10.30am–noon and 1.45–5pm, Dec–Feb Wed, Thurs, Sat and Sun 2.45–4.15pm, Fri 1.45–6pm; adm €1.50.

This small museum contains mementos of the Begijnhof and presents a powerful evocation of how the interiors of the modest dwellings once looked.

Minnewater D8–9

The Minnewater – a broad stretch of water connected to the canals, and eventually the sea – was once a hive of activity as dozens of ships and barges jockeyed for position along the quays. The sluicegate had the important task of controlling the flow of water through the city. Today it is a quiet backwater, enjoyed by strollers and swans, perhaps now more atune to its popular name the 'Lake of Love'.

Minne means 'love' in Dutch, and so the Minnewater is often called the 'Lake of Love'. However, it seems that the tag is a case of mistranslation: Minnewater originally meant something like 'common water', or 'inner water'. It is a stretch of protected water off the outlying canals where the River Reie enters the city; it has served as a harbour since the 13th century, when the Brugse Vesten – the last, and largest, defensive ring of ramparts – was thrown up around the city and rimmed with a canal. This outer waterway became significantly busier after 1622, when it formed part of the Ghent–Bruges–Ostend canal.

Bust of Maurits Sabbe

Near the sluicegate house (*sashuis*) at the top end of the Minnewater is a bust of Maurits Sabbe (1873–1938), the Bruges-born academic and novelist who wrote several popular works set in the city, including *De Filosoof van het Sashuis* and *Aan 't Minnewater*. His vision of Bruges is upbeat and engaging, in contrast to the gloomy melancholy of Georges Rodenbach. It stands to reason that Sabbe gets a statue and Rodenbach doesn't.

Poedertoren

At the southern end of the Minnewater is the old Poedertoren (gunpowder tower), built in 1398. Formerly an arsenal, it was once part of the Brugse Vesten, and it used to form one of a pair guarding the entrance to the harbour. Its twin was dismantled in 1621 and until the First World War served as an icehouse, where winter ice from the Minnewater was stored for summer use.

There is a good view of the spires of Bruges across the water from the bridge at the base of the Minnewater and along Katelijnevest. As the term 'vest' suggests, this road follows the line of the old city ramparts, destroyed under the modernizing Emperor Joseph II in 1782–4.

Stedelijke Academie voor Schone Kunsten D8

Katelijnestraat/Arsenaalstraat.

The Academy of Fine Arts stands on the site where the old Bogaarden Convent once stood. This was originally a settlement for the *beghards*, the male equivalent of *béguines*, who spent their quiet lives mainly working with textiles. But the movement did not have the longevity of its female counterpart and died out in the early 16th century.

In 1513 the city fathers used the site to found the first Bogaarden School for poor children – a movement which went on to have a significant social impact across the Low Countries in the 16th and 17th centuries.

Almshouses D7–8

One of the prettiest sets of almshouses, called **De Vos**, is at Noordstraat 4–14 and is set around a garden. It was founded in 1683 by Christiaan de Vos. On Katelijnestraat is the **Godshuis Hertsberge** (1683), at Nos.87–101, and the **Godshuis de Generaliteit** (1572) at Nos.79–83.

On Driekroezenstraat you'll find the **Godshuis Onze-Lieve-Vrouw der Zeven Weeën** (Almshouse of Our Lady of the Seven Sorrows), founded in 1654, a set of seven houses said to symbolize the 'Seven Sorrows of Mary' – the seven trials of her life from the Flight into Egypt to the Crucifixion. And for yet more almshouses, on Nieuwe Gentweg are the **Godshuis Sint-Josef** (Nos.24–32), founded in 1634, and the **Godhuis de Meulenare** (Nos.8–22), founded in 1613.

Huisbrouwerij De Halve Mann 'Straffe Hendrik' D7

*Walplein 26, t (050) 33 26 97. **Guided tours** April–Sept daily 10am–5pm, Oct–March daily 11am and 3pm; **adm** €3.70 (including one free drink).*

The old Halve Mann Brewery is now the source of Bruges's powerful 'Straffe Hendrik' (Strong Henry) beer. Tours of the brewery are available. For details, *see* p.181.

Het Brugs Diamantmuseum D7

Katelijnestraat 43, t (050) 34 20 56, f 33 63 26, w www.diamondhouse.net. Open daily 10.30am–5.30pm; adm €5 (diamond polishing demonstration €7.50).

The Bruges Diamond Museum was opened in 1999. It offers a well-presented insight not only into the world of diamonds – mining, cutting, polishing, setting – but also into the role that luxury goods played in Bruges's past. It also has a section devoted to the general history of medieval Bruges, to set diamonds in their context, and translates details of jewellery from contemporary paintings into reality.

Bruges has a historic connection with diamonds, developing as a centre for diamonds before Antwerp and Amsterdam. In 1476 the goldsmith Lodewijk van Berquem is said to have invented the technique of cutting and polishing diamonds by using diamond powder on a rotating disk.

KONINGIN ASTRIDPARK AND AROUND

The Koningin Astridpark was named after Queen Astrid (1905–35), wife of Leopold III, King of the Belgians. A Swedish princess, she was cherished by the Belgians for her elegant beauty, common touch and charitable works. Mother of two young children, Prince Baudouin and Prince Albert (the current king), she died tragically young when a car driven by her husband crashed near Lake Lucerne. Her funeral in Brussels attracted 1.5 million mourners; many have pointed to the similarities with the death of Princess Diana in 1997.

With its bandstand and pond and attractive landscaping, the Koningin Astridpark (known locally as the Botanieken Hof) is the prettiest park in Bruges. There's also a children's adventure playground.

Sint-Magdalenakerk F6

Open Easter holiday and 15 Jun–15 Sept Mon–Sat 9am–noon and 2.30–5.30pm, rest of year Mon–Sat 9am–noon.

The Koningin Astridpark fills the site left by the destruction of a Franciscan monastery in the late 18th century. Now the only reminder of its former religious role is the large Sint-Magdalenakerk, built in neo-gothic style between 1851 and 1853, to designs by the British architect Thomas Harper King. Although a pupil of Augustus Pugin, author of the sumptuous neogothic interiors of the Palace of Westminster in London, this church is restrained – austere even. But there is some fine Victorian stained glass, and relief polychrome sculptures of the stations of the cross, placed in a medieval setting.

Pedestrian Bridge over the Coupure G6

Linking the Boninvest to the Kazernevest.

The Coupure (French for 'Cut') is a broad canal built in the mid-18th century to relieve the city centre of heavy canal traffic. The city authorities took the opportunity of the Brugge 2002 celebrations to span the southern end of the Coupure with a pedestrian and cycle bridge, and thus to fill the last remaining gap in a circuit of roads and paths around the egg-shaped outer limits of the city. They commissioned the Swiss designer and engineer Jorg Conzett for the task. A specialist in footbridges, he came up with a characteristically striking design, a confection of strident horizontals and verticals made of pipes and cables, which serve to raise the bridge when barges need to pass underneath.

Gentpoort F7

Closed to the public.

This imposing city gate, built in 1401 to serve the road to Ghent, was one of the four that survived the demolition of the city's outer perimeter of ramparts during a drive for modernization in the late 18th century.

Northeastern Bruges

Northeastern Bruges

Northeastern Bruges is agreeably quiet, with spacious streets lined with cottages and terraced houses, and infrequent cars rumbling over the cobbles. Although known as Bruges's Verloren Hoek ('lost corner'), it would be an exaggeration to say that it is off the beaten track, but you will be surprised how busy the centre of Bruges seems after visiting this neighbourhood.

The area encompasses a number of small museums and churches, which all have a slight note of quaint eccentricity about them. The row of windmills lining the earth bank along the canal also lends a rustic air, freshened by breezes that drive in across the polders from the North Sea. Having seen all the big sights in the city centre, you will find here the relaxed mood that is the authentic beat of the city.

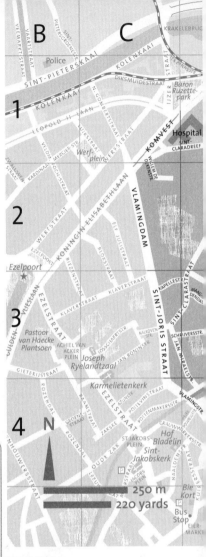

1 Lunch

De Karmeliet, Langestraat 19, **t** (050) 33 82 59. **Open** Tues–Sat noon–2pm and 7–10pm, Sun noon–2pm (closed 2 weeks in June–July). **Expensive.** Treat yourself to a divine lunch in one of Belgium's finest restaurants.

2 Tea and Cakes

Café Vlissinghe, Blekersstraat 2, **t** (050) 34 37 37. **Open** Mon–Wed 11am–midnight. An atmospheric old pub.

3 Drinks

Café 'De Versteende Nacht', Langestraat 121, **t** (050) 34 32 93. **Open** Tues–Thurs 7pm–late (at least 1am), Fri and Sat 6pm–late. Lively bar (with good bistro food) which doubles up as a jazz club.

Highlights

Couples' City: Investigate the domestic charms of old Bruges at the Museum voor Volkskunde, p.98

Beer: The Brugse Brouwerij-Mouterijmuseum, home of De Gouden Boom beer, p.102

Venice of the North: Wander along the key waterways, the Sint-Annarei and Potterierei/Langerei, see map

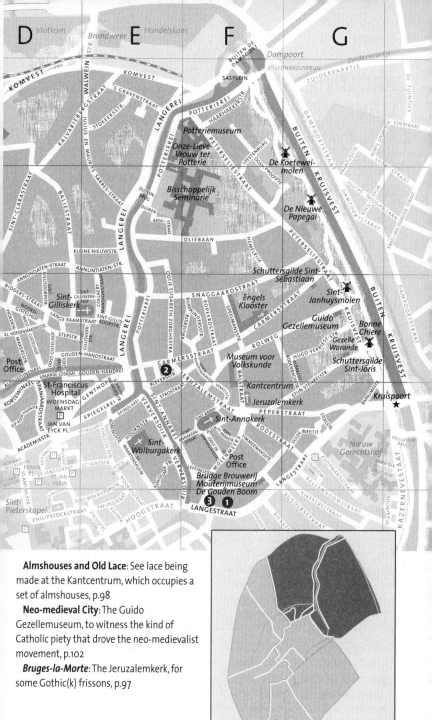

D Vlotkom · *Brandweer* **E** *Handelskom* **F** **G**

Dampoort
ST-LEONARDUSBRUG · Zuidervaartje

KOMVEST · WALWEIN · KOMVEST · BUITEN DE DAMPOORT · SASPLEIN · ZUIDERVAARTJE

LANGEREI · POTTERIEREI · HAARHAKKERSTR. · BUITEN KRUISVEST

Potteriemuseum

Onze-Lieve Vrouw ter Potterie

De Koetewei-molen

Bisschoppelijk Seminarie

De Nieuwe Papegai

OLIEBAAN · HEMELRIJK · PETERSELIESTRAAT

KLEINE NIEUWSTR. · ANNUNTIATEN-STRAAT · ANNUNTIATEN-STR.

Schuttersgilde Sint-Sébastiaan

Sint-Gilliskerk · SNAGGAARDSTRAAT · Engels Klooster · CARMERSSTRAAT · Sint-Janhuysmolen

Guido Gezellemuseum · Bonne Chiere

Post Office · CARMERSSTRAAT · ROLWEG · Gezelle Warande

Museum voor Volkskunde · Schuttersgilde Sint-Joris

St-Franciscus Hospital · WOENSDAGMARKT · JAN VAN EYCK PL. · Kantcentrum · Kruispoort

Jeruzalemkerk · PEPERSTRAAT

ACADEMIESTR. · Sint-Annakerk

Sint-Walburgakerk · Post Office · Nieuw Gerechtshof

Brugge Brouwerij Mouterijmuseum De Gouden Boom

Sint-Pieterskapel · HOOGSTRAAT · LANGESTRAAT

Almshouses and Old Lace: See lace being made at the Kantcentrum, which occupies a set of almshouses, p.98

Neo-medieval City: The Guido Gezellemuseum, to witness the kind of Catholic piety that drove the neo-medievalist movement, p.102

Bruges-la-Morte: The Jeruzalemkerk, for some Gothic(k) frissons, p.97

AROUND ONZE-LIEVE-VROUW TER POTTERIE

Onze-Lieve-Vrouw ter Potterie E–F1

Potterierei 79, t (050) 44 87 77; wheelchair accessible. **Open** *April–Sept Thurs–Tues 9.30am–12.30pm and 1.30–5pm, Oct–March Thurs–Tues 9.30am–12.30pm and 1.30–5pm;* **adm** *€2.50.*

This was the site of a medieval hospital, founded outside the city walls in 1276 as a refuge for the sick and poor, and for shelterless travellers and pilgrims. In 1359 it acquired its own church, possibly on the site of a chapel attached to the potters' guild, hence the name, Our Lady of the Pottery.

The Lady Chapel

From 1623 to 1625 the church was revamped in lavishly ornate Baroque style, and a Lady Chapel was added in the form of a second nave. The result is richly intense.

The most important possession of the Lady Chapel is a 14th-century stone statue, the Madonna and Child, which is believed to have miraculous powers. It is now surrounded by an extravagant Baroque altar and silver ex-voto offerings. A fine set of folksy 17th-century tapestries recording the miracles of Our Lady of the Pottery hangs between the columns of the nave. The remains of St Idesbald, abbot of Ter Duinen (d. 1167), were brought here in the 19th century and placed in a neogothic mausoleum on the south side of the chapel.

Potteriemuseum

A small but agreeable museum contains furniture, paintings (including a number of fine triptych altarpieces) and various church treasures accumulated over the centuries – an interesting showpiece of Bruges craftsmanship. Look out for the elegantly carved wooden leper's clapper by the reception desk. But the charm of this place is less the

> ## The Miracle of the Well
>
> On the corner of Korte Speelmansstraat and Carmersstraat, near the Engels Klooster (*see* p.104), is a crucifix dating from 1760, one of the city's more elaborate and charming street-side shrines which commemorates a local miracle. On a cold winter's day, a girl called Anna went to fetch water for a sick neighbour. She was attacked by a pair of thugs and thrown into the well, and her mother, in despair, set off on her knees to appeal to the famous Madonna at the church of Onze-Lieve-Vrouw ter Potterie, a kilometre away. When she returned, she found that Anna had miraculously emerged from the well, safe and sound. Some cynics pointed out that the well was frozen over, but why allow a scientific explanation to get in the way of a good miracle?

content and more the enclave as a whole, where the almshouses still serve as part of an extensive old people's home.

Bisschoppelijk Seminarie E–F2

Potterierei 72. **Closed** *to the public.*

The Episcopal Seminary was established when Bruges became a bishopric again in 1834 (with Sint-Salvator as its cathedral). It lies on the site originally developed by the Cistercian Abbey called Ter Duinen (the Dunes), founded in the 12th century at Koksijde, near Veurne, to the west of Bruges. Following the religious turmoil of the 16th century, and unsustainable encroachment by the coastal dunes, the abbey moved to Bruges in 1629, and developed this massive new complex around a fine Baroque church.

Duinenbrug E2

Potterierei.

This drawbridge takes its name from the Ter Duinen Cistercian Abbey that was established nearby. Rebuilt in 1976, it is one of the few drawbridges left in the city, designed to lift up to allow tall barges to pass.

Sint-Gilliskerk D–E3

Sint-Gilliskerkhof. **Open** *May–Sept Mon–Sat 10am–noon and 2–5pm, Sun 11am–noon and 2–5pm.*

This parish church takes the typical Bruges form, with a hall-like interior formed by three robust parallel aisles. A single nave was built around 1277, and two additional aisles were added in the late 15th century. The remarkable wooden barrel vault is original.

The interior was devastated and stripped by Protestant iconoclasts in the 1570s, only to be restored with Baroque flourishes in the Counter-Reformation, and in neogothic style in the 1880s. Its most interesting feature is the series of four paintings by the Bruges artist Jan Garemijn (1712–99) commemorating the work of the Bruges Trinitarian Brotherhood, founded in 1642, for whom this church served as headquarters.

Following in the footsteps of the 12th-century Trinitarian movement, the Brotherhood collected money to raise the ransom for soldiers and travellers held captive in the Muslim Ottoman Empire, especially in North Africa where they were sold as slaves. Among those rescued was Francis van Mulder, the son of a Bruges potter; one of the paintings shows his happy return to Dunkirk in 1780. The Brotherhood was suppressed in 1786 by the Austrians.

Outside, to the left of the door, is a modern memorial stone to Hans Memling. He was a resident of the parish, and was buried in the church in 1494, although no part of his tomb has survived. He had several properties in Sint-Jorisstraat and his studio was in Jan Miraelstraat, west of the church.

JERUZALEMKERK AND AROUND

Jeruzalemkerk F4

Peperstraat 3. **Open** *Mon–Fri 10am–12pm and 2–6pm, Sat 10am–12pm and 2–5pm;* **combined adm €1.50 with the Kantcentrum.**

The Jeruzalemkerk is a splendidly odd-ball 15th-century church for several reasons, not

---

The Adorno Family

The Jeruzalemkerk was built as a private chapel for the distinguished Adorno (or Adorni) family, scions of one of the leading families of Genoa in Italy. Oppicino Adorno (d. 1307) joined the crusader forces of Guy de Dampierre, Count of Flanders, and settled in Bruges. In 1427 brothers Pietro and Jacob Adorno, returning from a visit to the Holy Land, refurbished the family chapel as a replica of the Church of the Holy Sepulchre in Jerusalem, including a reconstruction of Christ's tomb (with a life-size naked body of Christ) in the crypt. The crypt also contains a fragment of the Holy Cross in a gilded silver cross (behind the ornate grille). The altar reinforces the theme: it is dominated by a macabre carving of a skull-laden Golgotha, and three stark crosses.

Pietro was a leading figure in Bruges's political life and carried the torch for Renaissance humanism, but he was also deeply pious, and his intention was to recreate a slice of the Holy Land in Bruges which the public could share in.

His son Anselmo (often referred to as Anselm Adornes) maintained this tradition. He became treasurer of Bruges, and likewise visited the Holy Land, adding to the collection of holy relics in the church. In the service of Charles the Bold, Duke of Burgundy, he travelled on a number of diplomatic missions, including to Scotland.

In 1472 he was appointed governor of the guild of Scottish wool-traders, and became an adviser to King James III of Scotland. This led to an involvement in Scottish politics, which resulted in his murder in 1483 by armed assassins in North Berwick. His effigy appears next to his wife's (d. 1472) on their fine black-marble tomb in the church; it has a sword hilt in his ribs to indicate the foul means of his death, and the tomb in fact contains only his heart.

least its polygonal tower surmounted by two tiers of wooden lanterns and crowned by a tin orb. It could be mistaken for a water tower, but in fact its influence is Byzantium. It heralds an even more eccentric and remarkable interior, which contains replicas of various sacred places in the Holy Land (*see* 'The Adorno Family', above). The church is still privately owned by the descendants of the family for whom it was built, the Adornos, and retains the distinctive atmosphere of a family chapel. Stained glass, dating from 1560 and commemorating the family, is amongst the earliest and best in Bruges.

Kantcentrum F4

Peperstraat 3a, t (050) 33 00 72, f (050) 33 04 17, e kantcentrum@yucom.be; wheelchair accessible. Open Mon–Fri 10am–noon and 2–6pm, Sat 10am–noon and 2–5pm; combined adm €1.50 with the Jeruzalemkerk.

The Lace Centre is a small museum, housed in 14th-century almshouses formerly sponsored by the Adorno family. It contains examples of Belgian lace – tablemats, handkerchiefs, collars, cuffs and borders – and underlines the important role that lace has played in fashion over time. But it's the afternoon demonstrations that bring this museum to life: a crowd of local practitioners sit chatting and laughing as they operate with lightning speed the numerous bobbins and pins on the cushions on their knees.

Museum voor Volkskunde F3

Rolweg 40; wheelchair accessible, t (050) 33 00 44. Open daily 9.30am–5pm (Oct–March closed Tues); adm €2.50.

Part of the charm of this rich and entertaining folklore museum is its location, in the former almshouses of the Shoemakers' Guild. Its comprehensive collection of artefacts includes furniture, tools, domestic implements, toys, lace, paintings and clothes, as well as replicas of a hatter's and a cobbler's workshop, an old grocery, an Empire-style pharmacy, and so on – all evoking strong impressions of craft techniques and the daily lives of ordinary people and craftworkers, mainly from the 19th century (labels in Dutch).

De Zwarte Kat

The museum also has its own pub (open same hours), created in 1894 by a Bruges social and cultural society to emulate the Parisian cabaret bar called Le Chat Noir, made famous by the singer Aristide Bruant.

Sint-Annakerk F4

Sint-Annaplein. Open April–Sept Mon–Fri 10am–noon and 2–4pm, Sat 10am–noon.

This is one of Bruges's most endearing parish churches; a fine barrel-vaulted church, originally consecrated in 1497, but wrecked by the iconoclasts in 1581. It was completely refurbished after 1624, and has retained its authentic 17th- and 18th-century interior, complete with chandeliers, marble rood screen, and carved oak panelling, with statues and barley-sugar columns in sombre oak. It may not have many great treasures, but the Sint-Annakerk has a sense of decorative unity unmatched by any other church in Bruges. It is easy to picture in your mind's eye the nave filled with the kind of well-to-do burghers portrayed in paintings by Jacob van Oost in the Groeningemuseum (*see* p.82) (also represented in the church), and perhaps members of Charles II's entourage swaggering in for a refreshing dose of confession and penitence. Guido Gezelle, the Bruges poet, was baptized and made his first communion here. The vast *Last Judgement* (over the entrance) by Hendrik Herregouts (1685) has the distinction of being Bruges's largest painting, measuring over 100 sq m.

Sint-Walburgakerk E4

Sint-Maartensplein. Open Easter–Sept daily 8pm–10pm.

This fine Baroque Jesuit church, built in the early 17th century, belongs to the era when Bruges had passed its medieval heyday.

Lace-making in Bruges

Since the 16th century the wealthy of Europe – men and women – have decked themselves in lace: lace cuffs, lace collars, lace caps, lace handkerchiefs, all fashioned in exquisite patterns wrought from hours of painstaking labour. Lace-making has always been a cottage industry, but in the old days it was also a pastime for women from virtually every social rank, notably the hundreds of women living in the *béguinages* and convents of the Low Countries.

Various lace-making techniques have been used over the centuries. In the 16th century it was essentially a form of embroidery; a hundred years later, the dominant technique was needlepoint (point lace), which had evolved in Venice. Bobbin lace developed during the 17th century in Genoa and Milan, as well as in Flanders, where the main centres were Brussels, Mechelen and Bruges. The bobbin technique is the one most widely seen today, especially in Bruges.

Handmade bobbin lace is extremely slow to make, requiring thousands of carefully planned movements of the bobbins and pins. The intricate patterns are created by moving the threads attached to the bobbins around the pins, which are pressed into a cushion. Complex lace calls for more than a hundred separate threads and bobbins. With the Victorian passion for lace with everything – from women's collars and lappets (ribbon-like hair adornments), and even underwear, to dining-room tablecloths and bedlinen – production grew exponentially in the 19th century, but by this time much of the demand was being met by lace-making machines. Bruges lace was originally made from linen from the flax fields of central Flanders, but at this time cotton took over.

Postcards seen in Bruges today show smiling elderly women sitting outside their cottages in the sunshine (for better light), quietly clicking away at their bobbins. However, there was once a more pitiful side to lacemaking: Bruges's textile industries were never mechanized, and during the 19th century unemployment soared. Lace was seen as a way to earn at least some income, and thousands of women and children laboured long hours to produce lace by hand, usually for a pittance. Girls as young as five in orphanages and convents were taught to make lace as a training for a profession, and they received no payment at all. By 1840 there were over 10,000 lacemakers in Bruges out of a total population of 45,000. The number dwindled only in the last 30 years of the century, as Victorian fashions became less flouncy.

Fine lace production has been further undermined in recent decades by cheap imports from the Far East, but in Bruges the tradition lives on – as a hobby and as a cottage industry. Genuine handmade lace is available in the more respected outlets (*see* p.189), where the staff will be happy to reassure you of its provenance; it should also come with a quality-control label. Handmade lace is always expensive: expect to pay at least €25 for a table doily. Cotton lace is more robust and less pricey; linen lace is much finer, and a larger piece with a complex design can cost many hundreds of euros. As well as at the Kantcentrum, collections of lace can be seen at the Arentshuis (*see* p.83).

Effectively, it is a political statement, a triumphant beacon of the Counter-Reformation designed to put the puritanical modesty of the Protestants in the shade. Unfortunately opening hours are restricted to the evening (when the church is evocatively lit and music is played) but there is a glass door at the entrance which usually allows you to peer into the interior. The church is sometimes used as a venue for concerts.

Sint-Walburgakerk has a chequered history. Among the leading forces in the Counter-Reformation were the Jesuits, members of the 'Society of Jesus' founded in the 1530s by the Spanish-born St Ignatius of Loyola. St Ignatius visited Bruges between 1528 and 1530, when studying in Paris, and stayed with

Guido Gezelle

Guido Gezelle (1830–99) pops up time and again in Bruges, a mysterious figure to English speakers, few of whom have ever heard of him. In Flanders, however (and to all Dutch speakers), this is equally surprising, since he is one of the leading figures of 19th-century Dutch literature, and one of its most popular poets.

Guido Gezelle was a priest as well as a poet, and almost all his work is suffused with religious wonderment. He is best known as an observer of nature, looking at reeds in a river, cherries on a tree or birds bringing up their chicks in a nest, and transforming these small details into symbols that reflect the extraordinary variety of the world and the infinite imagination of God.

In English translation his verse seems rather insubstantial, anodyne even, but in Dutch it has a powerful, melodic cadence, exploiting the cut and thrust of Dutch clicking consonants and chewy vowels coupled to poetic innovation. This is clear even if your Dutch is minimal. The following verse is from a poem about a bird's nest, from which the hatchlings have just emerged, and are now bouncing around on the twigs in a way that makes the poet burst out laughing.

Een meezennestje is uitgebroken,
dat, in den wulgentronk
gedoken,
met vijftien eikes blonk;

ze zitten in den boom te spelen,
tak-op, tak-af, tak-uit, tak-in, tak-om,
met velen,
en 'k lach mij, 'k lach mij, 'k lach mij bijkans krom.

Gezelle was also famous for reasserting Dutch (or Flemish, in this case) as a valid literary language, at a time when French predominated in Belgium as the language of education and culture.

Guido Gezelle born in the modest little house that is now his museum, on the eastern edge of the city. He was the eldest of five children; his father was a gardener, and his mother came from a farming family. He spent his childhood in the neighbourhood, and at the age of 16 went to a junior seminary school in Roeselare to begin studies for the priesthood. By the age of 18 he was writing and publishing poetry. He returned to Bruges to complete his studies at the Bishoppelijk Seminarie, where he was ordained in 1853. He developed a strong belief that the unity of religion and poetry (and art generally) could achieve a revitalization of Christian culture, as it had done in medieval times. He learnt to speak perfect English – he always retained a close bond with the English community in Bruges – and travelled frequently to Britain. In fact, one of his early ambitions as a priest was to become a missionary for the Roman Catholic faith in Britain (he hoped for a rapprochement between the Anglican and Roman Catholic Churches).

Gonzalez d'Aguilera, a leading figure in the Basque community. The Jesuit movement had a strong following in Bruges, and Sint-Maartensplein became their focus, with a monastery and college. Sint-Walburgakerk was the monastery church, built between 1619 and 1643 to designs by the Bruges-born Jesuit lay-brother, Pieter Huyssens (architect also of the Sint-Carolus Borromeuskerk in Antwerp). It was the first church to be dedicated to St Francis Xavier, the great Jesuit missionary who died in China in 1552, and

was canonized in 1622; his statue looks down from the façade. The Jesuits were suppressed under the Austrians in 1773, and this then became the parish church of St Walburga, taking over that role from another church nearby that was demolished in 1781.

St Walburga was an 8th-century English nun who accompanied St Boniface of Crediton on his missionary work to Germany. She was abbess of Heidenheim, but after her death her remains were transferred to

His first post was as deputy rector of the Anglo-Belgian Seminary on the Potterierei (now the Sint-Leocollege), where English Catholics were trained for the priesthood. Then from 1865 to 1872 he was parish priest at the Sint-Walburgakerk, just over the canal to the west. At this time he also began to broaden his cultural and journalistic endeavours, launching *Rond den Heerd* (*Around the Hearth*), the first of three cultural magazines that he founded. (One of these, *Biekorf*, still exists today.)

His work (often written under pseudonyms and using the old west-Flemish dialect) had a strong Flemish-nationalist bent, which was supported by several of Bruges's leading figures. However, his attitude brought him into conflict with the Francophile cultural elite, who accused him of being obsessed by Flemish issues to the point of 'fetishism'. His work for the English community, many of whom were Roman Catholics, drew much praise and thanks, but malicious rumours that a close relationship with the mother of an English family had exceeded the bounds of discretion persuaded his seniors to transfer him, and Gezelle was appointed parish priest at the Onze-Lieve-Vrouwekerk at Kortrijk (Courtrai).

Gezelle remained in Kortrijk for the next 27 years. During this period he developed as a poet, helped to found the Flemish Academy of Language and Literature, and personally collected thousands of Flemish words, sayings and proverbs. He also joined in the general vogue for folklore revival, and gradually came to be seen as a leading figure in the Flemish Movement. He translated Longfellow's *Hiawatha* into Flemish (1886) to great acclaim, and published his two most celebrated collections of poems, *Tijkrans* (*A Crown for the Year*; 1893), and *Rijmsnoer om en om het jaar* (*A Wreath of Rhymes Roundabout the Year*; 1897).

Driven by great energy, he also maintained broad contacts and correspondence with literary and religious figures and former pupils. In 1899 he was invited back to Bruges to translate some theological works, and also took up the post of Director of the Engels Klooster (English Convent; *see p.104*), with its attached convent school for English girls, in Carmersstraat, close to his birthplace. Already in declining health from diabetes, he became ill during one of his trips to England, this time to visit a sister convent set up at Haywards Heath. Shortly after his return to Carmersstraat, he died, on 27 November 1899.

It is not easy to gain an appreciation for Gezelle's work unless you can read Dutch. However, there is an excellent dual-language text called *The Evening and The Rose*, with English translations of 30 poems set beside the Dutch, which reveals the unusual charm of his work. Gezelle's poetry does not range widely across life's broad experiences, but within the narrow focus that he set himself it excels, and is cherished for its calm and innocent wonder, and its radiant spiritual balm.

Eichstätt on the eve of May Day – bad luck for the blameless Walburga, for this was a pagan festival associated with witchcraft, which subsequently became known as *Walpurgisnacht*.

During the French occupation the Sint-Walburgakerk had a spell as a Temple of Law. Despite this varied history, the Jesuit heritage remains very much in evidence – exuberant Baroque decorations, swags, garlands, cherubs and broken pediments, all elegantly modulated. The fine wooden pulpit (1667–69) was made by Artus Quellinus the Younger at about the time that his gifted pupil, Dutch-born Grinling Gibbons, went to England to start his career as one of the great master-carvers of all time. The high altar is an equally elaborate piece by Jacob Cocx, with a painting of the Resurrection (1783) by Bruges-born artist Joseph B. Suvée, who went on to become the director of the French Academy in Rome.

Guido Gezelle was a priest at the church for seven years from 1865, which is why he lived at Korte Riddersstraat (and later at 20 Ververdsijk, on the canal).

Brugse Brouwerij-Mouterijmuseum De Gouden Boom F4

Verbrand Nieuwlandstraat 10, t (050) 33 06 99, f (050) 33 46 44. Open May–Sep Thurs–Sun 2–5pm; adm €3.

The brewery museum is housed in an old malthouse belonging to De Gouden Boom (45 Langestraat), one of the city's leading breweries, which was founded in 1587. Visits can be combined with tours of the brewery (*see* p.181).

GUIDO GEZELLEMUSEUM AND AROUND

Guido Gezellemuseum G3

Rolweg 64; wheelchair accessible. Open April–Sept daily 9.30am–12.30pm and 1.30–5pm, Oct–March Wed–Mon 9.30am–12.30pm and 1.30–5pm; adm €2.

This is the birthplace of Guido Gezelle (1830–99), one of Flanders' most celebrated 19th-century poets (*see* pp.100–101). The fetching brick house, where he also spent his childhood, is now a museum.

Some of the house contains simple reconstructed rooms as Gezelle might have known them as a boy, leading a family life of thrift and piety, studying plants and flowers – and stuffing birds. But the collection, although admirably presented, consists primarily of his manuscripts and mementoes, and is of limited interest unless you know his work. The large garden is believed to have played a major role in shaping his abiding love of nature.

Schuttersgilde Sint-Sebastiaan G3

Carmersstraat 174, t (050) 33 16 26. Open April–Sept Tues–Thurs 10am–noon and 2–5pm, Oct–March Tues–Thurs and Sat 2–5pm; adm €2.

The Marksmen's Guild of St Sebastian is a fine red-brick guildhouse dating from 1565 that still boasts its rocket-shaped tower. These marksmen were longbow archers who formed a key element in the city's medieval defences and were also crusaders (their coat of arms includes the Cross of Jerusalem).

Founded in the 13th century, the guild far outlived the age of bows and arrows as military weapons, and continued its existence as a celebrated club. When Charles II, future king of England, was in Bruges between 1656 and 1658 he was awarded the title 'King of the Archers' by the guild, and he founded the Grenadier Guards here. Since he was penniless at the time, he pledged 1,000 crowns as his entrance fee, payable on his death; in fact he paid it back after his restoration, with interest.

The royal connections have been maintained by the guild: all British sovereigns have been members since the days of Charles II; Queen Victoria and Prince Albert came here in 1843, and duly signed the register.

The Kings' Room

The guild's grand assembly hall, or Kings' Room, is now essentially a small museum, crammed with paintings, fine empire-style chandeliers, drums, cannons and various royal mementoes, including a marble bust of Charles II (1660–1) by François Dieussart.

The Archery Club

The guild is still an active archery club. Beyond the covered shooting gallery parallel to the Kings' Room rises the white-painted 'standing perch' – a traditional archery game of ancient origin. The perch is lowered on a hinge, and the top is fitted with a frame holding 50 or so feather 'birds', which are then raised as a target for archers below.

Charles I in Bruges

The future Charles II, son of the beheaded Charles I, took refuge in Bruges in 1656. Initially, after the Battle of Worcester (1651), he had gone to the court of King Louis XIV in France, but in 1656 Oliver Cromwell made a treaty with France, and Charles became *persona non grata*. From a new base in Cologne he made an agreement with the Spanish king Philip IV, then barged his way uninvited into the Spanish Netherlands.

Charles was unpopular just about every-where he went, mainly because he, and his entourage of some 70 officials and house-hold staff, plus 800 soldiers and camp-followers, were almost universally penniless. His close coterie of advisers had lost their estates in England, and were dependent on hand-outs from supporters on the Continent, who became decreasingly generous as the prospects of Charles's restoration faded. It was a hard game to play. Charles was a flam-boyant, affable aristocrat in his 20s, with a reputation for grand living to uphold, and a string of mistresses. Cromwellian spies lurked, reporting back on the antics of the English exiles in lurid detail. 'Fornication, drunkenness and adultery are esteemed no sins amongst them,' reported one. Charles was desperate for money: funds promised by the Spanish king were sporadic and quickly consumed, shopkeepers would no longer give him credit, and he was forced to sell his silver and his horses.

A further cause of disapproval was the fact that Charles was a Protestant; the Council of Flanders was outraged to learn that Protestant services were held for his entourage, and declared that it would permit services only for Charles and Charles alone, in the privacy of his own chambers. Meanwhile, against a backdrop of poli-ticking, negotiations, and failed hopes of English rebellions, Charles contrived to have a jolly enough time. For much of his stay, his base in Bruges was the previously grand Huis de Zeven Torens in Hoogstraat, close to the Burg, but it was rented unfurnished, and

furnishing it caused yet another worrying drain on funds.

He and his youngest brother, Henry, Duke of Gloucester, liked to spend time at the three archers' guilds (two of these, the Schuttersgilde Sint-Sebastiaan and Sint-Joris, survive; *see* pp.102 and 104), practising shooting and carousing, and in 1656 he founded the First Regiment of Foot Guards at the Schuttersgilde Sint-Sebastiaan, as his personal guard – a regiment that after 1815 was renamed the Grenadier Guards. But as the numbers of his soldiers swelled to five regiments, and then found themselves idle and unpaid, they turned to begging and robbery, and terrified the locals. This continued until 1657, when Cromwell attacked Spanish possessions in northern France, and Charles's troops, led by his more austere younger brother, James, Duke of York (the future James II), were sent into action.

Charles apparently found some female company in Bruges. Lord Taafe wrote to him to recommend a Mademoiselle d'Imercell of the Brussels court, but added, 'If your Majesty be libre, which Mme Renenbourg saies you are nott, having gott a new wan at Briges.' The Brussels court nonetheless regu-larly lured Charles away from Bruges, and in the summer of 1658 he finally moved, first to Brussels, and then to Hoogstraten on the Dutch border. Oliver Cromwell died later that year, and England soon tired of the turmoil and lacklustre quality of the Commonwealth; Charles was invited home as king in 1660.

A strange footnote to this story appeared in 1963, when a Flemish fisherman, Victor De Paepe, was arrested off the coast of England. He claimed that in 1666 Charles II, as a way of repaying Bruges's hospitality, had granted 50 of its fishermen the right to trawl English coastal waters. This was strongly denied by the British government, and the matter faded from the headlines. But in 1999 newly released documents showed that the British might have lost the case if De Paepe had pushed it through the courts, for it appears that such a charter does indeed exist.

Schuttersgilde Sint-Joris G3

*Stijnstreuvelstraat 159, t (050) 33 54 08. **Open** Mon, Tues, Thurs and Fri 3–5pm (can vary, phone ahead to check); **adm** €1.50.*

Set in a small park, the Marksmen's Guild of St George is a guild house for cross-bowmen. The guild was disbanded in 1872, and the original building was demolished, to be re-established in this new building in the 1930s. What looks like a tall radio mast in the garden is in fact its 'standing perch' target. Charles II was also a member of this guild, and made a name for himself at the opening of a gala by hitting a 'bird' with his first shot.

The Schuttersgilde Sint-Joris also has its own museum of mementoes, housing paintings, archives and a collection of crossbows.

Engels Klooster F3

*Carmersstraat 85, t (050) 33 24 24. **Church open** Mon–Sat 2–3pm and 3–4pm (can vary, phone for details).*

This imposing building is the English Convent, distinguished because it contains Bruges's only domed church. Religious strife in England during the 16th century caused many Roman Catholics to flee to Europe, and to the Spanish Netherlands in particular, where Catholicism was reasserted after 1585. English sisters had gathered at the Augustinian convent of St Ursula in Leuven, but in 1629 a number of them relocated to Bruges and founded their own order here, in a settlement they called 'Nazareth'.

The convent was well funded: Catherine of Braganza, wife of Charles II of England, took a particular interest in its welfare. In 1739 it was able to renovate its church in Baroque style, to designs by the distinguished Bruges-born architect Hendrik Pulinx (1698–1781), but when the French revolutionaries took over Bruges in 1795, the convent was closed down and the nuns fled. They returned in 1802, and the complex became a boarding school for English girls from wealthy Catholic families. For more on the English in Bruges, see 'The British in Bruges', p.116.

Guido Gezelle – who always maintained close ties with the English – became rector of the convent in 1899, and it was here that he died seven months later. It still serves as a convent.

KRUISPOORT AND AROUND

Kruispoort H4

This mighty hulk of a gate (1403) once protected the city with a drawbridge and portcullis, and is set apart from the other surviving gates by its composition: white brick. Its castellated city side looks far more benign than its altogether more daunting exterior, overlooking what was the moat. The scale of this gate gives an indication of the colossal size of the old outer city walls, the Brugse Vesten, built after 1297. The moat became part of the Ghent–Bruges–Ostend Canal, and the massive 100m-long barges that ply Europe's inland waterways can often be seen moored at the canalside. Today virtually all that remains of the walls themselves is an earth embankment, now the site of a series of four historic windmills.

Windmills G1–3

*Kruisvest. **Open** May–Sept daily 9.30am–12.30pm and 1.30–5pm; **adm** €2 for each mill.*

There used to be over 20 windmills on the earth ramparts around the city, before they became redundant in the age of steam. Only one, the Sint-Janshuysmolen, still occupies the site on which it was originally built; the others have been moved here to form a kind of open-air museum. From north to south they are: **De Koeleweimolen** (a flour mill, brought here in the 1990s), **De Nieuwe**

The City Ramparts

Bruges has had three sets of city ramparts, if you include the palisades that surrounded the fort built by Baldwin Iron-Arm in c. AD 865. The first set of proper city walls was constructed in about 1127, around what is now the city centre. The next set, built after 1297, threw a loop 7km long around the city, underlined by a double set of moats-cum-canals, with further fortifications on the intervening embankment. A hundred years later, the eight city gates were enlarged, not just as a defensive measure, but also to control and tax incoming trade.

These outer city walls, the Brugse Vesten, were reinforced with bastions during the 17th century. They would have been turned into earth and stone ravelins, to contend with the increased power of cannon, had Bruges adopted the plans drawn up by the energetic French fort-builder Marshal Vauban. But lack of funds was cited, and Bruges's fortifications had become totally obsolete by the time they were demolished by the Austrians in the 1780s, in the interests of modernity.

Four gates escaped demolition – the Kruispoort (1403), the Gentpoort (1401), the Smedenpoort (1367) and the Ezelpoort (1615) – and they only survived because in the late 18th century they still served a tax-raising function, levying the *octrois* paid by traders bringing goods into the city.

Papegai (an oil mill, brought here in 1970), **Sint-Janshuysmolen** (a flour mill, built here in 1770 and in use until 1914; restored in 1964), and **Bonne Chiere** (a flour mill, brought here from Olsene, East Flanders, in 1911).

Two of these, De Koeleweimolen and Sint-Janshuysmolen, are still operational and can be visited (opening times given above); in addition they offer fine views over Bruges.

Muur der Doodgeschotenen H4

Kazernevest.

Next to the new courts of justice, formerly the barracks (*kazerne*), lies a tragic memento of the First World War. Behind a pair of large iron gates is the Wall of the Executed Prisoners, where 11 Belgians, one Frenchman and one Englishman were shot by the Germans during the First World War. Bullet marks can still be seen in the wall.

The Englishman killed here was Algernon Charles Fryatt, the captain of a merchant steamship called *The Brussels* that plied the North Sea. His death was a *cause célèbre*.

On 4 February 1915 the Germans unilaterally declared that the North Sea was a war zone, and that all enemy shipping would be vulnerable to attack. A month later, a German U-Boat stopped a British merchant ship called *The Falcon*, which slowed down to surrender. Perhaps due to a misunderstanding, the U-Boat nonetheless attacked *The Falcon*, and sank her, with the loss of 104 lives. This caused outrage in Britain.

When, three weeks later, on 28 March 1915, *The Brussels* was similarly stopped by a U-Boat, Captain Fryatt gave orders to ram it, and sank it, this being – he argued – the only form of self-defence available to him. Fryatt was congratulated by King George V and the Admiralty.

A year later *The Brussels* was captured on its way back to London from Holland, carrying Belgian refugees. The Germans discovered that the captain was Fryatt and he was taken to Zeebrugge, where he was court martialled (even though he was not in the military). He was sentenced to death. The commandant of occupied Bruges, Baron von Büttlar, arranged for the execution to take place at the barracks on 27 July 1916, determined to make an example of Fryatt, and even supplying a brass band to accompany the firing squad and prisoner to the place of execution.

The German High Command, however, had grave misgivings about the legitimacy – let alone the political wisdom – of the execution, and despatched a telegram to von Büttlar to cancel it. It arrived half an hour after the execution had taken place.

Western Bruges

Western Bruges

The area to the west of the city centre and the Markt has had its ups and downs over time. It was once the centre of power under the Burgundian dukes, who built their magnificent palace complex at the Prinsenhof (now utterly declined from grace) and worshipped at the church of St Saviour, which was only latterly upgraded to cathedral status. Today, western Bruges is the commercial heart of the city, and contains the main shopping streets, notably Steenstraat. This leads to the great open square at the western perimeter known at 't Zand, which again has a history of mixed fortunes. It now bustles with a large market on Saturdays, and is the site of the most exhilarating addition to Bruges's skyline in recent years, the Concertgebouw Brugge. For a century until the 1940s, 't Zand was the site of Bruges's station, and the old route of the Ostend–Ghent railway line sliced through western Bruges, effectively cutting off what lay beyond from the rest of city. Even now, these western reaches of the city still retain the air of dislocation, with tranquil streets, almshouses and a leafy park lining the canal.

1 Lunch
Patrick Devos, *Zilverstraat 41*, **t** *(050) 33 55 66*. **Open** *Mon–Fri noon–1.30pm and 7–9pm, Sat 7–9pm*. **Expensive**. Belgian high-art cuisine in suitably stylish surroundings.

2 Tea and Cakes
't Pallieterke, *'t Zand 28*, **t** *(050) 34 01 77*. **Open** *Wed–Mon 11.30am–9.30pm*. A pleasant restaurant-cum-tearoom.

3 Drinks
Lokkedize, *Kort Vuldersstraat*, **t** *(050) 33 44 50*. **Open** *Tues–Thurs 7pm–late, Fri–Sun 6pm–late*. A friendly bar – good for a relaxed evening get-together.

Highlights
Couples' City: Attend a concert in the new Concertgebouw Brugge, p.112

Beer: 't Brugs Beertje, a pub for devotees of Belgian beer, p.182

Venice of the North: Take in the ramparts at Boeverievest, p.113, and the city gate, the Smedenpoort, p.114

Almshouses and Old Lace: Explore the almshouses in Boeveriestraat, p.112, and around Onze-Lieve-Vrouw van de Blindekens, p.114

Neo-medieval City: Hof Bladelin, for an insight into the lifestyle of the wealthy in the Burgundian era, p.115

Bruges-la-Morte: The Sint-Salvatorskathedraal and museum, best on a gloomy day, for a taste of sombre devotions and relics, p.110

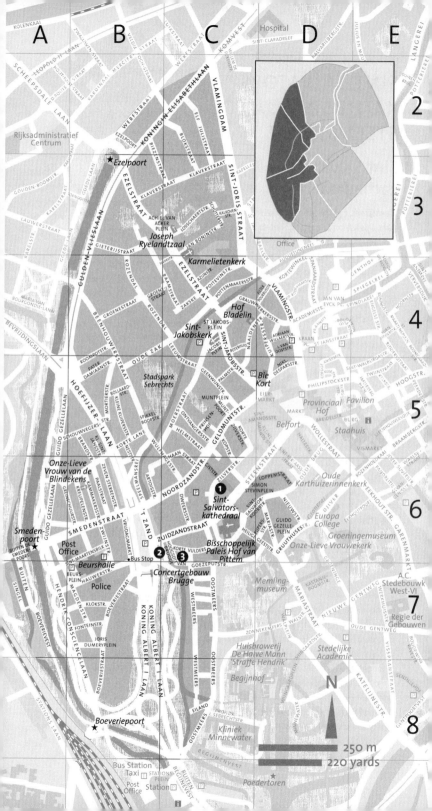

SINT-SALVATORS-KATHEDRAAL AND STEENSTRAAT

Sint-Salvators-kathedraal C6

Steenstraat, t (050) 33 61 88; wheelchair accessible. Open Mon 2–5.45pm, Tues–Fri 8.30–11.45am and 2–5.45pm, Sat 8.30–11.45am and 2–5.30pm, Sun 9–10.15am and 3–5.45pm.

Squat and built of yellow brick, this massive church is not quite the dominant building that its title would suggest, but then it only acquired the status of cathedral when Bruges became a bishopric in 1834. It then suffered a fire in 1839, which destroyed its roof and tower – subsequently rebuilt to a curious neo-Romanesque design by a British architect, Robert Chantrell. Its billing as a cathedral raises expectations too high, but it can be atmospheric, particularly on dark days.

The first church on this site was probably erected in the 9th century – although, according to an unlikely tradition, an even earlier church was founded here by Saint Eloi in about 640. A Romanesque church followed in 1127, and a Gothic one superseded this after 1275.

In the body of the cathedral there is an impressive pulpit (1778–85) by Hendrik Pulinx, as well as some large religious paint-ings by the Antwerp painter Erasmus Quellinus (1607–78), a pupil of and assistant to Rubens, who had considerable success after his master's death. The most arresting feature, however, is the remarkable Baroque organ (1682) at the base of the nave, a mighty confection topped by angels and cherubs playing celestial music. The central statue, of the Creator, is by Artus Quellinus the Younger (1625–1700). Some medieval painted stone tombs have been opened to view in the porch (under the organ).

The Choir

Today the oldest part of the cathedral is the choir, which contains original medieval choir stalls and carved misericords, above which are the painted coats of arms of the knights of the Order of the Golden Fleece, originating from a chapter meeting called by Maximilian of Austria in 1478; Edward IV of England was one of the knights in attendance. Above these, unusually, hangs a series of Brussels tapestries (c. 1731), depicting religious scenes such as the Nativity and the Adoration.

The Shoemakers' Chapel

The Shoemakers had a guild house in Steenstraat, just outside the church; their chapel in the north transept dates from 1372, although it was remodelled a century later. You can see their emblem, a crowned boot, beneath the barley-sugar columns on the Baroque altar (1667). The carved oak doors date from the mid-15th century.

The Museum

Open Mon–Fri 2–5pm, Sun 3–5pm; adm €1.50.

The cathedral has its own small museum just off the north transept, a mixed bag of church treasures, paintings, relics and other historic curiosities, set in a series of splendidly dingy neogothic ecclesiastical back rooms around a cloister. Its most important works of art – many of which were brought here after the church of St Donatian in the Burg was destroyed in 1799 – are currently in the Groeningemuseum (*see* p.82), including paintings by Dirk Bouts, Hugo van der Goes and Lancelot Blondeel.

St Gunhilde

One of the Sint-Salvatorskathedraal Museum's most curious treasures is an inscribed lead tablet found beneath the skull of Gunhilde in her tomb in the church of St Donatian. Gunhilde was the sister of Harold Godwinson, King of England. After he was slain by William the Conqueror at the Battle of Hastings in 1066, she fled to Bruges, where she spent the rest of her life doing good works. After her death in 1087, she was regarded as a saint and later canonized.

Simon Stevin

Born out of wedlock in Bruges in 1548, Simon Stevin was a tax inspector in his youth, before he went to the newly founded University of Leiden. He soon developed a reputation for mathematics and hydraulic engineering, but was also interested in astronomy, navigation, perspective and book-keeping.

He made a number of ground-breaking discoveries: in 1586, by dropping weights from a church tower in Delft, he disproved Aristotle's theory that weight determines the speed at which objects fall – three years before Galileo's experiment from the Leaning Tower of Pisa. He also discovered that the downward pressure of a liquid depends on its height and base, not on the shape of the container. He is credited by some as the inventor of the decimal point; if not the inventor, he certainly standardized its usage, and predicted that the future lay in the decimalization of units.

As adviser to Prince Maurits of Nassau, son of William of Orange, he undertook wide-ranging engineering projects, such as flood protection, and canal systems with sluices that had applications for military defence.

He taught at Leiden, and was instrumental in the creation of the world's first faculty of engineering. He was one of the first academics to publish scientific books in the vernacular, as opposed to Latin. He is also fondly remembered for his sand-yacht, a contraption with two sails that bowled along the seashore carrying 26 people.

Bisschoppelijk Paleis Hof van Pittem C6

Goezeputstraat. **Closed** *to the public.*

This neoclassical mansion is the former episcopal palace. It was built in 1740 on the site of the 16th-century Hof van Pittem, by the flamboyant bishop Hendrik van Susteren (1716–42). His grandiose tomb by Hendrik Pulinx can be seen in the Sint-Salvatorskathedraal.

Steenstraat C6–D5

Steenstraat is Bruges's main shopping street, lined with department stores, clothes shops, food shops and designer household stores (*see* p.188). In the past, a number of **guilds** had their headquarters here: the finest are the Shoemakers' at No.40 (still bearing its boot-and-crown emblem) and the Masons' at No.25 (1620).

Simon Stevinplein C–D6

This charming tree-lined square was once the site of a huge butchers' hall, the Westvleeshuis, dating back to the 14th century. It is now dominated by a bronze statue of Simon Stevin (1548–1620), made by Louis-Eugène Simonis and erected in 1847. Stevin was a remarkable figure, with a truly Renaissance breadth of talents – one of the outstanding figures of the age – but he joined the 16th-century brain-drain to the Protestant Netherlands, and as a result was disowned by Bruges for 250 years.

When his memory was honoured in the early 19th century by dedicating this square to him, there were still opponents who did not want to give such recognition to a heretic.

AROUND 'T ZAND

't Zand B6

Once a sandy hillock just outside the city walls, 't Zand (the Sand) served as a horse and cattle market, a gathering point and a place of execution. It became part of the city when the last set of city walls embraced it after 1297. The arrival of the railway in 1844 transformed the district. The Ostend–Ghent line cut through it along the path of what today is the Koning Albertlaan and Hoefijzerlaan (both busy highways). Bruges's main railway station was built on 't Zand,

The Sculpture in 't Zand

A great part of the success of 't Zand as a public square is due to its large modern statue, with fountains (1985–6). This is the most ambitious piece in the city by the local sculptors Stefaan Depuydt (b. 1937) and Italian-born Livia Canestraro (b. 1936), whose work can be seen at various points in Bruges.

The four groups of figures in the composition represent a composite image of Flanders: the *Bathing Women* symbolize the cities of Antwerp, Ghent, Kortrijk and Bruges; the *Fishermen* represent life on the North Sea; *Ducks flying over Flat Land* represent the Flemish sea polders; and the *Cyclists* express youth and the future. (Indeed, this is a gathering place for throngs of schoolchildren on bicycles at either end of the day.) On the top of a column sits the sprightly figure of Tijl Uilenspiegel (Till Eulenspiegel), the legendary prankster made famous in a novel (1867) by the Belgian writer Charles de Coster (1827–79), who cast him as a local hero born in Damme and fighting for Flemish independence from Spain.

and properties around the square were rapidly converted into hotels and cafés. The station was upgraded in the 1880s, with a grandiose neogothic building supported on a framework of iron. However, in 1948 the railway was rerouted around the outer rim of canals, leaving 't Zand without its *raison d'être*.

Today the square is the lid on a giant bunker, with the main-road traffic running beneath it through a tunnel flanked by a vast underground car park. This has freed up the ground level into an unusually large, empty and rather refreshing urban space.

Saturday Market
Held *Sat 8am–1pm.*

More recently, one of 't Zand's main functions has been to host Bruges's sprawling Saturday morning market, transferred here from the Markt in 1993. In fact from medieval times up until 1939 a regular Friday market was held here, and the western side of the square is still called the Vrijdagmarkt.

Concertgebouw Brugge C4

't Zand, **t** *(050) 47 69 99,* **w** *www. concertgebouw-brugge.be.*

The grandest project devised for the Brugge 2002 celebrations was this ultra-modern, state-of-the art concert hall, a symbol of Bruges's self-confidence and prosperity. The Belgian architects Robbrecht & Daem won an international competition with their innovative design, which includes a 1200-spectator main Concert Hall (with the largest stage in Belgium) and, more controversially, a 300-seater courtyard-style Chamber Music Hall overlooked by a spiralling balcony rising up through five levels inside the glass-walled 'Lantern Tower'. The terracotta-tile cladding is said to echo the tradition of Flemish brickwork architecture. The café-restaurant at the top of the Lantern Tower promises roof-terrace views over Bruges and as far as the coast. The building was inaugurated in February 2002.

Boeveriestraat B7–8

Boeveriestraat, at the southwestern corner of 't Zand, used to lead to the old city gate called the Boeveriepoort, which was finally demolished in 1863. It is now a quiet and pretty street, flanked by numerous almshouses, *Godshuizen*, and a handful of chapels. There are more almshouses on the cobbled Gloribusstraat.

At No.4 is the **chapel** of the former convent of the Capuchin nuns (*Kapucijnen*), and at No.18 is the 19th-century **monastery** of the Capuchin friars. The Capuchins were a reformist order of Franciscans, set up in 1525 to revive St Francis' traditions of frugality and austerity; they became a major force in the Counter-Reformation, noted for their self-sacrifice. Their original monastery (now the site of the Sofitel hotel; *see* p.166) was founded in 1592, but they had to make way for the expanding railway and moved here in 1869.

At No.34, there's a **wall shrine** to Onze-Lieve-Vrouw van Salette (1866), which is named after the pilgrimage site in eastern France where the Virgin Mary appeared to two young shepherds in 1846.

The **Abbey of St Godelieve** at No.45 (*open, in principle, Mon–Sat 9am–noon and 2.30–6.30pm, Sun 10.30am–noon and 2.30–6.30pm*) is a modest but attractive convent church, mainly in 18th-century Baroque.

No.73 used to be the **Sint-Juliaanshospitaal**, founded in 1290 by the Filles Dieu (Daughters of God), from northern France, as a hospital and refuge for the homeless, assisted by monks of the Sint-Juliaan Brotherhood. After 1600 it served as a mental home and foundling hospital.

In 1480 the governor of the Sint-Juliaanshospitaal, Donaas de Moor, founded a set of **almshouses** at Nos.52–76, for the use of former staff of the hospital and for members of the carpenters', masons' and coopers' guilds. Three years later, he was thanked by banishment from Bruges for siding with Archduke Maximilian in the growing crisis of the 1480s, and he died in exile on his estates outside the city limits.

On the corner with Van Voldenstraat is a **bell**, once the fire bell in the Belfort. It recalls the fact that there used to be an important bell foundry in Klokstraat (two streets back), run by the Dumery family, which produced, among many others, 26 bells which are still in the Belfort carillon (*see* p.70).

Hendrik Consciencelaan A6–B8

Running north at an angle from Boeveriestraat, the name of this residential street commemorates Hendrik Conscience (1812–83), an Antwerp-born novelist, whose best-known work is *De Leeuw van Vlaanderen* (*The Lion of Flanders*), a stirring account of the Flemish revolt before the Battle of the

St Godelieve

St Godelieve was born near Boulogne in about 1045, and at the age of 18 she was married to Bertulf, Lord of Gistel (to the west of Bruges). The ruffian promptly deserted her, leaving her in the hands of her cruel mother-in-law. Seeing her plight, Godelieve's father, assisted by the Bishop of Tournai, leant upon Bertulf to return to her, but Bertulf wasn't one to do another's bidding. He hatched a plan to rid himself of Godelieve by getting a couple of his retainers to strangle her and drown her in a well, making it look like an accident. It worked: Bertulf got off scot-free. But he hadn't counted on divine intercession. Locals were convinced that Godelieve was the victim of skulduggery; her story as an innocent victim of male oppression struck a chord, and she was elevated to sainthood, and a number of miracles were attributed to her. St Godelieve became the focus of a cult at Gistel, and a nunnery was founded.

During the Protestant rampages of 1578, the nuns fled to Bruges and settled here. In 1623 they were joined by Benedictines, and established this abbey. In 1723, to celebrate its centenary, its modest but appealing church was refitted in Baroque style.

Golden Spurs in 1302. The book did much to popularize a sense of pride in Flemish heritage and was a bestseller; however, one place where it was not so enthusiastically received was Bruges itself, where Flemish nationalism was a controversial issue. In 1983 it was made into a film.

Boeverievest A7

The Boeverievest, once part of the old city walls, the Brugse Vesten, has now been rehabilitated as a pleasantly wooded canal-side park, which includes the last remnant of the city's old water system, devised to pump water into the pipes that fed the city. Bruges had an underground water distribution system as early as the 13th century. A water-wheel driven by horses was used at the old

'Venice of the North'

Canals have played an integral role in the life of Bruges since its very foundation. In the 9th century the River Reie was the most reliable means of transport across the marshlands, and was soon given the additional role of defensive moat.

The canals that were developed from this river served the dual purpose of transport and defence, and the shape of the canals today corresponds closely to the circles of the three successive sets of city walls.

The River Reie still flows through the city, from the Minnewater to the Dampoort (city gate) in the northeast. The canal to Damme, cut in 1180, was the main artery to the sea throughout the medieval period. After the silting of the Zwin, new lifelines were forged to Ghent (in 1613) and to Ostend (in 1622), and the linked Ghent–Bruges–Ostend canal looped almost all the way round the city, on the outer ring.

By the 18th century the small canals winding through the city proved inadequate for commercial traffic, and by 1753 a new canal called the Coupure (the Cut) had been forged across the southeastern quarter to relieve congestion and improve the link to the centre.

Finally, in 1907, the Boudewijnkanaal was cut to the new port of Zeebrugge, linking Bruges's new and extensive docks, just to the north of the city, to the sea. Each set of canals had become in turn larger and more industrialized, with a proportionate loss of charm.

Despite this, it only takes one glance at a map of Bruges to see that the title 'Venice of the North' is ridiculous – if, that is, you are only referring to the canals. Bruges has nothing like the profusion of canals in Venice, nor in Amsterdam, the other 'Venice of the North', but in another sense the epithet was perfectly apt – in the magnitude of the city as a trading centre.

The last word goes to Pero Tafur, a 15th-century Spanish traveller, writing in 1438:

It is said that two cities compete with each other for commercial supremacy, Bruges in Flanders in the west, and Venice in the east. It seems to me, however, and many agree with my opinion, that there is much more commercial activity in Bruges than in Venice.

pumphouse (*oud waterhuis*) next to the path. Feeding the water pumps and fountains of the city, it was considered wondrous enough in its day to rank as one of the 'Seven Wonders of Bruges'.

Around the Smedenpoort at the northern end of the street, the park becomes an **arboretum** with labelled species of a broad range of trees.

Smedenpoort A6

The Smedenpoort (Blacksmiths' Gate) is the earliest surviving city gate, dating from 1367 (rebuilt in 1615). Picturesque it may be, but a bronze skull set into the wall on the city side is a reminder of its deadly serious role. The skull was put here in 1911 to replace the genuine skull of a man who was accused of betraying the city by trying to open the gate to the French forces of Louis XIV.

Onze-Lieve-Vrouw van de Blindekens B6

Kreupelenstraat (Cripple Street) 8, t (050) 34 12 03. Open only 1 hour before services, Sat 6pm and Sun 9am, or by appointment with the rector.

From the 14th century on, the chapel of Our Lady of the Blind was at the centre of a settlement for the blind, who lived in the attached almshouses. The complex was rebuilt in 1415, and again in 1651.

The Onze-Lieve-Vrouw van de Blindekens contains a number of curiosities, including the 14th-century wooden statue (with silver frame) of Our Lady, said to have miraculous powers. During the Protestant era (1578–84), the chapel was desecrated by iconoclasts. By 1588 the city was suffering from famine, while the countryside was controlled by armed gangs. Starving parishioners pleaded for relief before the statue, and subsequently a ship, St Michael, broke through the blockade on the canals to bring grain. A model of the ship hanging from the vault commemorates this 'miracle'.

On 15 August each year parishioners take part in the Blindekensprocessie (see p.198). The procession celebrates the safe return of Flemish soldiers after the Battle of Pevelenberg in 1304, following a pledge made by their womenfolk to carry a 16-kilo candle each year on that day to the chapel of Onze-Lieve-Vrouw ter Potterie.

AROUND SINT-JAKOBSKERK

Sint-Jakobskerk C4

Sint-Jakobsplein. Open July and Aug Mon–Fri and Sun 2–5.30pm, Sat 2–4pm.

Sint-Jakobskerk (the church of St James) is the richest of the parish churches in Bruges, but unfortunately it has very limited opening hours. The first building on this site was a 13th-century chapel, but it was enlarged in the 15th and 16th centuries, and remodelled in Baroque style in the 17th century in the wake of the destruction by the iconoclasts in 1580. It had an impressive range of benefactors in the Burgundian era, including Charles the Bold and Tommaso Portinari, as well as a dozen guilds, whose altars animated the side chapels and pillars. The church once contained paintings by Rogier van der Weyden, Hugo van der Goes and Hans Memling, but these were rescued from the iconoclasts and never returned.

The church still contains a good collection of some 80 paintings, including *The Legend of St Lucy* (c. 1480) by the Master of the St Lucy Legend, and work by Pieter Pourbus and Jacob van Oost the Elder. It also has one of the most ornate side chapels in Bruges to the right of the choir, containing the polychrome tomb of Ferry de Gros, treasurer of the Order of the Golden Fleece, who died in 1544. This tomb is curious because it includes both his wives: a statue of his first wife, who died in 1521 after producing 16 children, lies beside his effigy; his second wife also died before him in 1530 (after just three children), so she has been slotted in on the level below.

Hof Bladelin C4

Naaldenstraat (Needle Street) 19; ring the doorbell for access. Courtyard open April–Sept Mon–Sat 10am–noon and 2–5pm, Sun 10.30am–noon, Oct–March Mon–Sat 10am–noon and 2–4pm, Sun 10.30am–noon.

This is one of the great private mansions of the Burgundian era, complete with a tower. It was built in about 1450 by Pieter Bladelin

The Wealth of Bruges

In 1438 the Spanish traveller Pero Tafur recorded his impressions on a visit to Bruges: *In the whole of the west there is no other great mercantile centre except Bruges... and thither repair all nations of the world, and they say that at times the number of ships sailing from the harbour of Bruges exceeds seven hundred a day...The people of this part of the country are exceedingly fastidious in their apparel, very extravagant in their food, and much given to all kinds of luxury... Without doubt the goddess of luxury has great power there, but it is not a place for poor men, who would be badly received. But anyone who has money and wishes to spend it, will find in this town alone everything which the whole world produces. I saw there oranges and lemons from Castile, which seemed only just to have been gathered from the trees, fruits and wine from Greece, as abundant as in that country. I saw also confections and spices from Alexandria and all the Levant just as if one were there; furs from the Black Sea, as if they had been produced in the district. Here was all Italy with its brocades, silks and armour, and everything which is made there; and indeed there is no part of the world whose products are not found here at their best.*

The British in Bruges

Britain has had close links with Bruges for over 1,000 years. Flemish mercenaries took part in the Norman Conquest in 1066, and English wool became the mainstay of Bruges's textile industry. During the Hundred Years' War (1337–1453) Flemish loyalties wavered between England and France. During the Reformation, hundreds of English Roman Catholics fled to Flanders; English monks and nuns joined Flemish religious institutions, or set up their own.

A new breed of British visitor arrived after 1815: tourists on their way to see the battlefield of Waterloo, just south of Brussels. Many of the visitors stopped off at Bruges on their way, and were pleasantly surprised.

They also found Bruges remarkably cheap. Many impecunious middle-class families, unable to maintain standards in Britain, relocated to Bruges. In his *Tour through Belgium* (1816), James Mitchell remarked that over 40 British families were already resident in the city, enjoying cheap rents – a good house with garden, coach house and stable for £25 a year, 'a mere nothing'. But he also pointed out that 'the main secret of the economy of living... is this, that a family may here, where they are unknown, lower their style of living'.

This is what brought the writer Fanny Trollope (1780–1863) and her family to the city. She had taken up writing in an effort to escape the debts incurred by her barrister husband, Thomas; in 1827 they had been forced to flee the threat of debtors' prison by leaving England for the United States. After four years in Cincinnati she produced *Domestic Manners of the Americans* (1832), a critical exposé of a hypocritical, slave-owning society. She followed this up with a travelogue called *Belgium and Western Europe* (1833), an account of a journey she took with two of her sons. But in 1834 her husband's creditors were again pressing hard and they fled to Bruges. Here she embarked on a Gothic novel, *Tremordyn Cliff*, which was coloured by the laudanum she was taking to sustain her strength as her family collapsed into ill health. Her son Henry died of

tuberculosis aged 23 on Christmas Eve 1834, and her husband, Thomas, who had become unsociable and reclusive, died in October 1835. Both are buried in the Protestant section of a cemetery to the south of Bruges, near the Katelijnepoort. After her husband's death, however, the threat of imprisonment was lifted, and Fanny was able to return to England, where her youngest son, Anthony Trollope, embarked on his career as one of the great 19th-century English novelists.

Bruges by now had also attracted a handful of English antiquarians and art collectors who were to have a profound effect on its subsequent history. They included the print collector John Steinmetz; the architect and painter William Brangwyn; Thomas Harper King, a pupil of the great neogothic designer Augustus Pugin; the architect Robert Chantrell; and the art historian James Weale, who did much to establish the fame of the great Bruges artists of the late Middle Ages, such as van Eyck and Memling. They were avid supporters of Bruges's restoration, and helped to see a number of the key historic buildings saved and then embellished in neogothic style. They also laid the foundations for the collection in the Gruuthusemuseum.

By 1870 the English community in Bruges numbered some 1200, and warranted its own schools and church. The Anglicans used the old church of the Carmelite nuns (now the Josef Ryelandtzaal; see p.118) in Ezelstraat. The Catholic community was larger: there was a Catholic girls' school at the Engels Klooster in Carmersstraat (see p.104), and Catholic boys could go to the Xavier Institute in Mariastraat, where they were taught by British brothers. The former trading house of the Genoese merchants in Vlamingstraat was used as an English reading room, and English was widely spoken in the town. Today more British people come to Bruges than ever before, but they are by and large unaware of the important role their compatriots have played in the evolution of the city.

(1410–72), municipal treasurer and councillor to Philip the Good, treasurer of the Order of the Golden Fleece, and one of the wealthiest men in the city. The sculpture (1892) over the main entrance depicting Pieter Bladelin kneeling before the Virgin is by the neo-gothic architect Louis Delacenserie, who also designed the Provinciaal Hof (*see* p.71) in the Markt.

In 1469 the house was bought by the Medici Bank of Florence, hence the terracotta medallions on the walls of the courtyard, depicting Lorenzo de' Medici ('The Magnificent') and his wife Clarissa Orsini. One of its representatives, Tommaso Portinari, lived here from 1473 to 1497, and exercised a powerful role in the city as the banker who could underwrite the extravagances of Charles the Bold's court. He was also a patron of Hans Memling and Hugo van der Goes (whose triptych featuring the Nativity, now in the Uffizi Museum in Florence, is called the *Portinari Triptych*). After Charles the Bold's death in 1477, on his ill-advised military adventure against France, the Medici Bank dismissed Portinari for financial recklessness. He stayed in Bruges and worked on his own account, until bankrupted in 1497 – a sign of the failing economy of the city.

Muntplein C5

This pretty square was once the site of the old city mint, which produced coins from 1300 to 1786. The bronze statue, *Flandria Nostra* (1901), by Jules Lagae, depicts Mary of Burgundy, wife of Charles the Bold.

The frontage of the shop at No.9 Geldmuntstraat nearby, now the De Medici Sorbetière, is a rare example in Bruges of Art Nouveau/Jugendstil architecture.

Prinsenhof C5

Off Noordzandstraat. **Closed** to the public.
For 60 years the Prinsenhof was the epicentre of Burgundian rule, a glamorous and extensive ducal palace that witnessed

The Discalced Carmelites

In 1630 a mendicant order of friars called the Discalced (barefooted) Carmelites came to Bruges. Because there was a large population of mendicant monks and nuns in a city already economically stretched, they were not made very welcome. However, the following year Bruges was struck by plague. The Discalced Carmelites acted with selfless charity and tended to the sick, and they were rewarded with the unenviable honour of being appointed the official plague priests, led by the 'Pest-Pater', who carried a red warning stick with a cross on top. The plague continued for seven years, but the Discalced Carmelites never shrank from their duty. As one caught the plague and died, another would volunteer to take over his task, even putting on the dead man's habit. The grateful city granted them property in Ezelstraat in 1633, where a new convent was built after 1680. The order continued to do good works through the hard decades that followed, but it was suppressed in 1798, and many of the friars were transported to western France. They were allowed to return after 1800; their numbers rapidly dwindled before a revival in the 1840s, and they still form a community attached to the Karmelietenkerk in Ezelstraat (closed to the public).

the great set pieces of the era. Built originally in about 1350, it became an enclave of power, set around a series of courtyards stretching from here to Gheerwijnstraat and the mint, and north to Moerstraat. There were fountains, flower gardens, tennis courts and heated bath houses. The palace itself was crowned by turrets and had an eight-storey *donjon* attached to it, with a parapet and minstrels' gallery. An engraving of 1641 still shows it in good condition, but by this time it was well past its heyday.

After the death of Mary of Burgundy in 1482, and the humiliation of her unpopular husband Maximilian in 1488, political power shifted elsewhere, and gradually parts of the complex were sold off. In 1662 the remaining buildings were turned into a boarding school for English girls run by Franciscan nuns, and in 1795 they were sold off as national property by the French. Part of the complex was rebuilt in neogothic style in the 1880s, when it was taken over by a French community of nuns from Boulogne. Today little remains of the original palace.

AROUND EZELPOORT

Ezelpoort B3

The Ezelpoort was one of eight city gates built in the late 14th century to reinforce the outer defences of the city. With its weathered brick, a backdrop of trees and shallow arches spanning the canal, it is the prettiest of the four surviving gates, and also the latest, having been rebuilt in 1615. Note the bell on the roof, which would announce when the gate was closing.

Joseph Ryelandtzaal C3

Achiel van Ackerplein.

The convent church of the Discalced Carmelite nuns became an Anglican church in 1820, a measure of the growing English community in the city. In 1983 it was converted into the Joseph Ryelandtzaal, a municipal concert hall named after the Bruges-born composer (1870–1965), who became a professor at the Conservatoire of Ghent and wrote various symphonic works and an opera called *Sainte Cécile*. The sculptures (1987) on the façade are by Stefaan Depuydt and Livia Canestraro, creators of the large sculpture on 't Zand.

Achiel van Acker (1898–1975), after whom the adjacent square is named, was a Bruges-born socialist politician who was prime minister between 1945 and 1946 and between 1954 and 1958, and who was instrumental in establishing the welfare state in post-war Belgium.

A Walk Around Mercantile Bruges

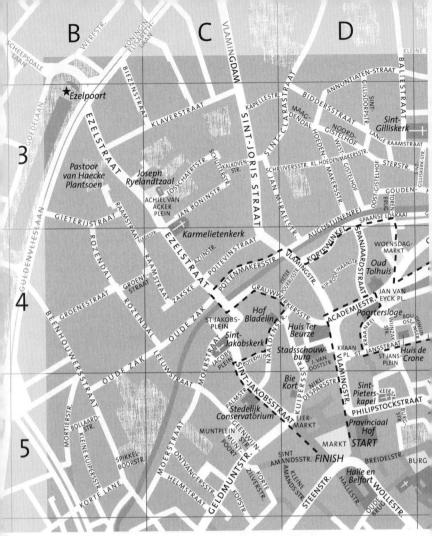

In the Middle Ages, Bruges was one of the wealthiest cities in the world, prospering from the vibrant activity of its traders. It was an international and cosmopolitan city, with a web of contacts stretching across Europe to the Baltic and Russia, the Mediterranean and the Middle East, and North Africa. The engine room of this business culture was the network of streets that lies to the north of the Markt. This is where the deals were struck, and where the barges came to unload their cargoes of wool, cloth, dyes, salted fish, wine, spices, silks, oriental carpets, jewellery and live exotic animals. This walk will give you a glimpse of this world and the rewards that it generated.

Start at the **Provinciaal Hof** in the Markt. The Waterhalle in the Markt (the great covered market hall) ran the length of its eastern flank where the Provinciaal Hof now stands, and the main canal through the city ran through it. This canal, the Kraanrei, was filled in at the end of the 18th century, but if you look at a map you can trace its path: start at the canal to the south of the Markt and the Burg, and follow the truncated spur that leads north, parallel to Wollestraat. Imagine it continuing beneath the Provinciaal Hof, then to the east of Vlamingstraat, then curving eastwards beside the street still called Kraanrei to meet the Spiegelrei on the other side of Jan van Eyckplein. Now picture this filled with barges loaded with cargo, and

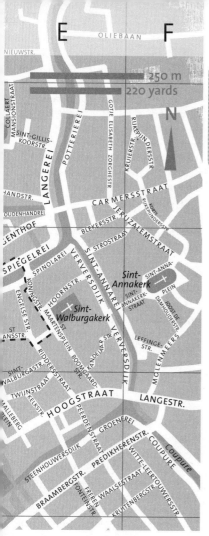

Start and finish: The Markt.
Walking time: 1½hrs. The total distance is about 3km.
Lunch and drinks stops: De Witte Poorte, *see* p.177; 't Voske Malpertuus, *see* p.173; Boterhuis Brasserie, *see* p.179; Lotus, *see* p.173; Het Dagelijks Brood, *see* p.173.

A little further up the street, in what is called **Beursplein** (Bourse Square), at No.33 Vlamingstraat, is the **Genuese Loge** (Genoese Lodge), the trading house of the merchants from the Italian city of Genoa. Not a lot of the 1399 building has survived, apart from the entrance (with a 19th-century relief sculpture of St George, patron saint of Genoa, slaying his dragon, a replica of the original preserved inside). During the 16th century, serge (a light woollen cloth) became a leading product of the town. After the Genoans abandoned Bruges in 1516 to join the other traders in the new trade centre, Antwerp, the serge-weavers took over their building, and it was renamed the Saaihalle (Serge Hall). In 1720 it acquired a Dutch-style bell gable. In the 19th century the building became the Café Rosimont, with boarding house and billiard hall, and the façade was emblazoned with lettering advertising its non-stop beefsteaks and other provender.

Next to the Genoese Lodge is the **Huis Ter Beurze**. This was the site of the inn run by the Van Ter Beurze family, where money-changers, bankers and merchants gathered to do business from the 13th century on. It was the world's first stock exchange, giving rise to the international term 'bourse' (*see* p.76). The building looks very much as it did in the mid-15th century, but has been largely reconstructed. It is currently being used as the organizational headquarters for the Brugge 2002 celebrations.

It was no accident that the Huis Ter Beurze became a centre for financial transactions: the entry point to the Kraanrei canal lay 200m away, and the Beursplein was flanked by the lodges of the Genoans, the Florentines and the Venetians, who won the privilege of constructing the first national lodge in 1322,

the next part of this walk begins to make more sense.

Leave the Markt by the northeastern corner and head up Vlamingstraat. After 150m you will reach the **Stadsschouwburg**, on the left-hand side. The Stadsschouwburg (Municipal Theatre) was built in 1868 in the grand neo-classical style considered essential for the era. It stands on the site of an inn called De Koorneblomme, where the American poet Henry Wadsworth Longfellow stayed. His poem *The Song of Hiawatha* (1855) was translated into Dutch to great acclaim in 1886 by Bruges's poet Guido Gezelle (*see* pp.100–1). The statue outside the theatre represents the bird-catcher, Papageno, from Mozart's *The Magic Flute*.

The Rules of the Trade

Foreign traders in Bruges during medieval times were allowed considerable freedoms, such as the right to purchase or rent property, and to carry arms unchallenged. The most important general restriction, however, was that they were not allowed to undertake retail trade, nor to resell within the city goods that they bought there: they were strictly import-and-export merchants and the main export was Flemish textiles. The trading houses (or 'lodges') – which became increasingly extravagant architecturally – offered their nationals a common meeting place, protection and representation, an information service for newcomers, and in some cases a chapel. They also took responsibility for policing their own compatriots, and laid down the etiquette of trade and general rules of behaviour, governing drinking, gambling and even bedtimes. As a result, this trading environment tended to be orderly, businesslike and civilized. By and large the atmosphere within the city was trusting and peaceable.

at right angles to the Huis Ter Beurze. The crumbled remains of their house were removed in 1965. Next to that, separated by a narrow continuation of Vlamingstraat, was the Florentine lodge, described in 1926 as 'a beautiful building flanked by four graceful turrets, now entirely spoilt'. That too has gone, but a **marble plaque**, on the side of No.1 Academiestraat, recalls it with a verse about Flemish dike-building from the *Inferno* by the Florentine poet Dante (1265–1321).

Turn right into Academiestraat, which broadens out into Jan van Eyckplein. At the end of the street, on the right, is the **Poortersloge**, built in the 14th century but much restored. It is one of the few buildings that has retained its tower (rebuilt after a fire in 1775), a common feature of prestige architecture in the medieval period. This was a meeting place for a select group of successful city burghers, and the Society of the White Bear, charged with organizing jousting tournaments, was also based here, hence the statue of a bear in one of the niches.

According to legend, when Baldwin Iron-Arm first built his castle and founded Bruges, the only living creature on the site was a bear – the city's first inhabitant. In 1739 the building was bought by the city and was home to its Academy of Arts for 150 years (hence the street's name). The Poortersloge was cited as one of the 'Seven Marvels of Bruges' in the 16th century, when it appeared in prints very much as it does today.

Diametrically opposite, overlooking Jan van Eyckplein, is the **Oud Tolhuis** (Old Customs House). Over the arched entrance is the coat-of-arms of Peter of Luxembourg, the receiver of the toll, who ordered the reconstruction of the building in 1477. The extremely narrow building next to the Tolhuis is the **Huis de Lastdragers** (1470), the guildhouse of the Stevedores. Both have been heavily restored. The location of these buildings is significant, for they overlooked the Sint-Jansbrug where there was a weighhouse belonging to the Tolhuis, and where, after weighing, customs were levied on all incoming cargoes. However, the bridge has gone, and the canals were removed in the 18th century to be replaced by **Jan van Eyckplein**, with a statue (1878) of the great 15th-century painter by the Bruges sculptor Henry Pickery (1828–94). The southern part of the square has retained its old name, Biskajersplein, after the trading house of the Biscayan (or Basque) merchants at **No.6a** – built in 1494 and much restored.

We now trace the path of the old canal a short distance by taking the Kraanrei west from the top of Biskajersplein to the **Kraanplein**. *Kraan* means crane. The 'town crane' in question was a herculean contraption, pictured in 16th-century prints and maps. It was built like a wooden barn, but with a triangular projection rising from it – the crane arm. The pulleys were driven by a pair of human treadmills and the whole machine swivelled round to lift heavy cargo from barges on to the quayside.

Turn left at Kraanplein into Sint-Jansstraat (St John's Street). You will soon come to Sint-Jansplein. The most striking feature of the square is the brick **Huis de Crone**, at the corner with Wijnzakstraat, a late-Gothic house, formerly a wine tavern, built in about 1500. At the centre of the square is a late 18th-century monumental **water pump**.

Continue along Sint-Jansstraat to Engelsestraat. **Engelsestraat** was so named because this was the heart of Bruges's English community. As purveyors of the high-quality wool on which the Flemish textile trade was based, they occupied a pivotal position in Bruges's business affairs. To facilitate business, the English were granted the privilege of having their own weighhouse, set up in this street in the 1330s, which meant that they could weigh their goods near their trading house without recourse to the public weighhouses.

Turn right into Engelsestraat, then first left into **Korte Ridderstraat**. The Bruges poet Guido Gezelle lived at **No.5** from 1865 to 1872. The street brings you swiftly to **Sint-Maartensplein**. Sint-Maartensplein used to be called Schottenplaats, after the Scottish contingent who had a consular house here. Today the dominant feature is the baroque façade of the **Sint-Walburgakerk** (*see* p.98; open Easter–Sept daily 8pm–10pm only, but a glass door allows you to glimpse the interior at other times). This is Bruges's most elegant Baroque church, reflecting the bravado of the Counter-Reformation and the Jesuits. Continue northwards from Sint-Maartensplein, following Koningstraat (King St) to the canal. Cross the Koningbrug to **Spiegelrei** (good view of the Poortersloge). *Spiegel* means 'mirror', and now that this stretch of canal no longer has through traffic of boats and barges it often is mirror-still.

No.15 Spiegelrei is now a school, but in the 15th century it was the headquarters of the English Merchant Adventurers who ran English business in Bruges, dealing mainly in wool, hides and tin. In 1464 the governor of the Adventurers was William Caxton, the man who brought printing to England (*see* p.25). At No.17 is a rare surviving example of a **spy mirror**, projecting from the window frame. This allowed people inside the house to see what was going on in the street outside. The

Bruges streets were once full of them, and visitors used to complain that it gave them the eerie feeling of being constantly watched.

Walk back westwards along the Spiegelrei to head back towards Jan van Eyckplein. The house on the corner with Genthof, called **Roode Steen**, used to bear a plaque commemorating Georges Rodenbach. On the death of the Belgian writer in 1898 there was talk in Bruges of erecting a statue in his honour. However, the suggestion was greeted with an outcry by many of the great and the good – including Guido Gezelle – who felt strongly that Rodenbach's most famous work, the novella *Bruges-la-Morte* (*Bruges the Dead*; 1892) had done a shameful disservice to their city. Yes, it had put Bruges firmly on the tourist map by being such a literary success, but it had painted such a gloomy, sickly, decaying, moribund image of Bruges that the people who actually lived there, and those who were actively trying to restore and renovate it, felt irked and offended by it. In the end, a small plaque was put up 50 years after his death – but his family had to pay. It has since been removed. But Gothic and ridiculous it may seem today, *Bruges-la-Morte* deserves its reputation as a masterpiece of Symbolist fiction. Its sustained mood of *fin-de-siècle* melancholy is achieved with admirable elegance. It was also, in its day, highly experimental: for Rodenbach, Bruges itself was one of the main characters in the plot. To this end, he insisted that the novella should contain photographs of the city, the first time photography had been used to enhance fiction.

Turn right at the end of Spiegelrei into **Genthof**. At No.7 is one of the very few surviving wooden houses in Bruges, dating from the 16th century. During the medieval era most houses in the city were made of wood – hence the importance of the Scottish timber trade, but fire was an ever-present hazard. Thatch was progressively banned after 1417, but the parallel restrictions on wooden houses were not introduced until the 1600s.

Continue to **Woensdagmarkt**. Woensdagmarkt is the site of the old

Wednesday market. The statue of the German-born painter Hans Memling (see p.88) is by Henry Pickery, completed four years before his Jan van Eyck to the south. To the north, Woensdagmarkt merges with **Oosterlingenplein**. This is named after the Oosterlingen, 'easterners' (in other words the Germans), representatives of the powerful trading cities of the Hanseatic League.

Formed during the 13th century, the Hanseatic League bound together German trading associations (Hanse) by treaties of mutual protection. It grew to include about 100 German cities and German merchant groups located outside Germany. They traded across the Baltic and north Europe, and as far east as Novgorod in Russia, dealing in a huge range of goods that included iron ore, timber, grain, furs, salt, fish, beer, beeswax, honey and amber. The Hanseatic League was so powerful that it had a fractious relationship with the city, with continual disputes over import taxes. Although it was one of the first foreign groups to be established in Bruges, it was also one of the last to be granted the privilege of building a trading house. Late in the day, in 1470, as an inducement to keep it in Bruges, it was at last given property by the town, and between 1478 and 1481 built the finest lodge of them all, the Oosterlingen-huis, a massive late-Gothic enclave with a crenellated castle topped with a soaring tower. This was one of the 'Seven Marvels of Bruges', the list of the finest buildings selected in the 16th century. Nonetheless, the Germans were among the first to relocate to Antwerp. The Oosterlingenhuis fell into decay and was demolished in the 18th century; all that remains of this building is at **No.1 Krom Genthof** (brick house with flag).

A little further north, Oosterlingenplein meets the canal. Take the street running westwards along the canal, **Spaanse Loskaai**. This part of town was effectively the Spanish quarter: the Spanish trading house was in Spanjaardstraat, just beyond Spaanse Loskaai. Their main trade was in wool, hides and fruit. After Bruges's decline in the 16th century, the Spanish were the only foreign

traders who maintained a large presence in the city, as part of the ruling elite; Flanders remained part of the Spanish Netherlands until 1713. The canal here traces the path of the second set of city walls, built in about 1127.

Continue westwards to Kortewinkel. **No.2 Kortewinkel** is another of Bruges's rare wooden houses. Cross to the north side of the canal by the **Vlamingbrug**, which has pretty views. Head west, following Pottermakkersstraat (Potters St). If you look south from here over the canal, you can see the last remnant of the 1127 **city walls**: part of a tower, now set in the garden wall of a house in Pieter Pourbusstraat.

At Ezelstraat (Donkey St), turn left along Grauwwerkerstraat, then first right into Naaldenstraat (Needle St). At No.19 is **Hof Bladelin**, one of the great private mansions of the Burgundian era, complete with a tower (see p.115), owned by the Medici Bank of Florence in the late 15th century.

Opposite Hof Bladelin on the corner of **Kuipersstraat** (Coopers St) is the site of the trading house of the Italian city of Lucca, built in 1394. Only the cellars remain. The tower at **No.7** marks the site of the Hof van Gistel, a palace built in 1444 by Antoine de Bourbon, Duke of Vendôme, Lord of Gistel. It was later owned by the head of the Spanish community in Bruges, Jean de Matance of Burgos.

Take the arched alley by No.9 Naaldenstraat, Boterhuis, so-called because it passes beneath the arch of the **Boterhuis** (Butter House), a market for dairy produce from the 16th century to the mid-19th century. Opposite the end of Boterhuis, at No.41 Sint-Jakobsstraat, is the **Hotel Navarra**. In the 16th century this was the consulate of Navarre, a kingdom that straddled the Pyrenees between Spain and France, before being absorbed by those countries in 1515 and 1589 respectively.

Turn left at Sint-Jakobsstraat, which opens up into Eiermarkt (Egg Market) – with its monumental **water pump** (1761) designed by Pieter Pepers – and leads you back to the Markt.

Day Trips

08

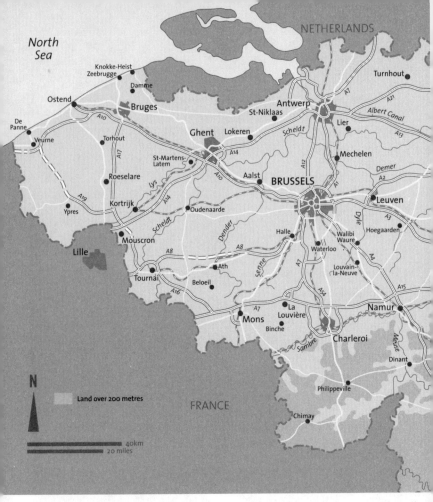

Belgium is a small country, and Belgians think nothing of travelling the length and breadth of their country for the day. However, these day trips all lie within 80km of Bruges.

DAMME

Apart from the canal that still connects it to Bruges, it is hard to believe that Damme was once a major port. Today it is a pretty little village surrounded by fields of grazing horses and sleepy dairy cows, and the polders stretch out for miles in all directions, divided only by roads and waterways lined with tall poplars.

One of Damme's most celebrated sons was the writer Jacob van Maerlant (or Maerlandt,

c. 1225–92), who translated popular tales and fables from Latin into Flemish. Belgian writer Charles de Coster (1827–79) also had connections to the town. He claimed that this was the home of the trickster Tijl Uilenspiegel in his picaresque tale of the fight for independence from Spain during the religious wars of the 16th century. The tale features three main characters: Tijl, his fiancée Nele, and their loyal pal Lamme Goedzak, all very much a part of the Damme landscape today. A monument to Tijl Uilenspiegel (1979) by Jef Claerhout was erected on Daamse Vaart-Zuid, on the centenary of Charles de Coster's death. It shows Tijl with various allegorical animals representing aspects of human nature.

Damme's literary tradition continues with its reputation as a bookworm's paradise, with

Getting There

Damme is just a 7km **walk** or **cycle** northeast of the centre of Bruges along the road that follows the canal. Alternatively, **Sightseeing Line/City Tour** buses leave from the Markt (*April–Sept departures daily at 2pm and 4pm; €17; historical commentary included*). You can also journey by **canal** aboard the *Lamme Goedzak*, leaving from Noorweegse Kaai, at Dampoort (*bus no.4 from the Markt*).

Quasimodo (*see* p.56) organizes a daily 25km bicycle tour, which includes Damme, departing from the Burg at 1pm, returning 5pm (*adults €17, under-26s €15*).

Tourist Information

Huyse de Grote Sterre, Jacob van Maerlantstraat 3, **t** (050) 35 33 19. **Open** *16 April–15 Oct Mon–Fri 9am–noon and 2–6pm, Sat and Sun 10am–noon and 2–6pm, 16 Oct–15 April Mon–Fri 9am–noon and 2–5pm, Sat and Sun 3–5pm*. Can arrange bicycle hire.

Eating Out

Bij Lamme Goedzak, *Kerkstraat 13*, **t** (050) 35 20 03. **Open** *Fri–Wed*. **Moderate**. Flemish traditional décor for gastronomic regional food, as well as lighter meals and snacks. Has a large garden terrace.

De Drie Zilveren Kannen, *Kerkstraat 9*, **t** (050) 35 56 77. **Open** *daily (closed Mon and Wed in winter)*. **Moderate**. Panelled interior richly adorned with antiques, and inspired French cooking. Also has a tea-room for light snacks.

De Lieve, *Jacob van Maerlantstraat 10*, **t** (050) 35 66 30. **Open** *Wed–Mon (closed Mon eve)*. **Moderate**. One of the most celebrated restaurants of West Flanders, with a relaxed, tastefully rustic setting. Inventive French cuisine, with seasonal notes.

Eetcafé De Spieghel, *Jacob van Maerlantstraat 1*, **t** (050) 37 11 30. **Open** *Wed–Sun*. **Inexpensive**. Snacks, tea and cakes, or a full meal. Terraces front and back.

Gasthof Maerlant, *Markt 21*, **t** (050) 35 29 52. **Open** *Thurs–Tues (closed Tues eve)*. **Moderate**. The 1920s are recalled in Art Deco style, as a backdrop for Belgian-style cuisine, and local produce. Terrace in summer.

Taverne 't Hemeltje, *Kerkstraat 46*, **t** (050) 36 07 07. **Open** *Thurs–Mon*. **Inexpensive**. Terrace in summer, open fire in winter. Specializes in eels.

over 10 bookshops crowding out all other forms of commerce, and a book market in the market square every second Sunday of the month.

The Stadhuis

Marktplein. **Open** *July–Sept daily 10am–noon and 2–6pm; guided tours in winter; adm €1*

The town hall was built between 1464 and 1468, as a scaled-down version of Bruges's Gothic Stadhuis. During rather over-zealous restoration work in the 19th century, the exterior was furnished with statues of the Counts of Flanders. The two stones hanging from the façade are known as the 'stones of justice' – to be hung around the neck or feet of adulterous women or scolds. The interior contains some atmospheric rooms where the aldermen met and worked. In the Marktplein outside is a statue (1860) of Jacob van Maerlant by the Bruges sculptor Henry Pickery, who was also responsible for the statues of Jan van Eyck and Hans Memling in Bruges.

Huyse De Grote Sterre (Maerlant-Uilenspiegel Museum)

Jacob van Maerlantstraat 3. **Open** *16 April–15 Oct daily 9am–noon and 2–6pm, 16 Oct–15 April daily 9am–noon and 2–5pm; adm €2.50*.

Huyse De Grote Sterre is a fine 15th-century building, which also served as the residence of the Spanish military governor during the 17th century. It contains not only the tourist office but also a small museum dedicated to Tijl Uilenspiegel and Jacob van Maerlant.

Huis Saint-Jean-d'Angély

(Huis Sint-Jan) Jacob van Maerlantstraat 11. **Closed** *to the public.*

Huis Saint-Jean-d'Angély is a 15th-century house built by the town of Saint-Jean-d'Angély in southwest France, one of 19 wine-trading enterprises located in Damme. It was in this house that Charles the Bold, Duke of Burgundy, and Margaret of York were married in 1468, before entering Bruges for their grand *Blijde Intreden* (Joyous Entry).

Sint-Janshospitaal

Kerkstraat 33. **Open** *April–Sept Tues–Thurs and Sat 10am–noon and 2–6pm, Mon and Fri 2–6pm, Sun 11am–noon and 2–6pm, Oct–March Sat and Sun 2–6.30pm;* **adm** *€1.*

According to tradition, the Sint-Janshospitaal was founded in 1249 by Margaret of Constantinople, who also founded the Begijnhof in Bruges. Some of the buildings date from the 13th century, while the chapel is largely Baroque. The museum contains a mixed collection of church treasures, paintings and medieval and Renaissance furniture and ceramics.

Onze-Lieve-Vrouwekerk

Open *May–Sept Tues–Sun 10–noon and 2.30–5.30pm;* **adm** *€0.50.*

The Onze-Lieve-Vrouwekerk has been left in a semi-ruined state since partial collapse in 1725, when the parishioners could not afford to repair it. It still has its 13th-century triple aisle in the style called Scheldt Gothic, with 16th- and 17th-century furnishings. The statues of the apostles date from the 14th century. Jacob van Maerlant lies buried beneath the tower, which now stands separate from the body of the church. There are fine views across the polders from the summit of the tower (43m tall; and from here it is possible to detect traces of buildings long since gone, indicating how the town has shrunk over the past 500 years).

Haringmarkt

The Herring Market was once a key centre for the herring trade, which, at its height in the 15th century, was shifting 28 million salted or smoked (and barrelled) herrings a year.

Schellemolen Windmill

Damse Vaart-West. **Open** *July–Aug daily 10.30am–12.30pm and 2–5pm, June and Sept Sat and Sun 2–5.30pm.*

The white-painted Schellemolen windmill dates from 1867, but a windmill has operated on this site since 1267.

OSTEND

There is a contented, prosperous air to Ostend (Oostende in Flemish). This is the place to come and enjoy a fine platter of seafood, straight out of the chill North Sea; to breathe in the air on the Zeedijk promenade that lines the north of the city, overlooking the broad beach of powdery sand bespangled with windbreaks and deckchairs and sandcastles; and to relish a unique mix of tasteful elegance and seaside tat. There are bleak days when the sea churns grey, and a biting wind whisks sand along the seafront. On others, the skies open up into aquamarine blue, the wind drops, and the town is bathed in glorious, bronzing warmth.

It is not all buckets and spades, oysters and waffles. Ostend is an active seaport, for ferries linking Britain and for its fishing fleet, the largest in Belgium. It also has a rewardingly strong line in art. This was the home of that great artist James Ensor, Post-Impressionist, precursor of the Expressionists. Local galleries include examples of his work, plus work by many of the great Belgian Symbolists, as well as a dynamic modern collection.

Getting There

By Car: Ostend is just 20km northwest of Bruges, reached in about 20 minutes, either on the N9, or on the A10/E40 motorway. There are car parks and plenty of parking meters in the centre of town as well as free 'periphery' car parks.

By Train: There is a direct and frequent train link between Bruges station and Ostend, departing at least every half an hour. The journey takes just 14 minutes and adult fare costs €2.90 each way. Trains arrive at the harbour, which is a short walk from the town centre.

Getting Around

By Tram: The Flemish Coastal Tram, **t** (059) 56 53 53, runs right the way along the coast, a total distance of 69km passing through Ostend. This is a fun, inexpensive and relaxing way to explore the coast when you are in Ostend.

Tourist Information

Toerisme Oostende, Monacoplein 2, **t** (059) 70 11 99, **f** 70 34 77, **e** *toerisme.oostende @flanderscoast.be*, **w** *www.oostende.be.* **Open** *June–Aug Mon–Sat 9am–7pm, Sun 10am–7pm, Sept–May Mon–Sat 10am–6pm, Sun 10am–5pm.*

Festivals

With a name like **Le Bal du Rat Mort** (Dead Rat Ball), perhaps it is no surprise to find that James Ensor was among the organizers of the first ball, back in 1896. The ball is a noted high-point on the social calendar and takes place on the first Saturday after Shrove Tuesday in the casino, with participants wearing masks and fancy-dress based on the chosen theme, which changes each year. Tickets cost about €23.

Eating Out

Art Café, Romestraat 3, **t** (059) 80 56 86, *wheelchair access.* **Open** *Mon–Fri.* **Moderate**. Conveniently located in the Museum of

Provinciaal Museum voor Moderne Kunst

*Romestraat 11, **t** (059) 50 81 18, **w** www.pmmk. be.* **Open** *Tues–Sun 10am–6pm; adm €2.50.*

This is Ostend's fine modern art museum: three floors of paintings, sculpture, prints, installations and video work, attractively presented in bright, well-designed galleries. It includes work by many of the leading Belgian artists of the 20th century, such as Léon Spilliaert, Edgard Tytgat and Jean Brusselmans, some Dadaists and Surrealists (René Magritte, Paul Delvaux), Pierre Alechinsky, and an interesting and satisfyingly provocative selection of contemporary work. It also holds temporary exhibitions of distinction.

Museum voor Schone Kunsten

*Wapenplein, **t** (059) 80 53 35.* **Open** *holidays Wed–Mon 10am–noon and 2–5pm; adm €3.50.*

The city's fine art museum (on the second floor of the Stedelijk Feesten Kultuurpaleis), is not extensive, but for anyone with an interest in Belgian art, especially the Belgian Symbolists and James Ensor, it is deeply rewarding. It contains mainly late 19th-century and early 20th-century paintings, prints and drawings, and, most notably, works by Ensor, Léon Spilliaert, and artists of the Sint-Martens-Latem School, such as Albert Servaes, Constant Permeke and Gustave de Smet.

James Ensorhuis

*Vlanderenstraat 27, **t** (059) 80 53 35.* **Open** *during the holidays daily 10am–noon and 2–5pm, outside the holidays Sat and Sun only, 2–5pm; adm €1.50.*

This was the house of James Ensor, and makes a fascinating visit for anyone interested in his work. James Ensor (1860–1949) is one of Belgium's most celebrated – and oddball – painters. He was born to an English father and Flemish mother, who ran a novelty and souvenir shop selling – among other things – the kind of carnival masks that

Modern Art (PMMK), a stylish, modern café offering substantial meals, as well as lighter fare throughout the day, and late into the night.

Au Vigneron, *Koningstraat 79, t (059) 70 48 16. Open Fri, Sat, Mon–Wed. Expensive.* A famous Belgian restaurant, in the reconstructed royal villa, overlooking the sea. An elegant and historic setting for respected and inventive fish gastronomy.

Fort Napoleon, *Vuurtorenweg, t (059) 33 21 60. Open daily; closed Mon outside school holidays. Moderate.* Stylish restaurant and bar in a recently restored Napoleonic fortress. You can combine a gastronomic meal or just a drink with a visit to the fort.

Le Grillon, *Visserskaai 31, t (059) 70 60 63. Open Fri–Wed. Moderate.* A smart but relaxed restaurant with above-average cooking at moderate prices (three course meal for about €25), specializing in fish.

Lucullus, *Louisastraat 19, t (059) 70 09 28. Open Tues–Sat. Moderate.* Elegant modern restaurant in the heart of town, offering a range of dishes, from lobster to beef stewed in beer.

Savarin, *Albert I-Promenade 75, t (059) 51 31 71. Moderate. Open daily.* Something of an institution, with its titanium and glass veranda overlooking the sea. Specializes in fish, but offers a wide variety of fare throughout the day.

Se@site, *Alfons Pieterslaan 86, t (059) 56 88 18. Open Tues–Sun. Moderate.* A sleek, airy, modern restaurant with a nautical theme, serving well-cooked and inventive seafood and meat dishes.

Villa Maritza, *Albert I-Promenade 76, t (059) 50 88 08, wheelchair access. Open Tues–Sat. Expensive.* One of the most revered restaurants of Ostend, with fine all-round cuisine, and an unusual setting: the Edwardian-style dining room of a splendid 1885 *maison de maître*, overlooking the sea.

appear in Ensor's paintings. He began his art career as a gifted Impressionist before he allowed a wild streak in his character to take voice in the mid-1880s. Thereafter he created a bizarre, brightly-coloured, carnival-like world of caricatures, skeletons, mock religious figures – unsettling, macabre and satirical, and foreshadowing the Expressionist movement. His eccentric work alienated him from the Brussels avant-garde, of which he had been a leading figure, as a member of the Le Cercle des Vingt. He spent most of the rest of his life painting in relative isolation in Ostend, although he was recognized publicly when made a Baron in 1929. He lived in this house from 1917 until his death. There are no original paintings by Ensor here, but the rooms, his studio, the artefacts and reproductions of his work create a strong evocation of his world (real and imagined).

Mercator

Jachthaven Mercator. Open July–Aug 10am–6pm; April–June and Sept 10am–12.30pm and 2–5.30pm; Oct–March Sat–Sun only 10am–12.30pm and 2–4.30pm; adm €3.50.

The Mercator is a beautiful three-masted schooner, used as a sail-training ship by the Belgian merchant navy from 1932 to 1960. It now serves as a museum (although it still leaves harbour from time to time on sailing trips), and presents the story of its many voyages and scientific expeditions. It is named after the Flemish geographer Gerard Mercator (1512–94), who devised the Mercator projection – a way of making maps of the world look flat.

Kursaal (Casino)

Oosthelling, t (059) 70 51 11. Open daily 3pm until late.

The grand old Casino and Spa built by Leopold II was destroyed in the Second World War. This replacement, built in 1953, offers a welcoming gaming hall for those who fancy a flutter on roulette, blackjack, craps and other games. The dress code is smart casual (no jeans). Beginners are welcome and are offered introductory courses. The casino also has a concert hall, hosting classical, pop and rock concerts of note, and Friday-night party-discos in July and August. The Kursaal retains its name, but is no longer a health spa: there is the separate 1930s 'Thermae Palace' on the promenade, 500m to the west, which still offers sauna and other thermal bathing facilities.

Zeedijk (Sea Dike)

Part of the 15km-long dike built to protect Ostend from the North Sea has been turned into a 30m-wide promenade that lines the beach along the north of the city. It's a pleasant place to walk. The oldest part includes the Albert I Promenade, the site of the Kursaal and the Chalet Royal. In summer, you can rent pedal carts (for up to 10 people) to trundle along the walkway.

Westerstaketsel (West Pier)

The stone jetty lining the harbour mouth (the Havengeul) is a popular place for a stroll and for fishing, with fine views. Stand back and admire from a distance in rough weather.

Bloemenuurwerk (Flower Clock)

Leopoldpark (on the Leopold II laan).
A famous sight of Ostend, based on a tradition dating back to 1748: a huge clock on the edge of the Leopoldpark, with the clock face composed of flowers, which is redesigned and planted afresh each year. The idea is said to have been inspired by the great 18th-century Swedish botanist Linnaeus, who claimed that he could set his clock by the opening of the passion flower at noon. The minute hand of today's mechanism (installed in 1963) is 4m long. During the summer months, the date is formed in digital

style by flower boxes, which are moved manually each day.

The Beaches

Broad sandy beaches, fronting a shallow, tidal sea, line the northern flank of Ostend, and stretch east and to the west along the coast. Ostend has five beaches, one to the east of the harbour, and the remainder adjoining each other to the west. During the summer season, the western beaches lining the Zeedijk offer freshwater showers, public toilets and deckchair hire, and the sea is under the surveillance of life-guards operating a safety-flag system.

GHENT

Of all the great Flemish cities, Ghent wears the robes of its prosperous and noble past with the most dignity. Stately step-gabled façades line the tranquil canals, while the pinnacled and gilded spires of its great monuments shape the skyline.

A number of Ghent's museums surpass expectations; its begijnhof (*béguinage*) is one of the most charming and evocative in Belgium; and there is a dazzling jewel in this crown: within its fine cathedral is one of the great masterpieces of European art, Jan van Eyck's *Adoration of the Mystic Lamb*.

As night falls the atmosphere relaxes in expectation of pleasure, and the welcoming lights of the numerous bars and excellent restaurants – many housed in centuries-old historic buildings – glow across the canals and in the recesses of the crooked streets.

Sint-Baafskathedraal

St Baafsplein. Open 8.30am–6pm; closed (except for worshippers) Sun am and ecclesiastical festivals; adm free.
Ghent's cathedral, one of the finest in Belgium, was named after the city's most cherished early-Christian saint, St Bavo (or Bavon). The present cathedral was founded

originally in the 10th century as a church dedicated to St John the Baptist, but was rebuilt in Gothic style from 1290 to 1569. It was renamed after St Bavo in 1540, when Charles V had the old Sint-Baafsabdij pulled down in order to build a castle on the site.

The great treasure of the cathedral is the **Adoration of the Mystic Lamb**, displayed in a rather cramped room to the left of the west (main) door to the cathedral (*adm €2.50*). It is a large polyptych of 12 panels, painted by Jan van Eyck between 1426 and 1432. Given that this is one of the earliest known oil paintings, the proficiency with which the new medium was used is astonishing.

In the nave of Sint-Baafskathedraal is a fine **pulpit** (1741–5) by Laurent Delvaux (1696–1778) made of an unusual mixture of oak and marble – Baroque, but with a Rococo lightness of touch.

The stark beauty of the 13th- and 14th-century **choir**, built of grey-blue Tournai stone, has been compromised by the monumental 18th-century neoclassical screen erected in its midst to draw focus to the **altar**; this altar was designed by Hendrik Verbruggen (creator of the extraordinary pulpit in the cathedral of Brussels) and shows the *Apotheosis of St Bavo*.

The ambulatory of Sint-Baafskathedraal has been divided up into a series of atmospheric, dimly lit **chapels**, one of which (to the left of the altar) contains *The Vocation of St Bavo* (1623–4) by the master painter Pieter Paul Rubens.

Belfort

Open 10am–1pm and 2–6pm daily; adm €2.50. Carillon concerts mainly in the summer, Fri and Sat 11.30am–12.30pm; also July and Aug Sat 9–10pm.

The belfry of Ghent is one of the city's great landmarks. It rises majestically to the gilded copper dragon at 91m, and has a weather-vane that can trace its history back to 1377, set above a crescendo of black-tiled pinnacles and rooftops, dappled with gilded crockets.

Hotel and Restaurant Key	
13	Brooderie
4	't Buiske Vol
16	Chez Jean
11	Het Cooremeterhuys
17	Cour St-Georges
3	De Draecke
7	Dulle Griet
12	Guido Meerschaut
14	Hotel Gravensteen
6	Keizershof
1	't Klokhuys
10	De Kruik
15	Het Pand
5	De Pepermolen
8	Pink Flamingo's
9	Sofitel
2	Togo

Built originally between 1380 and 1381, it was heavily restored in the 19th century.

Today the tower contains not only its clock, but also a 52-bell carillon, 37 of which date back to 1660. Visitors can reach the parapet at 65m by lift, from where there are good views of the city.

Stadhuis

1 Botermarkt, t (09) 266 5211. Open May–Oct Mon–Thurs; English tours at 3pm from the tourist office beneath the Belfort; adm €2.50.

This imposing town hall has three faces: overlooking Hoogstraat is the flamboyant Gothic façade (1518–60); overlooking the Botermarkt is the newer, more restrained Renaissance façade of 1581, which reflects the cooler outlook of the then Protestant administration. The third façade is a complex of antique wonky rooflines which can be glimpsed only from the Gouden Leeuwplein.

Still serving as a centre for city administration – and still the focus of the occasional demonstration – the interior mainly dates from the restoration that took place after 1870. However, among the rooms is the 16th-century Pacificatiezaal where the Pacification of Ghent was signed in 1576.

PATERSHOL

Museum voor
Volkskunde

Gravensteen

GELDMUNT

ST VEERLEPL.

BURGSTRAAT

Museum voor
Sierkunst

St Michielsbrug

St Niklaaskerk

KOREN-
MARKT

HOOGSTRAAT

KTE MUNT
LANGE MUNT

KRAANLEI

ONDERSTRAAT

HOOGPOORT

Stadhuis

GOUDEN
LEEUWPL.
Belfort

Het Pand

ZWARTEZUSTERS
STR.

ONDER BERGEN

VOLDERSSTR.

VELDSTRAAT

GEBR.
VANDEVELDE
STRAAT

KOOP
HANDELSPL.

KOUTER

NEDERKOUTER

BAGATTENSTRAAT

LINDENLEI

IEPENSTRAAT

COUPURE RECHTS

COUPURE LINKS

Bijlokemuseum

Leie

IZERLAAN

BIJLOKEKAAI

KORTRIJKSE POORTSTR.

CH. DE KERCHOVELAAN

Citadelpark

KONING LEOPOLD II LAAN

ORTLAAN

E.CLAUSLAAN

Plantentuin
Universiteit
Gent

Museum voor
Schone Kunsten

Museum van
Hedendaagse Kunst

ST.AMANDSTR.

OVERPOORTSTR.

ST. PIETERSNIEUWSTRAAT

MUINKKAAI

FRANKLIN ROOSEVELTLAAN

Kon. Albertpark

LAMMERSTR.

GR. VAN
VLAANDERENPLEIN

BRABANTDAM

RENSTR.

ST. ANNAPL.

ZUIDPARKLAAN

LANGE VIOLETTENSTRAAT

TWEEBRUGGENSTRAAT

HUBERT FRÈRE ORBANLAAN

KASTEELLAAN

Klein
Begijnhof

VIOLETTENSTRAAT

KEIZER KARELSTRAAT

KOEPOORTKAAI

FERDINAND LOUSBERGS KAAI

GANDASTR.

St. Baafsabdij

Station
Ghent-
Dampoort

DAMPOORTSTR.

HAGELANDKAAI

SCHOOLKAAI

VOORHOUTKAAI

Leie

OUDE
BEESTENMARKT

NIEUWBRUGKAAI

ST.JACOBSNIEUWSTR.

BELFORTSTR.

ST.
BAAFSPL.

St-Baafskathedraal

LIMBURGSTR.

HENEGOUWENSTR.

VLAANDE-

BISDOMKAAI

REEP

Duivelsteen

VRIJDAGMARKT

OTTOGRACHT

BIBLIOTHEEKSTR.

STEENDAM

N

300 metres
300 yards

Getting There

By Car: Ghent (Gent) is a mere 40km south-east of Bruges. The quickest route is via the A10/E40 motorway (which also goes to Brussels), joined from the road leading southwest out of Bruges, passing the station. Alternatively, there is a marginally longer road, the N9, via Eeklo, joined by driving east out of Bruges. Parking is fairly easy in Ghent, and signs on the access roads to the city tell you where space is available in the public car parks (€1.25/hr).

By Train: Ghent is on the main line between Bruges and Brussels, and is served by regular trains, departing at least every half hour. The journey takes 20 minutes and adult fares cost €4.70 each way. The main station (Gent-Sint-Pieters) is 2.5km south of the centre, with connecting trams (1, 11 and 12) and taxis. For travel details, see the Belgian railways Web site w www.nmbs.be.

Getting Around

Ghent has a good **bus and tram** network. Maps are available from the ticket office on the Korenmarkt, at the western end of Sint-Niklaaskerk. **Boat trips** on the canals depart from the Graslei and Korenlei. The city centre trip lasts about 30mins (*April–Nov 10am–7pm; €3 per person for an open boat*). **Horse-drawn carriages** make half-hour trips around the main sights, starting at Sint-Baafsplein (*Easter–Sept/Oct 10am–7pm; €20 per carriage*).

Tourist Information

Beneath the Belfort, **t** (09) 225 3641, w www.gent.be. *Open April–June daily 9am–8pm, July–Nov daily 9.30am–6.30pm, Nov–March daily 9.30am–4.30pm.*

Festivals

Ghent's most spectacular festival is its flower show, the **Gentse Floraliën**, at the Flanders Expo (huge international trade fair centre) in late April, every five years.

The Flanders-wide **Festival van Vlaanderen** is a major European festival of classical music that takes place from April into the autumn.

Where to Stay

Cour St-Georges, 2 Botermarkt, **t** (09) 224 2424, **f** 224 2640. *Moderate*. Dated 1228, this is one of the oldest hostelries in Europe. neobaronial in style but unspectacular rooms. Good restaurant.

De Draecke, 11 Sint-Widostraat (Gravensteen), **t** (09) 233 7050, **f** 233 8001. *Inexpensive*. Youth hostel, €10–15.

Flandria, 3 Barrestraat, **t** (09) 223 0626, **f** 223 7789. *Inexpensive*. Agreeable family-run hotel with 22 rooms, near the centre.

Hotel Gravensteen, 35 Jan Breydelstraat, **t** (09) 225 1150, **f** 225 185. *Expensive*. Elegant 19th-century 'Second Empire' town house. Close to the city centre.

Sofitel, 63 Hoogport, **t** (09) 233 3331, **f** 233 1102. *Expensive*. Smart, modern hotel in the historic city centre.

Bed and Breakfast: A list of selected accommodation, including full descriptions, is published by GGG (*Gilde der Gentse Gasten Kamers, 81 Baliestraat, B-9000 Gent,* **t** (09) 221 2054). Many are handsome, central *maisons de maître*, and cost around €40 per night for two persons.

Eating Out

Brooderie, 8 Jan Breydelstraat, **t** (09) 225 0623. *Open Tues–Sat. Inexpensive*. Bakery selling delicious cakes, crusty loaves and healthy lunches for around €7.50.

Chez Jean, 3 Catalioniëstraat, **t** (09) 223 3040. *Open Tues–Sat. Expensive.* Stylish restaurant, in a gabled house dated 1634 serving seasonal food, such as pheasant in *millefeuille* pastry with endives.

De Kruik, 5 Donkersteeg, **t** (09) 225 7101. *Open Mon–Wed and Fri–Sun am*. Excellent French cuisine (notably fish), served with the chef's choice of wine for an astounding €35 all-in.

De Pepermolen/Moulin à Poivre, 25 Kraanlei, **t** (09) 224 2894. *Open Thurs–Tues. Expensive*. Sociable canal-house restaurant. Choose anything from *Magret de canard, sauce aigre-douce* to a slab of Scotch beef.

Guido Meerschaut, *3 Kleine Vismarkt, t (09) 223 5349*. **Open** *Tues–Sat and Sun pm*. **Expensive**. Modern restaurant run by a master-fishmonger; delicious fish at sensible prices.

Het Cooremeterhuys, *12 Graslei, t (09) 223 4971*. **Open** *Mon, Tues and Thurs–Sat*. **Expensive**. Elegant restaurant in a fine old guildhouse. Sophisticated French cuisine.

Het Pand, *1 Onderbergen, t (09) 225 0180*. **Open** *Mon–Sat*. **Expensive**. Stylish restaurant on upper floor of a former monastery. Expect gastronomic excursions based on ingredients such as lobster and goose liver.

't Buiske Vol, *17 Kraanlei, t (09) 225 1880*. **Open** *Mon, Tues and Thurs–Sat*. **Expensive**. Inventive *haute cuisine française*, in a beautifully decorated canal house. Menu from €25.

't Klokhuys, *65 Corduwaniersstraat, t (09) 223 4241*. **Open** *Tues–Sun and Mon pm*. **Moderate**. Modern brasserie, in an old, gabled building in Patershol, serving tasty dishes such as eel and lamb chops cooked with basil.

Togo, *Coco de Mer, 19 Vrouwebroersstraat, t (09) 223 6551*. **Open** *daily*. **Moderate**. African dishes, such as stew with dried prawns and manioc for €13.50.

Bars

Dulle Griet, *50 Vrijdagmarkt, t (09) 224 2455*. **Open** *daily; closed Sun eve*. Candlelit bar, dripping with beer-drinkers' mementos. 250 varieties of beer – claims to be a *bieracademie*.

Keizershof, *47 Vrijdagmarkt t (09) 223 4446*. **Open** *Mon–Sat*. Popular tavern serving beers from the barrel and good home-cooked food.

Pink Flamingo's, *55 Onderstraat, t (09) 233 4718*. **Open** *Mon–Sat*. No food, but a spendidly oddball café/bar with kitsch décor.

Shopping

The main shopping districts are south of the Belfort, down Magdeleinstraat and Volderstraat, along Koestraat, around the Kalandenberg square, and along the Lange Munt north of the Groentenmarkt. A market is also held on Fridays (*7am–1pm*) and Saturdays (*1–5pm*) in the large Vrijdagmarkt.

Sint-Niklaaskerk

Open *Tues–Sun 10am–5pm, Mon 2–5pm*.

This fine church, built mainly in the 13th century in what is known as Scheldt Gothic, is currently emerging from two decades of renovation, and the entrance for the time being is on the southern side. It has an atmospheric interior, with plain walls and columns of nibbled stone set against concertinaed ranks of dressed-stone buttresses and side chapels and the elegant curvature of the Gothic arches. This was once the church of the guilds (St Nicholas was the patron saint of merchants). The astonishing Baroque **altarpiece**, which blocks off most of the east end with its statues, ornate pediment and candy-twist columns in black-and-white marble, centres on a painting by Niklaas de Liemakere (1601–46), a pupil of Rubens. It shows the appointment of St Nicholas (far left) as Bishop of Myra.

Sint-Michielsbrug

This bridge is Ghent's most famous viewpoint, and justly so. To the east is the spectacular line-up of the towers of Sint-Niklaaskerk, the Belfort and Sint-Baafskathedraal. To the north of Sint-Michielsbrug is the city's beautiful stretch of canal, with the Graslei to the right and the Korenlei to the left.

Graslei and Korenlei

The waterway (the canalized River Leie) leading between these two quays was at the heart of the old port of Ghent. The **Graslei** on the eastern side is a fetching jumble of step-gables, stone carving and ranks of elegant windows. The buildings go as far back as the 12th century, added to slowly over 500 years, but are mainly Flemish Renaissance in style. To the south, the last and the finest of the buildings is a beautifully designed Renaissance house (1531), **Gildehuis der Vrije Schippers** (Free Boatmen), with an elaborately sculpted gable, a façade filled with windows, and a relief sculpture of a ship over the doorway.

Museum voor Sierkunst

5 Jan Breydelstraat, t (09) 267 9999. Open Tues–Sun 9.30am–5pm; adm €2.50.

This museum of the decorative arts is one of the most rewarding and delightful in Belgium. It is set out in a series of rooms in a grand 18th-century town house built for a wealthy family of cloth merchants and has an excellent collection of antique furniture. The modern annexe contains a superb collection of modern design, from Art Nouveau to Postmodernism.

The suggested route through the museum takes you initially past rooms of 17th–19th-century furniture and artefacts. It then leads to the lower floor of the modern section, and here the real feast begins. There is Art Nouveau glassware, perfume bottles by René Lalique, furniture, textiles and a 1925 version of the **Wassily Chair**, the first to be made of tubular steel, by Marcel Breuer. There is also a 1929 version of the X-frame **Barcelona Chair** by Ludwig Mies van der Rohe.

Look out for the work of the British designer **Christopher Dresser**, a leading campaigner for industrial design against the tide of the Arts and Crafts movement. The collection has been kept fresh by some skilful buying which demonstrates vividly how Postmodernism has the same kind of appeal, élan and shock that Art Nouveau and Art Deco had in their day.

Het Gravensteen

Sint-Veerleplein. Open April–Sept daily 9am–6pm, Oct–March daily 9am–5pm, last entry 45mins before closing; adm €5.

This grim and muscular fortress comes as something of a shock after the more dainty Gothic architecture of Ghent's other prominent monuments. Its name means 'Castle of the Counts', and it was built in 1180 by Philip of Alsace, Count of Flanders, on the site of the original 9th-century castle of Baldwin Iron-Arm. Restored with a decidedly heavy hand, it is at its best when seen from a distance over the water of the River Lieve.

Museum voor Volkskunde

Kraanlei 65, t (09) 223 1336. Open April–Oct Tues–Sun 10am–12.30pm and 1.30–5.30pm, Nov–March Tues–Sun 10am–noon and 1.30–5pm; adm €2.

There are numerous folk museums in Belgium, but they don't come much better than this one in Ghent. It is housed in a dainty little cluster of whitewashed almshouses dating originally from 1363. Not all almshouses (also referred to as hospices) were created as acts of pure charity: the Rijm family was forced to fund this one as a form of punishment in settlement of a bitter dispute with a rival family, the Alijns. It contains an impressive collection of furniture, toys, dolls, tools, etc. There is also a **puppet theatre** where marionette shows are regularly performed.

Bijlokemuseum

Bijlokekaai. Open daily 10am–1pm and 2–6pm; adm €2.50.

This rich and pleasantly unfocused historical museum is housed in the Abdij (Abbey) van de Bijloke, which can be reached from the city centre by walking along the picturesque canals on the Recollettenlei and Lindenlei. The abbey itself is a beguiling set of red-brick buildings designed in a traditional Flemish style.

The museum is casually set out in the cloisters and former dormitories of the abbey with a vast array of historical objects of all kinds: furniture, paintings, donated collections of Chinese ceramics and costumes.

Museum voor Schone Kunsten

Citadelpark, t (09) 222 1703. Open Tues–Sun 9.30am–5pm; adm €2.50.

The grand neoclassical entrance to this museum, built in 1902, and Ghent's long artistic tradition promise much, but this municipal gallery of fine art is, alas, faintly disappointing. The collection is, however, punctuated by a few treasures.

The early section, from the Flemish primitives to Pieter Paul Rubens, contains one outstanding piece, the *Bearing of the Cross* by **Jeroen (Hieronymus) Bosch** (1450–1516), who worked in 's-Hertogenbosch in the Netherlands and whose imagery was immensely influential. Christ, painted with a sublime expression of suffering and inner peace, is surrounded by a dense throng of grotesque degenerates. Other notable works include *The Virgin with a Carnation* by **Rogier van der Weyden** (c. 1400–64); a *Pietà* by **Hugo van der Goes** (c. 1435–82); two pieces by **Pieter Bruegel the Younger** (1564–1638); market scenes by **Joachim Beuckelaer** (1530–74); and a splendidly sensual *Jupiter and Antiope* by **Antoon van Dyck** (1599–1641).

Among the 19th-century paintings there is the *Reading by Emile Verhaeren* by the Ghent-born painter **Théo van Rysselberghe** (1862–1926). A founder member of Les XX in Brussels, Rysselberghe adopted the Pointillist style of Seurat and Signac in the 1880s and 1890s and developed it as a technique for landscape, interiors and portraits. The Post-Impressionist **Henri Evenepoel** (1872–99) is represented by his striking *L'Espagnol à Paris*. There are also works by **James Ensor**, **Léon Spilliaert** and, from the 20th century, **Rik Wouters**, plus works by the idiosyncratic Flemish Expressionists **Jean Brusselmans** (1884–1953) and **Edgard Tytgat** (1879–1957).

A special emphasis is given to the artists associated with the Sint-Martens-Latem School, which was based around the Symbolist poet Karel van de Woestyne and the sculptor and painter George Minne (1866–1941). This collection includes work by the remarkable **Constant Permeke** (1886–1952), a chief figure in Flemish Expressionism. It also holds the marble version of **George Minne**'s *Fontein der Geknieden* – sculptures of six contemplative, naked boys kneeling around a fountain.

Museum van Hedendaagse Kunst

Citadelpark. **Open** *daily 10am–6pm;* **adm** *€2.50.*

The museum of contemporary art contains the largest collection of modern paintings and sculpture in Belgium, founded in the 1950s. The permanent collection includes not only work by post-1945 Belgian artists – such as the participants of La Jeune Peinture Belge and Cobra – but numerous pieces by leading figures of the international art scene, such as Francis Bacon, Andy Warhol and Gilbert and George. The museum's temporary exhibitions are generally major events.

Klein Begijnhof

Entrance on Lange Violettenstraat. **Open** *daily until 9pm.*

Of the many *béguinages* in Belgium, this is one of the most charming, with its neat and peaceful lines of little red-brick houses set around an open area of grass and trees and a Flemish-Baroque chapel. Founded in 1234 by Joanna of Constantinople, patroness to numerous early *béguinages*, it has changed little since the 17th century. There have been no *béguines* at the Klein Begijnhof for some years, however, and the houses are slowly being converted for secular use.

Outside Ghent

Groot Begijnhof

One of the largest *béguinages* in Belgium, situated a couple of kilometres to the east of the centre of Ghent, between E. van Arenbergstraat and Schoolstraat (look out for the needle-like spire of the church), it is not quite what it seems: it was in fact built in 1874 to house *béguines* from the St Elizabeth Begijnhof, founded in 1234. It is a fair re-creation of a medieval *béguinage* – but somehow lacks soul. It is still home to a couple of *béguines*, but most of the houses are now rented out to families.

Sint-Martens-Latem

Sint-Martens-Latem is a village famous for the school of artists which assembled here at the start of the 20th century. At Sint-Martens-Latem itself you can see the **Museum Gevaert-Minne** (*open Easter–Sept Thurs–Sat 2–6pm, Sun 10am–noon and 2–6pm, Oct–Easter Wed–Sun 2–5pm; adm €1.50*), which displays work by Edgard Gevaert and George Minne. At nearby Deurle there are three museums. The **Museum Dhondt-Dhaenens** (*open Wed–Fri 2–5pm [in summer 2–6pm], weekends 10am–noon and 2–6pm; closed Dec–15 Feb; adm €1.25*) contains a private collection of work by various members of the school. The **Museum Gustave de Smet** (*opening hours and adm charges as for Museum Gevaert-Minne*) shows the artist Gustave de Smet's work in his former home. And finally there's the **Museum Leon de Smet** (*open Easter–Sept Wed–Mon 2–6pm, Oct–Easter by appt only, t (09) 282 8693; adm free*).

ANTWERP

A bitter wind, straight off the North Sea, hurries down the wide estuary of the River Scheldt, rattling the old store-sheds that line the riverside quays, and briskening the heart-beat of this invigorating city. Once, upon this wind, came Antwerp's fortunes: goods from around the world were brought and traded with products from the whole of northern and central Europe. Antwerp was one of the great cities of the continent: proud, powerful and adventurous.

This is the city where Rubens lived and worked, the brightest star in a galaxy of artistic talent. The manifestations of Antwerp's artistic tradition can be seen in the city gallery (one of the great collections of art in Belgium), in many of the churches and in a handful of small, charming museums. The tradition lives on. Antwerp has earned a name for itself as a city where things are happening. The city's strength has, today, been rekindled by new industry and the

mighty, sprawling docks to the north of the city centre. Antwerp is awakening from a period of neglect and is in tune with the new Europe. Its recent successes in the fashion world are a symbol of its new mood, with clothes designed by, among others, Dries van Noten, Ann Demeulemeester and Martin Margiela.

There is something in the air in Antwerp: go on a weekend and the streets positively zing. Youthful crowds pack out the bars and

cafés hosting live music; literary cafés hum to earnest debate; and families fill the restaurants that serve anything from steaming casseroles of mussels to *sashimi* to some of the most recherché cooking in Belgium.

Grote Markt and Stadhuis

*Stadhuis open for **tours** Mon, Tues, Thurs and Fri 11am, 2 and 3pm, Sat 2 and 3pm.*

Hotel and Restaurant Key

Getting There

By Car: Antwerp (Antwerpen) is about 80km due east of Bruges, and less than an hour's drive. The most direct route is via the N9 east out of Bruges, then the N49/E34. Alternatively there is the motorway link via Ghent, on the A10/E40, then A14/E17.

By Train: Trains leave for Antwerp every half-hour; some are direct (leaving at 05 past the hour), and some require a change of trains at Ghent (Gent-Sint-Pieters), but both take about 1 hour 20 minutes, and an adult fare costs €10.80 each way. For travel details, see the railways Web site **w** *www.nmbs.be*

Getting Around

To get to the centre by **car**, follow the signs to Stadhuis and Schelde. There are plenty of paying **car parks** around the old quayside sheds along the River Scheldt, close to the centre, and a number of underground car parks in convenient places (€12 *per day*).

Antwerp has an efficient **public transport system** (called De Lijn) consisting of trams, buses and the underground Premétro tram line. A 'Netplan' of the system is available from the tourist office (*see* below) and main stations. **Taxis** are available from designated taxi ranks, or by calling **t** (03) 238 9825.

Horse-drawn carriages make tours of the centre, starting from the Grote Markt. You can also take **boat trips** on the River Scheldt and to the Port of Antwerp.

Tourist Information

15 Grote Markt (corner of Wisselstraat), **t** (03) 232 0103, **f** 231 1937. *Open Mon–Sat 9am–5.45pm, Sun 9am–4.45pm.*

Where to Stay

Antigone, *11–12 Jordaenskaai*, **t** *(03) 231 6677*, **f** *231 3774*. **Moderate**. Well-appointed hotel (Ikea meets Art Deco) overlooking the River Scheldt.

De Witte Lelie, *16–18 Keizerstraat*, **t** *(03) 226 1966*, **f** *234 0019*, **w** *www.dewittelelie.be*. **Expensive**. Delightful city hotel. Cool, elegant décor and antique furniture, plus numerous discreet touches of luxury.

Diamond Princess, *Bonapartedok, St Laureiskaai*, **t** *(03) 227 0815*, **f** *227 1677*. **Moderate**. A 'flothotel' – hotel and restaurant on a converted ship. Napoleon's dock is somewhat forlorn, however.

Eden, *25–27 Lange Herentalsestraat*, **t** *(03) 233 0608*, **f** *233 1228*, **w** *www.diamond-hotels.com*. **Moderate**. Minimalist hotel in the diamond district.

Villa Mozart, *3–7 Handschoenmarkt*, **t** *(03) 231 3031*, **f** *231 5685*, **w** *www.best western.com*. **Moderate**. Small, tasteful hotel of just 25 Laura-Ashley-decorated rooms, opposite the cathedral.

Youth Hostels: Six in the city. Contact *Vlaamse Jeugdherbergcentrale, 40 van Stralenstraat*, **t** *(03) 232 7218*.

Eating Out

De Stoemppot, *12 Vlasmarkt*, **t** *(03) 231 3686*. *Open Wed–Sun; closed Sat lunch*. **Inexpensive**. The place to try out some *stoemp* (€9) – traditional Flemish dish of puréed meat and vegetables.

Het Vermoeide Model, *2 Lijnwaadmarkt*, **t** *(03) 233 52 61*. *Open Tues–Sun*. **Moderate**. Tavern ('The Sleepy Artist's Model') built into the side of the cathedral, with a pleasant atmosphere. Grilled fish for €12.50.

Kartini, *61 Oude Koornmarkt*, **t** *(03) 226 4463*. *Open Tues–Sun evenings*. **Inexpensive**. Indonesian serving authentic dishes, including a 12-course *Rijsttafel Kraton* for €37.

La Rade, *8 Ernest van Dijckkaai*, **t** *(03) 233 3737*. *Open Mon–Fri and Sat pm (closed 3 weeks in July)*. **Expensive**. Superior restaurant, founded in 1949, in the splendid late 19th-century neo-renaissance-style rooms of an old mansion, overlooking the Scheldt. *Haute cuisine française*, elegantly served.

Marrakech, *1 Wisselstraat*. **t** *(03) 231 3092*. **Moderate**. Exotic ambience, like the inside of a nomad tent, where hearty plates of couscous are served for €11–15.

Sjalot en Schanul, *12 Oude Beurs*, **t** *(03) 233 8875*. *Open daily*. **Inexpensive**. Combination of greengrocer and relaxed café. Vegetarian dishes and light salads.

Entertainment and Nightlife

Antwerp is famous for its vigorous clubbing scene. Clubs get going around midnight and don't close until 4am. Entry is usually €6–10.

Café d'Anvers, *15 Verversrui*, *t (03) 226 3870*. *Open Fri–Sun*. Old warehouse, very big and dark, popular venue for house music.

Le Palais, *12 van Ertbornstraat*, *t (03) 233 3515*. Large disco, formerly Jimmy's.

Paradox, *25 Waalse Kaai*. Club-discothèque famous for its regular parties.

Red and Blue, *13 Lange Schipperskapel-straat*. House and soul music. Entry before midnight free, thereafter €6.

Zillion, *4 Jan van Gentstraat*, *t (03) 248 1516*. *Open Thurs–Sat*. Vast disco: 3 floors and 10 bars. House/techno on Thurs, top international DJs on Fri and Sat.

Shopping

The main shopping street is the **Meir**. The eastern end, leading into Leysstraat and Teniersplein, includes some grand 19th-century neo-Baroque buildings, now occupied by boutiques and department stores. This procession continues eastwards along De Keyserlei up to Antwerpen Centraal Station. Pelikaanstraat, south of the station, is at the heart of the **diamond district**. There are varied **markets** on Theaterplein at the weekends, and on Wednesday and Friday mornings there's an antiques and jumble market at the Vrijdagmarkt, outside the Museum Plantin-Moretus.

Antwerp's famed **fashion** stores are found south of the Groenplaats (south of the cathedral). Dries van Noten (*16 Nationale-straat*) has a Modepaleis, and Louis (*2 Lombardenstraat*, *t (03) 232 9872*) stocks Ann Demeulemeester, Martin Margiela and Raf Simons. Closing Date (*15 Korte Gasthuisstraat*, *t (03) 232 8722*) stocks Walter van Beirendonck's Wild and Lethal Trash line. Further down the street the Nieuwe Gaanderij Arcade is packed with fashion shops. Coccodrillo (*9A–B Schuttershofstraat*, *t (03) 233 2093*) sells fashionable shoes.

The central square of Antwerp is one of the most attractive in Belgium, flanked by ornate guildhouses on the northern side and south-eastern sides and the famous **Stadhuis** (town hall). Built in 1564, the Stadhuis was designed by the architect and sculptor Cornelis Floris, also called Floris de Vriendt (1514–75). His training in Italy is apparent in this building: in the mathematical distribution of windows as well as in the Renaissance flair of the centrepiece. Completed in 1565, it was burnt out during the Spanish Fury of 1576, but restored after 1579. The interior was totally renovated in the 19th century, largely in retrospective historical styles.

Onze Lieve Vrouwe Kathedraal

Handschoenmarkt, *t (03) 213 9940*. *Open Mon–Fri 10am–5pm, Sat 10am–3pm, Sun and religious hols 1–4pm*; *adm €2*.

The largest Gothic cathedral in Belgium it may be, but the approach to it through a web of medieval streets gives it a charming, human scale. The earliest parts of the building date from 1352, but the cathedral took nearly three centuries to build, and was not completed until 1521. The first phase was designed by Jan Appelmans; in the last phase the main designers were the influential late-Gothic architects Herman de Waghemakere (1430–1503) and his son Domien (1460–1542) and Rombouts Keldermans (1487–1531).

When completed, the cathedral was the richest of the Low Countries. The interior was a dazzling treasure trove, glittering with the dozens of shrines and retables set up by the city's guilds. Many of these, however, were destroyed in a fire in 1553; the building was later sacked by iconoclasts in 1566. The cathedral was stripped of its surviving treasures during the French occupation after 1784. Only a part of its original collection of works of art was recovered from France after 1815.

Despite this history, the cathedral still contains a remarkably rich collection of paintings and sculpture, set against the elegant simplicity of the Gothic architecture.

It is famous above all for its paintings by **Pieter Paul Rubens**, notably the pair of powerful triptychs of *The Raising of the Cross* (1610) and *The Descent from the Cross* (1612) flanking the choir on either side of the transept. The former is a painting of dynamic anguish and tumult; the latter is filled with deep compassion and silence.

Etnografisch Museum

19 Suikerrui. **Open** *Tues–Sun 10am–4.45pm;* **adm** *€4.*

African masks, drums from New Guinea, a Maori war-canoe, an Inuit child's kayak, Indonesian jewellery, pre-Columbian American pottery, Japanese paintings, Tibetan Buddhas – these are just some of the hundreds of varied objects representing over a century of collecting, housed since 1988 in a new museum on three floors. The Central Africa collection is particularly strong.

Steen and the Nationaal Scheepvaartmuseum

Steenplein, t (03) 232 0850. **Open** *Tues–Sun 10am–4.45pm;* **adm** *€4.*

The Steen, the powerful old fortress at the river's edge, was built between the 10th and 16th centuries, originally as the residence of the Margrave of Antwerp – although legend said it was home of the giant Antigon. It was used as a prison until 1823, then rescued from that role and heavily restored in the late 19th century. It is now home to the National Maritime Museum. This contains an interesting and well-presented collection of ship-orientated artefacts, including numerous superb models of ships, plus a collection of barges and other small vessels.

Vleeshuis

38–40 Vleeshouwersstraat, t (03) 233 6404. **Open** *Tues–Sun 10am–4.45pm;* **adm** *€7.50.*

In a forgotten corner of central Antwerp, cheek by jowl with the small red-light district of Burchtgracht, is one of the city's most impressive buildings. This is the Butchers' Hall, the guildhouse and meatmarket of the Guild of Butchers, designed in Gothic style in 1503 by Herman de Waghemakere. Its walls, step-gables and the five hexagonal turrets running up the sides are built in alternating layers of stone and brick.

The Butchers' Guild was a powerful institution. The large and robust meat hall was, for decades, the only place in Antwerp where meat could be sold. The hall, and other rooms accessed from it, now contain a rewarding collection of historical odds and ends: medieval sculpture, paintings, musical instruments, and the mummy of a 10th-century BC Egyptian singer.

Sint-Pauluskerk

Veemarkt. **Open** *May–Sept daily 2–5pm;* **adm** *free.*

This strange, hybrid church, with a Flamboyant Gothic body dating from 1517 and a Baroque spire dating from 1679, rises out of a cluster of buildings (some of which are attached to it) in an attractive quarter of alleyways, small shops and atmospheric bars. The Baroque interior, with its elaborately carved wooden stalls, is an expression of a bold architectural style that sang of the triumph of the Counter-Reformation over iconoclasm. It contains a remarkable collection of paintings, including the series of 15 on the *Mysteries of the Rosary* (1617–19), by various artists such as Cornelis de Vos (*Nativity, Presentation at the Temple*), David Teniers the Elder (*Gethsemane*), Rubens (*Flagellation*), Van Dyck (*Bearing of the Cross*) and Jordaens (*Crucifixion*).

Sint-Carolus Borromeuskerk

Hendrik Conscienceplein, t (03) 233 0229. **Opening** *times vary;* **adm** *€12.50.* Guided **tours** *by arrangement.*

The façade of this church represents one of the great monuments of Jesuit Baroque architecture – a birthday cake of sculpture, pineapples and pepperpot domes, disposed with an elegant pace and rhythm (tradition holds that it was designed by Rubens). The church was built in 1615–21 and dedicated to St Charles Borromeo (1538–84), a church reformer who attempted to address the abuses of the Catholic Church in the face of the rising tide of Protestantism.

In 1620 the Jesuits asked Rubens to create three altarpieces and 39 ceiling paintings for the church. But in 1718 a fire caused by light-ning destroyed the lot. Given this history, it is barely surprising that the interior is disap-pointing, although it contains fine late-Baroque **woodwork** installed after 1718, and a **Lady Chapel** which survived the fire.

Rockoxhuis

Keizerstraat. **Open** *Tues–Sun 10am–5pm;* **adm** *€2.50.*

Nicolaas Rockox (1560–1640) was mayor of Antwerp during many of its years of revival in the early 17th century; he was also a noted humanist, philanthropist and art collector, and a friend and patron of Rubens. The ground floor of his large house, set around a courtyard garden, was converted during the 1970s into a gallery to house a handsome collection of paintings, tapestries and antique furniture from the era. There are sketches and paintings by all the Golden Age Antwerp artists – Rubens, Van Dyck, Jordaens and Frans Snyders, plus work by the preceding generation, including Joachim Beuckelaer and Pieter Bruegel the Younger.

Sint-Jacobskerk

73 Lange Nieuwstraat, t (03) 232 1032. **Open** *April–Oct daily 2–5pm, Nov–Mar 9am–noon;* **adm** *€2.*

Rubens lies buried in a family chapel in this yellow-sandstone church, designed in late-Gothic style during the 15th and 16th centuries by Herman de Waghemakere and his son Domien, and subsequently by Rombouts Keldermans. The interior is one of the richest in Antwerp and contains the tombs of wealthy Antwerp families and numerous works of art. There are **sculptures** by Hendrik Verbruggen, Artus Quellinus and Luc Fayd'Herbe; and **paintings** by Bernard van Orley, Otto Venius (Rubens' master), Rubens himself, Jordaens and van Dyck.

Museum Plantin-Moretus

22–23 Vrijdagmarkt, t (03) 221 1450. **Open** *Tues–Sun 10am–4.45pm;* **adm** *€2.50.*

This is one of Antwerp's most celebrated museums. In principle it has the ingredients for a fascinating visit – a 16th-century patri-cian house, set around a courtyard straight out of a painting by a Dutch master, original furnishings, and the workshop and book col-lection of one of the great masters of early printing, Christopher Plantin (c. 1520–89). French by birth, Plantin came to Antwerp in 1546 and his publishing enterprise became a hub of North-European learning and art.

On the ground floor are a pair of grand 16th- and 17th-century reception rooms, hung with tapestries and paintings, including some portraits and *The Lion Hunt* by **Rubens**. A door leads out into the pretty Renaissance courtyard, off which is a series of small rooms, including one that in the 17th century was a bookshop. A passageway leads to the **printing workshop**, a large room crammed with old printing presses.

Upstairs are a series of displays which demonstrate the scope of the Plantin family's printing achievements. These include the Polyglot Bible; engravings by Rubens; maps by Gerard Mercator (1512–94); and a priceless copy of Gutenberg's 36-line Bible. The upper floors are the most atmos-pheric, with a suitably dingy library lined with august leather-bound tomes, and a printers' workroom where the type was cast.

Rubenshuis

9–11 Wapper, t (03) 201 1555. **Open** *Tues–Sun 10am–4.45pm;* **adm** *€5.*

Pieter Paul Rubens (1577–1640) is considered to be the outstanding painter of Antwerp during a Golden Age of exceptional artistic endeavour. This was the house that he bought in 1610, when he was already a wealthy man, and in the service of the Archduke Albert and the Infanta Isabella as court painter. Over the next 17 years he transformed it into a kind of Italian villa.

The house has an illustrious past. Rubens was the centre of an elevated artistic circle that included his associates Antoon van Dyck (1599–1641) and Jacob Jordaens (1593–1678). His noble patrons, including Marie de Médicis (Queen of France) and George Villiers, Duke of Buckingham, also visited Rubens in this house. It later fell into sad neglect, and was only saved after 1937, when it was bought by the city and underwent massive renovation. The paintings and furnishings are designed to evoke Rubens' epoch, but are not his own. The Rubenshuis is considered a premier tourist sight of Antwerp, and its rooms are often inundated with visitors.

There are a few highlights, including Rubens' large **studio**, now used as a concert hall. The courtyard outside is separated from the small garden by a magnificent **Baroque portico**, with elaborate stonework designed by Rubens (the statues of *Mercury* and *Minerva* on the parapet are modern replicas). The dining room contains a self-portrait (1625–8) by Rubens, and an example of the still lifes which made the name of **Frans Snyders** (1579–1657). In the Kunstkammer, where Rubens would have displayed the pride of his collection of paintings, is the intriguing *Gallery of Cornelis van der Geest* by **Willem van Haecht**, a contemporary of Rubens.

Museum Mayer van den Bergh

Lange Easthuisstraat. **Open** *Tues–Sun 10am–4.45pm;* **adm** *€4.*

This is the most charming and rewarding of Antwerp's small museums – an Aladdin's cave of paintings, antique furniture and coins and much else. These were all the private possessions of Fritz Mayer van den Bergh (1858–91), who devoted himself to collecting.

The most famous painting of the collection is by **Pieter Bruegel the Elder** (c. 1525–69): *Dulle Griet* (Mad Meg) portrays this medieval allegory of disorder as an armed woman running from a burning town on which she has vented her rage. The painting may be a comment on the political and religious troubles that had begun to engulf the Low Countries in the mid-16th century.

The Diamond District

It is claimed that 85 per cent of the world's uncut diamonds are traded through Antwerp, and most of these are cut and polished in this city which boasts a tradition of diamond-processing that dates back to the late 15th century. Diamonds are big business, worth seven per cent of Belgium's total export earnings. The bulk of the business is carried out in a square mile area, to the southwest of the Centraal Station. To get an idea of the scale of the diamond trade, go to **Pelikaanstraat**, where there are dozens of jewellery and gold shops beneath the railway arches. There is nothing fancy about the diamond business here: they stack 'em high and sell 'em cheap. Notices in the windows boast 'Diamond-setting in 15 minutes'!

Provinciaal Diamantmuseum

31–33 Lange Herentalsestraat. **Open** *daily 10am–5pm;* **adm** *free (€5 for special exhibitions).*

This museum provides a good introduction to diamonds through photographic panels, models and exhibits. It shows how diamonds are found, explains their natural structure, and how they are cut and shaped.

Koninklijk Museum voor Schone Kunsten

1–9 Léopold de Waelplaats, t (03) 238 7809; wheelchair accessible. **Open** *Tues–Sun 10am–5pm;* **adm** *€4, free Fri.*

Antwerp's Royal Museum of Fine Art is housed in an overgrand neoclassical temple, built in 1878–90, topped by female charioteers (by the Antwerp-trained sculptor Thomas

Vinçotte), and standing in forlorn grounds. Don't let this put you off, for what lies within is an outstanding collection of north European art. The collection is divided into two parts: the Old Masters of the 14th–17th centuries are in the grand marbled galleries on the upper floor; the 19th–20th-century collection is on the ground floor.

Outstanding works from the early collection include **Jan van Eyck**'s unfinished portrait of *Saint Barbara* (1437), sitting with a book on her lap in front of a Gothic cathedral under construction. The crystal-sharp triptych *Altar of the Seven Sacraments*, by **Rogier van der Weyden** (c. 1400–1464), illustrates the seven key sacraments of the Christian Church, all being played out around a crucifixion set in a Gothic cathedral. A delightful triptych by **Hans Memling** (c. 1433–94) portrays Christ surrounded by angels and angelic musicians.

The early 16th-century collection is particularly strong. This was a period when Italian painting was beginning to influence Flemish art, through artists such as **Bernard van Orley** (1492–1542), whose *Last Judgement and Seven Acts of Mercy* contains figures in a neoclassical setting. Compare this, however, with the highly gruesome but vigorous *The Entombment of Christ*, a magnificent triptych which shows the greater assurance of the Antwerp painter **Quentin Metsys** (1460–1530). Look out also for the works of **Frans Floris** (1516–70), brother of Cornelis Floris, the architect of the Stadhuis.

The centrepiece of the 17th-century collection is the area devoted to **Pieter Paul Rubens** (1577–1640); this being his city, the rooms promise much, but are disappointing. However, there are two classic Rubens here: the *Enthroned Madonna and Child* surrounded by saints has a typically dynamic composition; and *Adoration of the Magi* is a masterpiece of composition, with at least four main centres of focus, in which swaggering kings, camel-riders and helmeted soldiers are stopped in their tracks by the sight of the Holy Child.

In a period of numerous stars illuminated by Rubens' talents, probably his most celebrated contemporary was **Antoon van Dyck** (1599–1641), who for a while worked with him as an assistant. He was famous as a portrait-ist, but he was a painter of considerably wider skills, as his intense *Lamentation of Christ* demonstrates. After the deaths of Rubens and Van Dyck in 1640 and 1641 respectively, **Jacob Jordaens** (1593–1678) – who had worked alongside Rubens for 20 years – was considered the greatest painter of Antwerp. Jordaens is well known for his voluptuous paintings of fertility and fun, of which *As the Old Sang, the Young Play Pipes* (1638) is a famous example.

The museum virtually dismisses the 18th century and early 19th century to launch into an excellent late 19th- and 20th-century collection. Just about every major figure in Belgian art since 1850 is represented: **Emile Claus**, **Théo van Rysselberghe**, **Léon Spilliaert**, **Henri Evenepoel**, **Henry van de Velde**, artists of the Sint-Martens-Latem School, Flemish Expressionists **Jean Brusselmans** and **Edgard Tytgat**, **René Magritte**, **Paul Delvaux** and the artists of Cobra, including **Pierre Alechinsky**. It is worth looking out in particular for the work of **James Ensor** (1860–1949), including the *Oyster Eater* of 1882, a watershed date when he began to pursue his idiosyncratic course. Never has oyster-eating been portrayed with such a pungent subtext of sensual pleasure.

There is also a major collection of work by **Rik Wouters** (1882–1916), the best known of a group called the Brabant Fauvists. Wouters' paintings are colourful, but judiciously balanced and full of light and joyousness.

Museum voor Hedendaagse Kunst (MUHKA)

Open *Tues–Sun 10am–5pm; adm €2.50.*

The interior of a huge fawn-coloured grain warehouse, built in the 1920s, has been broken up into a series of dazzling white spaces for this avant-garde museum, which presents a permanent collection of post-1970 works and temporary exhibits – sometimes exhilarating, sometimes bemusing, sometimes infuriating. The third-floor café is a gathering point for artists and writers at the cutting edge.

Provinciaal Museum voor Fotografie

Waalse Kaai. **Open** *Tues–Sun 10am–5pm;* **adm** *€2.50, free Fri.*

This modern museum tracks the history of photography in a series of well-explained exhibits. The exhibition begins with the very first experiments in photography by its pioneers in the 1820s and 1830s. It includes beguiling landscapes and portraits by **Julia Margaret Cameron**, who saw the artistic potential of photography in the 1860s. The work of the great American photographers such as **Edward Steichen** and **Ansel Adams** is also represented, and there are numerous classic photographs by other greats: **Henri Cartier-Bresson**, **Robert Capa**, **Irving Penn** et al. A large collection of cameras traces the technical development of photography.

YPRES (IEPER)

Like the Somme and Passchendaele, the name Ypres casts a long shadow. Ypres – Ieper in Flemish, 'Wipers' to the British Tommy – was a focal point of some of the most horrific destruction during the First World War. Battle raged around Ypres for four long years with the front line centring upon the Ypres Salient, a ridge that formed a half-circle to the east of the city. The statistics of Ypres are grim: about half a million young men lost their lives in the surrounding fields – of which 250,000 were British, and 50,000 from the Commonwealth. Most of the dead now lie in the 170 cemeteries scattered around Ypres. The city itself, once a glorious medieval centre of the weaving trade, on a par with Bruges, was virtually flattened. Then it was rebuilt, virtually brick for brick.

One might expect it to be a city haunted by this past, but it gets on with its life. The reconstruction is surprisingly convincing: it looks at first glance almost as old and authentic as Bruges. It has a breezy prosperous air, and the surrounding fields are now once again grazed by contented cattle. But clusters of neat rows of headstones and crosses, in their mute ranks and breathtaking numbers, are never far away.

Ypres has confronted this past by making a virtue of it. Its innovative museum of the First World War, entitled 'In Flanders Fields', alone justifies the trip, and opens the gates to an unforgettable and profound experience.

In Flanders Fields

Lakenhallen, Grote Markt 34, t (057) 22 85 84, f 22 85 89, w www.inflandersfields.be. **Open** *daily April–Sept 10am–6pm (last entry 5pm), Oct–March Tues–Sun 10am–5pm (closed 3 weeks in Jan);* **adm** *€7.50.*

The 13th-century Lakenhallen (Cloth Hall) was the centrepiece of Ypres' medieval past, a vast and magnificent Gothic building, with belfry, dominating the central square, the Grote Markt. This is where cloth was sold and stored, and the scene of the annual trade fairs. It was destroyed during the First World War, but reconstructed over three decades (1933–67). Its belfry contains a 49-bell carillon.

The interactive museum called 'In Flanders Fields' now occupies much of the western part of the Lakenhallen. It tells the story of Ypres in the First World War and, by so doing, reveals graphically what it must have been like to have taken part. It does this through a combination of archive film, touch-screen displays, soundtrack, recorded readings, artefacts and panels. But it also invites the visitor to follow the story of one particular participant from any of the four main warring parties (British and Commonwealth, French, Belgian, German), or a local resident. As you enter you are given a bar-coded card with the name of a real historical person: by feeding this into screens at three points along the way, you can see what fate had in store for him or her. The displays take you through various experiences – the build-up to confrontation, the trenches,

Getting There

By Car: Ypres (Ieper) is about 45km south-west of Bruges. The easiest route is via Kortrijk, about 60km on the A17/E403 and (after Kortrijk) the A19. There is a large public car park in the central Grote Markt.

By Train: Getting to Ypres from Bruges by train requires at least one change, at Kortrijk, or two changes, at Ghent (Gent-Sint-Pieters) and Kortrijk. The journey takes between 1½ and 2 hours and an adult fare costs €8.80 each way. There are about two departures an hour.

Tours

Quasimodo Tours (*see* p.56). Offers a much commended 'Flanders Fields' excursion, a 'laidback' minibus tour of Ypres and the battlefields, including Passchendaele, the Menin Gate, and a number of abandoned trenches, bunkers and craters. Commentary in English; picnic included. Sun, Tues and Thurs; pickup from your hotel in Bruges, or the station, 8.45–9.20am, returning 4.30pm; adults €37.50, under-26s €30.

Daytours, *Wijngaardplein 12*, *t (050) 34 60 60*, *w www.daytours.be*. Offers mini-bus day trips from Bruges (with hotel pick-ups), visiting Ypres, and various cemeteries, trenches and strategic positions (€59 with lunch).

Salient Tours, *t (0475) 910 223 (before 9pm)*; *w www.salienttours.com*. Easter–mid-Nov, no tours on Wed. Minibus tours with British guides, starting from Ypres (Menin Gate) and visiting the Salient, as well as British, Canadian and Anzac memorials and cemeteries (visits to relatives' graves can be included, free of charge). Standard tour 10am–2pm, €25; short tour 2.30–5pm €18.

Tourist Information

Toerisme Ieper, Lakenhallen, Grote Markt 34, **t** *(057) 22 85 84*, **f** *22 85 89*, **e** *toerisme@ieper.be*, **w** *www.ieper.be*. *Open Mon–Fri 9am–5pm, Sat and Sun 10am–5pm (April–Oct closes at 6pm)*. This is a first-class tourist office, producing a wealth of literature about Ypres, and the First World War. Its brochures include background history, plus recommended touring routes to visit the war zone.

Festivals

The Cat Festival (Kattentoet en Kattenworp) is celebrated every three years (next in 2003) on the second Sunday in May. In the Middle Ages, cats helped to control vermin in the Lakenhallen (Cloth Hall) during the winter months, but to keep their numbers down they were culled at the beginning of summer by casting them out of a window in the belfry. Today the ceremony is re-enacted with cloth cats, thrown from the belfry by the festival jester. An afternoon parade brings together marching bands, floats and horses, and plenty of cat costumes.

Eating Out

Den Anker, *Grote Markt 30*, *t (057) 21 12 72*. *Open daily*. *Moderate*. An upmarket restaurant, neatly decked in white linen, serving mussels cooked in every manner imaginable, plus local dishes such as eels, and steak. There's a good-value two-course daily menu at €8.60.

Old Tom, *Grote Markt 8*, *t (057) 21 15 41*. *Open Sat–Thurs*. *Inexpensive*. Pleasant, old-fashioned pub, serving snacks plus full meals, featuring local specialities, notably seafood (eels, lobster, oysters).

Regina, *Grote Markt 45*, *t (057) 21 88 88*. *Open Sat–Thurs (closed Sun eve)*. *Moderate/expensive*. A hotel and restaurant with a formidable reputation for its gastronomic cuisine, which includes home-made *foie-gras*, hop-shoots, consommé of langoustines, and king crab.

't Katerke, *Boomgaardstraat 10*, *t (057) 20 86 11*. *Open daily*. *Inexpensive*. Very Belgian: a trim, modern, no-fuss restaurant and tearoom. Inexpensive meals of Flemish dishes, steak, eel, plus good cakes and tarts.

Vivaldi, *Grote Markt 21*, *t (057) 21 75 21*. *Open Tues–Sun (closed 3 weeks from mid-July)*. *Moderate*. Handsome tearoom and restaurant in the main square, with a terrace in summer. Good-value lunches of mixed grills, fish and fish pie; menus from €22.

the first gas attack, the field hospital – all presented imaginatively and powerfully. It is of course harrowing, but also fascinating.

The Menin Gate

A large memorial arch in eastern Ypres, on the road to Menin (Menen), marks the start of the route on which some 5 million British and Commonwealth troops marched on their way to the Salient. Designed in Classical style by the British architect Sir Reginald Blomfield, it was built on the site of an old city gate and inaugurated as a Commonwealth war memorial in 1927. Inscribed on it are the names of the 54,896 soldiers who were reported missing on the Ypres Salient up to 15 August 1917, but who had no proper burial. (There were not enough panels in the arch to record all the names of the missing, so a further 34,957, reported missing after 15 August 1917, are listed at Tyne Cot cemetery.) At 8pm every evening the Last Post is played here by buglers of the Ypres Fire Brigade – as it has been since 11 November 1929 (with the exception of the years of WW2 German Occupation). There are pleasant walks to the south of the Menin Gate, around the periphery of the city.

Stedelijk Museum

Ieperstraat 31, t (057) 22 85 82. Open Tues–Sun 10am–12.30pm and 2–5pm (April–Oct closes at 6pm); adm €2.50 (free with tickets to 'In Flanders Fields')

Set in a 13th-century almshouse in the south of the city, this small museum presents a record of Ypres' pre-war past, seen through paintings, photographs, sculpture, domestic and church artefacts, furniture and ceramics. It also has a cherished collection of pastel drawings by the Ypres artist Louise de Hem (1866–1922).

War Graves

There are a terrifying number of cemeteries around Ypres. Many of these are maintained in immaculate condition by the Commonwealth War Graves Commission (*Elverdingsestraat 82, t (057) 21 01 18, f 21 80 14; open Mon–Thurs 8.30am–12.30pm and 1.30–5pm, Fri 8.30am–12.30pm and 1.30–4.30pm*); information on the position of individual graves can be obtained here. Its Web site (**w** *www.cwgc.org*) details all its cemeteries and what is known about those who are buried in them, and where they lie. Here are just a few of the larger cemeteries:

Tyne Cot Cemetery, near Passendale (Passchendaele). The largest Commonwealth war cemetery in the world (11,908 graves, 34,957 listed as missing).

Lyssenthoek Cemetery, near Poperinge. The largest Commonwealth cemetery associated with a field hospital or Casualty Clearing Station (18,000 dead).

Poelkapelle. A British cemetery (7,450 dead, including the youngest, aged 14).

No Man's Cot, Pilkem Ridge. A Scots' cemetery.

Caesar's Nose Cemetery, Pilkem Ridge. A Welsh cemetery.

Saint-Charles-de-Potyze Cemetery. A French cemetery (4,000 buried, 600 unknown soldiers in a mass grave).

Kemmel Hill. French Memorial and mass grave of 5,294 French soldiers.

Houlthulst. A Belgian cemetery (1,855 dead).

Langemark. German cemetery (graveyard for 44,061 soldiers, over 24,800 of them unknown, and including 3,000 student volunteers).

Vladslo, Diksmuide. German cemetery. The graves of 25,638 soldiers, and the heart-rending sculptures by Käthe Kollwitz, *The Mourning Parents*, in memory of her 18-year-old son.

Waregem, 40km east of Ypres. American cemetery (368 graves).

Hill 62, Sanctuary Wood Museum

Canadalaan 26, Zillebeke, t (057) 46 63 73 Open daily 10am–7pm; adm €4.

Has the only trenches in the area left unchanged, plus munitions, weapons, uniforms and photographs.

Brussels

09

Hotel and Restaurant Key

10	L'Amadeus
9	Les Bluets
4	Bonsoir Clara
1	Comfort Art Hotel Siru
8	Comme Chez Soi
2	Hôtel Métropole
5	Kasbah
7	't Kelderke
3	Pacific
6	Zebra

Ever since Brussels emerged from a bog in the Dark Ages (Brussels means 'settlement in the marshes'), the city has skulked in the shadow of Europe's ruling powers, and has been occupied time and again, until finally the Belgian nation was formed in 1831. Not suprisingly, 'Brussels' has never had the same ring to it as many of Europe's great cities, but today, as nominal 'Capital of Europe', you might expect the city to be laughing. And, yes, Brussels is proud of its grand new soubriquet, but it has served as a

mixed blessing: the city's role as a legislative and administritive centre has given it an unfair reputation for being boring.

Part of the problem is that Brussels' many graces are not served up on a plate and many fly-by visitors come away with an impression that the magnificent Grand' Place is the city's sole selling point. But it is a progressive city of multiple layers. Within easy walking distance of one another, the city's different quarters each have their attractions. Wander the maze of medieval

lanes; settle down in an Art Nouveau café; admire the work of Surrealist masters in a world-class museum; or shop in cutting-edge fashion boutiques. For those with a taste for more, there is also the city's energetic nightlife, sipping on one of the hundreds of beers brewed to perfection by generations of thirsty monks or dining on cuisine cooked with obsessive attention to detail. Then come away and consider whether you reckon Brussels is boring.

AROUND THE GRAND' PLACE

The Grand' Place is the jewel in Brussels' crown. Surrounding the square is a lively tangle of narrow medieval streets and it's a great place just to wander.

The Grand' Place

Metro *Bourse.* **Hôtel de Ville: t** *(02) 279 4365.* **Open** *Tues–Fri 9.30am–5pm, Sun 10am–4pm;* **adm** *€2.50.* Guided **tours** *in English, Tues and Wed 3.15pm, plus April–Sept Sun 12.15pm.*

The Grand' Place was the city's main marketplace and the names of the streets that lead into it today bear witness to this past: Rue au Beurre (butter), Rue Chair et Pain (meat and bread), Rue des Harengs (herrings), and so on. During the 15th century the *échevins* (assistants to the Burgomaster) organized the building of a grand Hôtel de Ville on the square – a bold statement of the city's wealth and pride which confirmed the Grand' Place's central role in the public life of Brussels. The guilds then wanted to be near the seat of civic authority, and during the 16th century the borders of the old market square began to fill up with their **guild houses**. Much of what you see today was rebuilt within five years of the bombardment by

Map Key

1–2	La Maison des Boulangers
3	La Brouette
4	Le Sac
5	La Louve
6	Le Cornet
7	Le Renard
8	L'Etoile
9	Le Cygne
10	La Maison des Brasseurs
11	La Rose
12	Mont Thabor
13–19	La Maison des Ducs de Brabant
20–22	Anna-Joseph and Le Cerf
24–25	La Maison des Tailleurs
26–27	Le Pigeon
28	La Chambrette de l'Amman
37	Le Chêne

French canons in 1695. The role of the Grand' Place as the city centre survived even after the guilds were disbanded in the 1790s by French Revolutionaries.

With the large-scale renovations to the Hôtel de Ville and the Maison du Roi during the 19th century and in recent decades, the Grand' Place could have become a museum piece, but it hasn't: today the old guild houses are occupied by cafés, banks, hotels and lace shops. You can go inside the **Hôtel de Ville**; tours take visitors through the grand public rooms.

Getting There

By Car: Follow signs for the A10/E40 motorway, leading southwest out of Bruges (past the station). Brussels is about 85km away, or about an hour's drive. Parking in Brussels is comparatively easy: in the centre of town there are a fair number of underground car parks and parking meters.

By Train: There is a direct and frequent link by train from Bruges railway station, taking you to the three Brussels stations: Gare du Nord/Centrale/Midi. The Gare Centrale is closest to the city centre, but the others are within easy walking distance. There are about two fast trains an hour, running from early in the morning to late at night; the journey takes about 50 minutes and adult fares cost €10.30 each way. For travel details, see the Belgian railways Web site *w www.nmbs.be*.

Getting Around

Brussels is a compact city and most of the museums and sights are within walking distance of the centre. The métro system has two lines: Line 1 crosses town from east to west and Line 2 curls around the centre. If you want to travel above ground, there is an extensive bus and tram network. Public transport tickets can be used on buses, métro and trams. Taxis can only be hired at designated spots or by phone.

Tourist Information

Hôtel de Ville, *Grand' Place*, **t** *(02) 513 8940*, **f** *514 8320*, **e** *tourism.brussels@tib.be*, **w** *www.tib.be*. **Open** *summer daily 9am–6pm, winter Mon–Sat 9am–6pm, Sun 10am–2pm*.

Where to Stay

Comfort Art Hotel Siru, *1 Place Rogier*, **t** *(02) 203 3580*, **f** *203 3303*, **e** *art.hotel.siru @skynet.be*, **w** *www.comfort hotel/siru.com*; *métro Rogier*. **Moderate**. 'Art hotel', with every room stylishly decorated by the work of contemporary Belgian artists – a lively and commendable concept. For the more aesthetically adventurous.

Hôtel Métropole, *31 Place de Brouckère*, **t** *(02) 217 2300*, **f** *218 0220*, **e** *info@metropole hotel.be*, **w** *www.metropolehotel.com*; *métro De Brouckère*. **Luxury**. Brussels' grandest old hotel: marbled halls and palm court – the picture of Belle Epoque elegance encountered only on film sets.

Les Bluets, *124 Rue Berckmans*, **t** *(02) 534 3983*, **f** *543 0970*, **e** *bluets@eudora mail.com*, **w** *www.geocities.com/les_bluets*; *métro Hôtel des Monnaies*. **Inexpensive**. This 19th-century home has been converted into an extraordinary guesthouse hotel. It is brimming with old paintings, figurines and plants; the bedrooms remain airy despite having been treated to a similar excess of decoration. If you like minimalism this isn't the place for you; otherwise, you might just love it.

Pacific, *57 Rue Antoine Dansaert*, **t** *(02) 511 8459*; *métro Bourse*. **Inexpensive**. More like a private home than a hotel, every room has bags of old-world character, down to the original 1910 plumbing. Charming.

The Manneken-Pis

*Rue de l'Etuve/Rue du Chêne; **métro** Bourse.*

'*Manneken*' is *bruxellois* for little man; '*pis*' speaks for itself. This bronze statue of a little naked boy peeing with happy abandon has long been held in great affection by locals and has become a symbol of their city. Whatever the legend behind the statue (and there are many), when the first bronze statue was cast by Jérôme Duquesnoy the Elder in 1619 it was probably based on an earlier model. Duquesnoy's version was much loved and even had a brocaded suit made – the first in his splendid collection of costumes. When an ex-convict stole the Manneken-Pis in 1817 the city was distraught; the culprit was caught and branded in the Grand' Place, then sentenced to 11 lifetimes' hard labour. The statue was in ruins and had to be recast. This, then, is the statue you see today. A programme listing which costume he'll be wearing over the current period is posted on the railings.

Eating Out

Bonsoir Clara, *22–26 Rue Antoine Dansaert,* **t** *(02) 502 0990;* **métro** *Bourse.* **Open** *daily.* **Moderate**. Deliciously stylish restaurant in Paul Klee colours with low lighting, animated by the in-crowd. Inventive cuisine with lunch menu at around €15.

Comme Chez Soi, *23 Place Rouppe,* **t** *(02) 512 2921;* **métro** *Anneessens.* **Open** *Tues–Sat; closed July.* **Expensive**. This is Brussels' premier restaurant – and with just 40 places you need to book weeks in advance. Exquisite concoctions of snipe, eel, truffle, lobster, all beautifully presented.

Kasbah, *20 Rue Antoine Dansaert,* **t** *(02) 502 4026;* **métro** *Bourse.* **Open** *daily.* **Moderate**. Theatrical Arabian Nights setting, under dozens of glowing glass lanterns, with top-notch Moroccan cooking. The *tajine aux pruneaux* (spiced Moroccan stew with prunes; €15) is particularly recommended.

L'Amadeus, *13 Rue Veydt,* **t** *(02) 538 3427;* **métro** *Louise.* **Open** *Tues–Sun and Mon eve.* **Moderate**. Sophisticated restaurant housed in Rodin's former studio. Boasts an extensive wine list and classic and modern dishes.

't Kelderke, *Grand' Place,* **t** *(02) 513 7344;* **métro** *Gare Centrale.* **Open** *daily.* **Expensive**. Medieval cellar setting for authentic and hearty shoulder-to-shoulder dining.

Zebra, *35 Place St-Géry,* **t** *(02) 511 0901;* **métro** *Bourse.* **Open** *daily.* **Inexpensive**. Trendy café-bistro in the most booming part of the city. Brick walls, candlelight, jazz music, inexpensive tasty snacks; nice terrace in summer.

Bars

L'Archiduc, *6 Rue Antoine Dansaert,* **t** *(02) 512 0652;* **métro** *Bourse.* **Open** *daily.* Authentic Art Deco gem and at the core of Brussels' nightlife. Designed like the interior of a cruise ship, it has irregular jazz nights.

L'Ultime Atome, *14 Rue St Boniface,* **t** *(02) 511 1367;* **métro** *Porte de Namur.* **Open** *daily.* A hugely popular café-bar at the heart of Ixelles. Wines and a good selection of beers are available.

P. P. Café, *28 Rue Jules Van Praet;* **métro** *Bourse.* **Open** *daily.* Brussels' first cinema, the Pathé Palace, refurbished in pre-1940s style, with an adjoining Art Deco bar. Trendy.

Shopping

The best-known shopping street is **Rue Neuve**, lined with large chain stores. The nearby shopping centres – **Anspach** and **Centre Monnaie** – peddle similar high-street wares. A bit more upmarket is the area around **avenues Louise and Toison d'Or** (including Galeries Louise and Toison d'Or). This neighbourhood is noted for its chic clothes shops, and is where you're likely to find that little number for the coming season. Despite its down-at-heel appearance, **Rue Dansaert** is the centre for serious avant-garde fashion – you'll find lots of local designers, including the Antwerp Six, on show. Brussels is famous for its *galeries*, the oldest and most famous of which is the elegant **Galeries Royales de St-Hubert**, with its marbled halls and luxurious boutiques.

La Bourse

2 Rue Henri Maus; **métro** *Bourse or De Brouckère.* **Open** *Mon–Fri on request.*

The former stock exchange is an impressive rectangle in neoclassical style but with little sense of neoclassical restraint. Decked with garlands of stone flowers and cherubs, it is typical of the retrospective style used for many of the grand buildings in the Brussels of Léopold II. Though it looks much earlier, the Bourse dates from 1873. It is now used to mount temporary exhibitions.

COUDENBERG

The Musées Royaux des Beaux-Arts sit on the summit of the Coudenberg, the high ground east of the city centre which was once the enclave for the rich. It still is a grand part of town, with long vistas, stately architecture and the large formally planned Parc de Bruxelles overlooked by the Palais Royal.

Musées Royaux des Beaux-Arts

3 Rue de la Régence for Musée d'Art Ancien, 1–2 Place Royale for the Musée d'Art Moderne t (02) 508 3211, e info@fine-arts-museum.be, w www.fine-arts-museum.be; métro Gare Centrale; wheelchair accessible. Open Tues–Sun 10am–5pm; adm €5.

This combines two superb museums, the **Musée d'Art Ancien** (15th to 18th centuries; blue and brown sections on the museum's map) and the **Musée d'Art Moderne** (19th and 20th centuries; green and yellow sections). By the standards of most major national art collections, the Musées Royaux des Beaux-Arts are refreshingly single-minded. The main focus is on Belgian art – or at least the art of the Low Countries, for those centuries before Belgium came into existence. Italy and Spain, even France, barely get a look in, but nonetheless the collection is a ravishing *tour de force* and a monument to the technical virtuosity and distinctive mood of North European art.

Pieter Bruegel the Elder and Rubens are the stars of the Musée d'Art Ancien, but there are also paintings by Antoon van Dyck, Jacob Jordaens and Dirk Bouts. The Musée d'Art Moderne also has an impressive line-up, including the Belgian Impressionists, Post-Impressionists and Symbolists (*see* pp.44–5), and the Magritte collection, mainly the legacy of his wife, Georgette.

Musée des Instruments de Musique (MIM)

2 Rue Montagne de la Cour, t (02) 545 0130, w www.mim.fgov.be; métro Gare Centrale. Open Tues, Wed and Fri 9.30am–5pm, Thurs 9.30am–8pm, Sat and Sun 10am–5pm; adm €2.50.

This museum is in a former department store called Old England – a throwback to the late 19th century when the British Arts and Crafts movement and Liberty style were all the rage. The building was designed by

Paul Saintenoy (1862–1952) and completed in 1899. The building still shows its cast-iron pillars with characteristic swirling Art Nouveau motifs, and steel joists painted with floral decoration. The interactive museum contains more than 6,000 musical items and is the biggest of its kind. The collection is mainly European, dating from the Renaissance onwards, and includes numerous interesting oddities, such as the 18th-century kits or *pochettes* – tiny violins which dancemasters could carry in their pockets. The building retains its top-floor tearoom, which is now the museum café, Du Mim, with views over the lower town as far as the Atomium.

Parc de Bruxelles

Metro Parc or Trône. Open daily 6am–9pm. Palais Royal: Place des Palais, t (02) 551 2020; wheelchair accessible. Open end July–early Sept Tues–Sun 10.30am–4.30pm; adm free.

This is Brussels' most attractive formal park. Ranks of mature trees stand over the broad avenues, which lead past statues, ornate cast-iron benches and fountains to vistas of the palaces at either end. Over-looking the park at the southern end is the **Palais Royal**, a grand if rather cold-looking building. The two wings date from the 18th century, but the central section was rebuilt in the French 18th-century neoclassical style in 1904–12. The interior is glittering with chandeliers, brocade curtains and polished marble, but rather soulless. It looks more impressive at night, under floodlights. It is no surprise that the royal family prefers to live at their other palace at Laeken.

MAROLLES AND SABLON

The old residential quarter of the Sablon is now the focus of Brussels' upmarket antiques trade, with a number of chic art galleries thrown in. From here it is only a short walk southeast to the area called Porte Louise, a showpiece of Euro-commerce with a roll-call of the top designer names. In the shadow of the grand Palais de Justice lies the Marolles district, the old artisans' quarter with a long and ragged history.

Palais de Justice

1 Place Poelaert, t (02) 508 6578; métro Louise. Open Mon–Fri 9am–3pm; adm free. Guided tours (€25) on written request.

The Palais de Justice is a monumental hulk of a building. The area that it covers, 180m by 170m, made it the largest construction in continental Europe in the 19th century. Its dome rises to 105m. It cost 50 million francs to build, a huge sum in its day. The plan was initiated under Leopold I in 1833 but not undertaken until the reign of Leopold II. It was the crowning achievement of the architect Joseph Poelaert, who paid for it with his sanity. You can wander the public hallways of the building, which consists mainly of one colossal atrium, with broad marble stairs rising on either side to the galleries. Almost as an afterthought, there are 25 courtrooms tucked away in the walls, including the Cour de Cassation, the highest court in the country.

Place du Grand-Sablon and Around

Métro Gare Centrale or Louise. Notre Dame du Sablon: Rue de la Régence. Open Mon–Fri 9am–5pm, Sat 10am–5pm, Sun 1–5pm. Notre-Dame de la Chapelle: Place de la Chapelle; wheelchair accessible. Open June–Sept daily 9am–5pm, Oct–May 11.30am–4.30pm.

This large, triangular square was laid out in the late 17th century and is still fronted by old step-gabled façades. At weekends an antiques market clusters around the foot of the **Notre-Dame du Sablon**. Also known as Notre-Dame des Victoires, this is Brussels' most beautiful Gothic church. It was built in the 15th and 16th centuries to accommodate

the cult of the miraculous *Madonna of Baet Soetken*, which stood in the chapel of the Guild of Crossbowmen. The statue itself, however, was destroyed by iconoclasts in 1580.

To the north of the square is the **Place du Petit-Sablon**, with its formal gardens in the centre laid out by Henri Beyaert (1823–94). They are dedicated to Counts Egmont and Hornes, and to the spirit of the struggle for liberty and enlightenment that marked the medieval and Renaissance periods. They led a rebellion of nobles against the repressive régime of Philip II. Statues of the counts stand over the central fountain, while 48 statues representing the medieval guilds stand on the pillars around the perimeter.

To the south of the Place du Grand-Sablon is the **Notre-Dame de la Chapelle**. The fortress-like grandeur of this church, with its orbed and black-shingled clock tower and its massive creamy-white stone walls, has made it one of the great landmarks of Brussels. Built originally in the 13th century, the choir and transept are essentially Romanesque, whereas the nave and aisles are Gothic, added in the 15th century. The curious clock tower was added after the church was damaged by the French bombardment of 1695. The interior is an elevating space of arching stone vaults, lit by Gothic windows, and has some fine carving: the apostles on the columns of the nave and the wooden pulpit, dating from 1721. This church is noted as the burial place of Pieter Bruegel the Elder and the third side chapel of the south aisle is dedicated to him.

NORTH CENTRAL

This area is a mish-mash of styles and very little is what it seems: beneath the sedate neoclassical square of Place des Martyrs lie the bodies of hundreds of revolutionaries, and what was once an Art Nouveau textile store is now a comic-strip museum. But most locals come here to shop: Rue Neuve is one of Brussels' busiest shopping streets.

Centre Belge de la Bande Dessinée

*20 Rue des Sables, **t** (02) 219 1980; **métro** Botanique or Rogier; wheelchair accessible. **Open** Tues–Sun 10am–6pm; **adm** €6.*

This old Art Nouveau textile megastore designed in 1903 by Victor Horta was stylishly renovated, and opened in 1989 as a shrine to the comic strip, consisting mainly of a large collection of original drawings.

The comic strip became popular in Belgium when *Les Aventures du Petit Nemo au Pays des Songes* by Winsor McCay appeared in French in 1908. It proved a wild success and Belgian artists soon became leaders of this new field. By far the most famous of these comic characters is Tintin by Hergé. He is accorded a special place here, with original drawings, historical notes and 3D models of famous scenes. Other characters like Lucky Luke the lackadaisical cowboy (by Maurice de Bevere), are only vaguely recognized by the English-speaking public, but are known to every Belgian.

Glasshouse of the Jardin Botanique

*Entrance on Rue Royale, **t** (02) 218 7935; **métro** Botanique; wheelchair accessible. **Open** daily 11am–6pm; **adm** free.*

The old botanical gardens have been transferred outside Brussels, but the glasshouse survives, built for the Brussels Horticultural Society in 1826–9 following drawings by a painter and theatre designer called Pierre-François Gineste (1769–1850). Although the exterior was cleverly preserved, the glasshouse was converted into the Centre Culturel de la Communauté Française Wallonie-Bruxelles (Cultural Centre of the French Community of Wallonia and Brussels) in the early 1980s, and now contains a series of spaces for temporary exhibitions, concerts and plays, as well as a cinema and brasserie. Only the main corridor retains its hothouse atmosphere, with small fishponds, ferns and papyrus plants. In the huge hollow in front of the glasshouse is a formal garden with box hedges and statuary, some of which is by Constantin Meunier (*see* p.159).

De Ultieme Hallucinatie

*316 Rue Royale, **t** (02) 217 0614; **métro** Botanique, then tram 92, 93 or 94. **Open** Mon–Fri noon–2.30pm and 7–10.30pm, Sat 7–10.30pm.*

This celebrated Art Nouveau restaurant and bar is in a building dating from 1856 but transformed at the start of the 20th century by Paul Hamesse (1877–1956), a pupil of Paul Hankar. Even the umbrella stand and piano in the hall have had the Art Nouveau wand waved over them, but the real triumph is the small restaurant. Nothing has been left to chance: the chandeliers, stencilled wall-hangings, fireplace, side cabinets, ceiling mouldings, stained-glass partitions – all have been redefined with the graceful curves of Art Nouveau.

QUARTIER LÉOPOLD

Brussels boomed under the rule of King Léopold II and a swathe of wealthy suburbs began to spread out from the old centre. In 1880 Belgium celebrated 50 years of independence with an International Exhibition in the newly laid-out Parc du Cinquantenaire. This now forms a grand setting for a series of museums. The same part of town has been adopted by the headquarters of the European Union and much transformation has taken place.

Musée Wiertz

62 Rue Vautier, t (02) 648 1718, e info@fine-arts-museum.be, w www.fine-arts-museum.be; métro Maelbeek or Schuman. Open April–Oct Tues–Sun 10am–noon and 1–5pm; closed Sat and Sun in July and Aug; adm free.

This museum offers the rare possibility of seeing inside a 19th-century artist's studio. But this was not just any 19th-century artist – this was Antoine Wiertz, who from an early age liked to compare himself to Rubens and Michelangelo. His ambitions and delusions were on a truly epic scale.

The main part of the studio is just high enough to hang several immense canvases. These are rather crudely executed and instantly forgettable. Wiertz's more remarkable works are on a smaller scale, technically very uneven, but stamped with his own peculiar vision. Some are a bizarre combination of the macabre and erotic; others are loaded with a crushingly blunt moral message. *Le Suicide* graphically illustrates a young man blasting his brains out with a pistol under the covetous gaze of good and bad angels. In *Une Scène d'Enfer* (*A Scene from Hell*) distraught men and women present severed limbs to a smouldering (literally) figure of Napoleon.

Parc du Cinquantenaire

Métro Schuman or Mérode.

The year 1880 marked the Cinquantenaire (the 50-year jubilee) of the Belgian nation. At Léopold II's insistence, a military parade ground was transformed into a park containing elegant exhibition halls. It is a pleasing area of sandy walkways shaded by mature trees, but sadly has never been the same since the Avenue J. F. Kennedy surfaced in its middle. In the grounds is the **Pavillion Horta**, an neoclassical temple designed by the young Victor Horta (*see* p.159) in 1889. The **Arcade du Cinquantenaire** was added in 1905 to mark Belgium's 75th anniversary. The copper-green quadriga on the top of the arch

is by Thomas Vinçotte (1850–1925), official sculptor to Léopold II: if it looks familiar, no doubt it reminds you of the more famous Brandenburg Gate in Berlin, created over a hundred years earlier. (In Léopold's Brussels, originality was not a criterion.) The buildings on either side are now home to two major museums:

Musées Royaux d'Art et d'Histoire

Entrance in right-hand wing, t (02) 741 7211, e info@kmkg-mrah.be, w www.kmkg-mrah.be; métro Mérode or Schuman; tram 81 and 82; wheelchair accessible. Open Tues–Fri 9.30am–5pm, Sat and Sun 10am–5pm. Salle aux Trésors is open 10am–noon and 1–4pm; adm €4.

Since its foundation in 1835, this museum, known as the Musée du Cinquantenaire, has accumulated many historical and anthropological artefacts, from Phoenician glass to Art Nouveau sculptures. You cannot hope to see everything. The best policy is to decide what you want to see, then use the confusing colour-coded map of the museum's three levels to plan your route. The **Salle aux Trésors** (Treasure Room) contains a superb collection of medieval pieces – gilded and bejewelled reliquaries and medieval church treasures, ivories, jewellery and textiles. Also worth seeking out are the ***arts décoratifs*** of the Middle Ages.

Don't miss the **Musée Boyadjian du Cœur** (Boyadjian Heart Museum): Dr Boyadjian, a leading contemporary heart surgeon, was interested in the heart as a symbol, and his extensive private collection of *objets d'art* was donated *en bloc* to the museum.

Musée Royal de l'Armée et d'Histoire Militaire

3 Parc du Cinquantenaire, under the arch, to the left, t (02) 737 7811, w www.klm-mra.be; métro Mérode or Schuman; tram 81 and 82. Open Tues–Sun 9am–noon and 1–4.50pm; adm free.

This is another huge collection, but fairly easy to assimilate. The oldest part of the exhibition (installed in 1923) contains cabinets stuffed with uniforms, weapons and military mementoes. Portraits of mustachioed generals and tattered regimental colours arranged on the walls, create the atmosphere of a baronial hall. Follow signs to the section '**Air et Espace**'. In a vast hall built for the 1910 International Exhibition is a jumble of aircraft. Outside is the '**Blindés**' section, a graveyard of tanks and armoured cars.

OUTSIDE THE CENTRE

Musée Horta

25 Rue Américaine, t (02) 543 0490, e musee. horta@horta.irisnet.be; métro Horta. Open Tues–Sun 2–5.30pm; adm €5.

The outstanding Art Nouveau architect Victor Horta (1861–1947) built this as his home and studio in 1899–1901, when he was at the pinnacle of his talent. The interior, which had remained more or less intact, has been carefully restored and is now furnished with pieces Horta designed for the house, as well as for other buildings. As soon as you walk through the front door, the motifs in the mosaic flooring and the flowing shapes of the coathooks, hatstand and door furniture tell you that you are entering one of the most complete and carefully thought-out Art Nouveau environments in Europe. Note in particular Horta's use of light, especially in stairwells lit by an overhead canopy of glass.

Musée Constantin Meunier

59 Rue de l'Abbaye, t (02) 648 4449, e info@ fine-arts-museum.be, w www.fine-arts-museum.be; métro Louise, then tram 93 or 94. Open Tues–Sun 10am–noon and 1–5pm; closed alternate weekends; adm free, ring the bell for admittance.

The painter and sculptor Constantin Meunier (1831–1905) is best remembered for his bronzes of industrial workers – notably the gaunt forge-workers called *puddleurs* (puddlers). In his early career, Meunier painted only monastic and religious scenes, but between 1879 and 1881 his visits to the industrial regions around Liège and the coal-mining Borinage district left a deep mark. Meunier thereafter became a social realist. Barring the odd lapse into sentimentality, Meunier's work has a deep sense of conviction. The museum consists of a collection of Meunier's paintings, drawings and sculpture set out on the ground floor and in his large, north-facing studio to the rear. One of his most famous paintings, *Le Retour des Mineurs*, is on show.

Musée David et Alice van Buuren

41 Avenue Léo Errera, Uccle, t (02) 343 4851, e museumvanbuuren@skynet.be, w www. museumvanburren.com; tram 23 or 90; bus 60. Open Sun 1–5.30pm and Mon 2–5.30pm; adm €7.50.

This Dutch banker's elegant private house was built and furnished in the Art Deco style. Exotic woods and ivory are among the materials integrated into the luxurious interior décor, every last item conforming to the harmony of the design. The house contains a remarkable collection of paintings, including works by Bruegel, Wouters, van Gogh, and the Sint-Martens-Latem School. The gardens, landscaped by René Pechère, contain hundreds of rare trees and a maze.

Maison d'Erasme

31 Rue du Chapitre, Anderlecht, t (02) 521 1383, e erasmushuis.maisonerasme@skynet.be, w www.ciger.be/erasmus; métro St-Guidon. Open Tues–Sun 10am–5pm; adm €1.25.

In 1521, the great Dutch humanist and Renaissance scholar Desiderius Erasmus (c. 1459–1536) spent five months at this house, as a guest of Canon Wijkman, enjoying the relaxation and country air. The brevity of his stay undermines the museum's claim to be the 'House of Erasmus', but don't let that put you off. Restored in the 1930s, after a century of neglect, it consists of a series of rooms containing a rich collection of books, furniture, paintings and engravings from the life and times of Erasmus. It provides a rare opportunity to see the interior of a 16th-century house.

Musée René Magritte

*135 Rue Esseghem, t (02) 428 2626; **métro** Pannenhuis. **Open** Wed–Sun 10am–6pm; **adm** €6.*

The house where Magritte and his wife lived from 1930 to the mid-1950s was bought in 1994 and the ground floor has been meticulously restored to show how it looked when they lived there, with other exhibits on the upper floors. Although Magritte painted for 25 years in this house, there are only a few sketches and letters on display, as well as the trademark bowler hat, pipe and chessboard. It provides an interesting insight into the master of the surreal, not least because the house and its contents are so plain.

Atomium

*Bvd du Centenaire, t (02) 474 8977, e info@atomium.be, w www.atomium.be; **metro** Heysel. **Open** April–Aug daily 9am–7.30pm, Sept–March daily 10am–5.30pm; **adm** €5, combined ticket with Mini Europe €13.50, and with Océade €15.50.*

The Atomium was designed as the centre-piece of the Exposition Universelle et Internationale de Bruxelles of 1958 – a show-piece of the then-powerful Belgian metal industry. During the 1950s the atomic structure was a popular design theme, first seen on a grand scale at the Festival of Britain Exhibition of 1951. In 1958 a group of Belgian designers went the whole hog, creating this giant-sized version of an iron atom. This is architectural kitsch on a grand scale, sorely compromised by the practical necessity of

grounding the structure to earth with fire escapes. It looks more like a space station than a conceptual image from particle physics. Inside, a glass-topped lift whisks you up the central shaft to the Panorama at 100m. From here you can see right across Brussels and look down on the Parc de Laeken. **Bruparck** is close at hand, with Mini Europe, containing models of all the major landmarks reduced to one-twenty-fifth of their actual size. There's also Kinepolis, the largest cinema complex in the world, and Océade, a complex of swimming pools.

Musée Royal de l'Afrique Centrale

*13 Leuvensesteenweg, entrance through gates at the back of the building, Tervuren, t (02) 769 5211, e info@africamuseum.be, w www.africamuseum.be; **métro** Montgomery, then tram 44 to the Tervuren terminus and a 200m walk. **Open** Tues–Fri 10am–5pm, Sat and Sun 10am–6pm; **adm** €2.*

This vast, domed Louis XV-style château was designed expressly as a museum at the end of the reign of Léopold II and first opened its doors to the public in 1910, a year after Léopold's death. The museum details the history of Belgium's colony in the Congo and contains a large and absorbing collection of historical, anthropological and zoological artefacts: fetishes, jewellery, baskets, weapons, sculpture, masks and headdresses, and stuffed wildlife – many of which were collected for the Congo exhibit at the Brussels Universal Exhibition of 1897. Among the most memorable exhibits are an enormous pirogue – a 22.5m-long canoe, big enough for 100 men, hewn out of a single tree – a battered trunk used by Dr Livingstone on his last voyage; and the peaked cap of the great adventurer Henry Morton Stanley. Since the 1960s, various artefacts from the Americas and Pacific Islands have been added to the impressive collection. After visiting the museum, you can walk down to the lakes at the foot of the park.

Where to Stay

Bruges has hotels to suit all tastes – and over 100 of them. They range from small family-run guesthouses, with their own ways of doing things and quirky charms, to the large, efficient, comfortable you-could-be-anywhere hotels of the international chains.

The really special hotels are the small and luxurious ones in the centre of town, occupying beautifully restored and converted historic mansions and town houses. The rooms look like photographs from glossy interior-design magazines, with plush and tasteful comfort down to the last pampered detail – backed by impeccable service. Cheaper hotels are more run-of-the-mill, but it may be worth sacrificing comfort for a more central location.

Most hotels offer family rooms, in which children can share with their parents; and most hotel rooms (except the very cheapest) have telephones and TV sets. For disabled visitors, the tourist office Web site (w www.brugge.be) offers more detailed information about hotels with wheelchair facilities.

Note that Bruges's cobbled streets are noisy with traffic, horse-drawn carriages and revellers. In summer you may want to insist on a room with double glazing and air conditioning, unless you can put up with the noise and mosquitoes coming through open windows.

Virtually everyone in the hotel business speaks English, so booking is easy. Check that the price quoted includes breakfast (charged separately, it can be surprisingly expensive). Establish if the hotel has its own parking or is close to a public car park. Parking can be very tricky anywhere in the city, especially in summer.

All hotels listed below have the central Bruges postcode (8000 Brugge), unless otherwise stated.

Reservations on the Internet

The Bruges tourist office offers a free reservations service on their Web site w www.brugge.be. The Web site w www.hotels-brugge.org allows you to refine your search by ticking a list of desired amenities. You can also book online using w www.flandersholidaystore.com.

Price Categories

Price for a double room:
luxury above €200
expensive €140–200
moderate €80–140
inexpensive €50–80
cheap under €50

Central Bruges

The historic centre of Bruges has some of the best places to stay in the city as they are often located in beautifully restored buildings.

Luxury

These hotels are right in the centre – set among the web of streets filled with atmospheric, medieval charm.

Die Swaene E5
Steenhouwersdijk 1, t (050) 34 27 98, f (050) 33 66 74, e info@dieswaene-hotel.com, w www.dieswaene-hotel.com. Part of the Small Luxury Hotels of the World group. Delightful 15th-century mansion, with a much-lauded gastronomic restaurant, overlooking the canal. Louis XV-cum-Laura Ashley style décor with four-poster beds. Has indoor swimming pool and sauna.

De Orangerie D6
Kartuizerinnenstraat 10, t (050) 34 16 49, f (050) 33 30 16, e info@hotelorangerie.com, w www.hotelorangerie.com. Delightful, elegant and sumptuous small hotel, sister to De Tuilerieën. Sixteenth-century former convent overlooking the canal with canalside breakfast terrace. Private garage.

Expensive

Holiday Inn Crowne Plaza D–E5
Burg 10, t (050) 44 68 44, f (050) 44 68 68, e hotel@crowne-plaza-brugge.com, w www.global-hotel.com. Sleek modern hotel, with pool, parking and an archaeological site in the basement. Children free if sharing with parents. One room has wheelchair facilities. Parking €15 a day.

Jan Brito E5
Freren Fonteinstraat 1, t (050) 33 06 01, f (050) 33 06 52, e info@janbrito.com, w www.janbrito.com. Sixteenth-century gabled mansion, near the centre, beautifully restored, in Louis XVI style. Breakfast only, no restaurant.

Romantik Pandhotel E6
Pandreitje 16, t (050) 34 06 66, f (050) 34 05 56, e info@pandhotel.com, w www.pandhotel.com. Fine central 18th-century burgher's house, now a cosy, elegant hotel, with canopied beds and Ralph Lauren fabrics. Part of the Romantic Hotels chain.

Walburg E5
Boomgaardstraat 13–15, t (050) 34 94 14, f (050) 33 68 84. Elegantly restored 19th-century mansion in the heart of Bruges with impossibly high ceilings and frothy neoclassical décor. Restrained and spacious; backs onto a sunny garden and terrace.

Moderate

Botaniek E5
Waalsestraat 23, t (050) 34 14 24, f (050) 34 59 39, e hotel.botaniek@pi.be, w www.hotels-belgium.com/brugge/hb-brugge-botaniek.htm. Small, comfortable 18th-century town house.

Bourgoensch Hof D5
Wollestraat 39, t (050) 33 16 45, f (050) 34 63 78, e info@bour

bourgoensch-hof.com.
Traditional Flemish architecture
overlooking the canal. Good
restaurant and brasserie serving
classic regional dishes.

Duc de Bourgogne E5
Huidenvettersplein 12, **t** (050) 33 20
38, **f** (050) 34 40 37,
e duc.bourgogne@ssi.be.
Hotel-restaurant with just ten
traditionally decorated rooms in a
very central historic house.
Excellent restaurant.

Patritius E4
Riddersstraat 11, **t** (050) 33 84 54,
f (050) 33 96 34, **e** hotel.patritius@
proximedia.be, **w** www.hotel
patritius.be.
A big old mansion, converted into
a medium-priced hotel, spacious
and central. Has one room with
wheelchair facilities.

Inexpensive

Central D5
Markt 30, **t** (050) 33 18 05, **f** (050)
34 68 78, **e** central@hotelcentral.be,
w www.hotelcentral.be.
The only hotel on the Markt: could
hardly be more central, with views
across the square to the Belfort.
Just nine rooms, not all with en
suite bathrooms.

Cordoeanier D5
Cordoeaniersstraat 16–18, **t** (050)
33 90 51, **f** (050) 34 61 11,
e info@cordoeanier.be,
w www.cordoeanier.be.
Small, central good-value family-
run hotel. Also has a 'family house'
for rent for up to 10/12 people.

't Koffieboontje D5
Hallestraat 4, **t** (050) 33 80 27,
f (050) 34 39 04, **e** hotel_koffie
boontje@online.be, **w** www.hotel-
koffieboontje.be.
Atrractive little hotel in the heart
of the city. Also reasonably priced
holiday apartments for
1–6 people.

Southern Bruges

Southern Bruges enjoys the
leafy tranquillity of the Begijnhof
and the Minnewater – but also

has the main thoroughfare linking
the city centre to the coach park at
the southern perimeter. The map
on pp.164–5 will show how several
of these hotels are in fact very
close to the centre.

Luxury

De Tuilerieën D6
Dijver 7, **t** (050) 34 36 91,
f (050) 34 04 00, **e** info@hotel
tuilerieen.com, **w** www.hotel
tuilerieen.com.
Pampered luxury in a 15th-century
town house on a pretty stretch of
canal near the centre. Private
garage and swimming pool. One
child under 12 stays free.

Expensive

De Snippe E7
Nieuwe Gentweg 53, **t** (050) 33 70
70, **f** (050) 33 76 62,
e desnippe@relaischateaux.com,
w www.relaischateaux.com.
Hotel-restaurant with celebrated
cuisine. Sympathetically restored
18th-century house; comfortable
elegance, polished wood floors,
soft drapes.

Moderate

Dante F6
Coupure 29A, **t** (050) 34 01 94,
f (050) 34 35 39, **e** info@hotel
dante.be, **w** www.hoteldante.be.
Large, imposing and modern with
mellow interior. The vegetarian
restaurant, Toermalijn, comes
recommended.

De Barge E9
Bargeweg 15, **t** (050) 38 51 50,
f (050) 38 21 25, **e** debarge@
online.be, **w** www.debarge
hotel.com.
A stylish and novel hotel on a
barge (with a restaurant) in the
far south of the city, close to the
Minnewater – 23 double or triple
rooms kitted out in nautical style
with en suite bath and WC.

Egmond D8
Minnewater 15, Brugge,
t (050) 34 14 45, **f** (050) 34 29 40,
e info@egmond.be.

Gabled, sprawling and utterly
romantic. Also surprisingly
reasonable. Beautiful gardens.

Ibis Brugge Centrum D7
Katelijnestraat 65A, **t** (050) 33 75 75,
f (050) 33 64 19.
Large hotel with all mod cons in a
15th century convent; near the
Begijnhof. One room has wheelchair facilities.

Novotel Zuid Off maps
Chartreuseweg 20, 8200 Brugge
(Sint-Michiels), **t** (050) 40 21 40,
f (050) 40 21 41, **e** H0466@accor
hotels.com, **w** www.novotel.com.
Functional family hotel with 101
rooms 4km south of the city.
Woodland setting with outdoor
pool (May–Sept). Near the A17
motorway but good double-
glazing. Two rooms have
wheelchair facilities.

Inexpensive

Breugelhof C8
Oostmeers 128, **t** (050) 34 34 28,
f (050) 34 34 47, **e** info@hotel-
breugelhof.be, **w** www.hotel-
breugelhof.be.
Cheerful hotel-cum-bistro, set in
leafy surroundings near the
Begijnhof, about four minutes'
walk from the station and ten
minutes from the centre.

Campanile Off maps
20 Jagerstraat, 8200 Brugge (St-
Michiels), **t** (050) 38 13 60, **f** (050)
38 45 42.
Friendly, modern family-run hotel,
south of the station. Two rooms
have wheelchair facilities.

Cheap

Rembrandt-Rubens D7
Walplein 38, **t** (050) 33 64 39.
A gabled 17th-century house set
back from the canals, near the
Begijnhof.

't Keizershof C8
Oostmeers 126, **t** (050) 33 87 28,
e hotelkeizershof@12move.be.
Useful budget guesthouse, clean
and presentable, next to the
Breugelhof, at half the price.
Shower and WC on the landings.

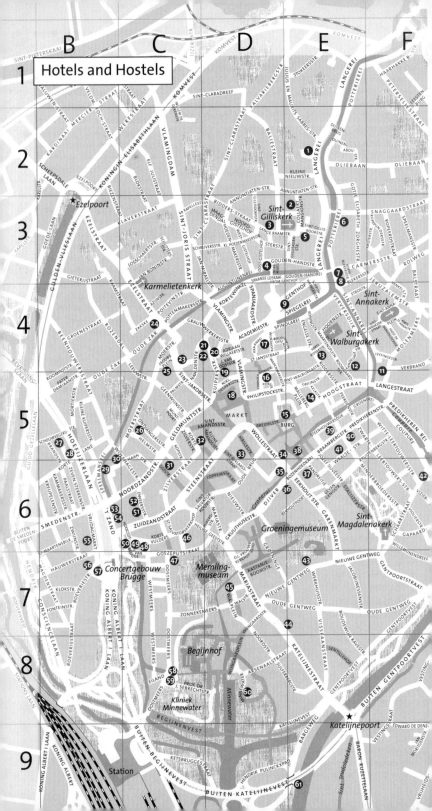

Map Key

8	Adornes	19	Hansa
57	Albert I	15	Holiday Inn Crowne Plaza
22	Aragon	29	Hotel Ensor
5	Asiris	52	Hotel Gran Kaffee de Passage
30	Azalea	44	Ibis Brugge Centrum
10	Bauhaus Budget Hotel	51	Imperial
17	Biskajer	3	Jacobs
41	Botaniek	40	Jan Brito
23	Boterhuis	28	Karos
34	Bourgoensch Hof	21	Lucca
59	Breugelhof	48	Lybeer
7	Bryghia	27	Montovani
20	Cavalier	25	Navarra
18	Central	55	Park Hotel
14	Charlie Rockets	13	Patritius
16	Cordoeanier	54	Portinari
42	Dante	26	Prinsenhof
61	De Barge	9	Relais Oud Huis Amsterdam
46	De Castillion	45	Rembrandt Rubens
53	De Markies	37	Romantik Pandhotel
6	De' Medici	24	Snuffel Sleep In
35	De Orangerie	56	Sofitel Bruges
2	De Pauw	4	Ter Brughe
43	De Snippe	1	Ter Duinen
36	De Tuilerieën	11	Ter Reien
39	Die Swaene	58	't Keizershof
38	Duc de Bourgogne	33	't Koffieboontje
60	Egmond	50	't Putje
47	Goezeput	32	Van Eyck
31	Grand Hotel du Sablon	12	Walburg
49	Groeninghe		

Northeastern Bruges

Many of these hotels enjoy canalside locations and views, and benefit from the fact that they are a little off the beaten track – although well within walking distance of the centre.

Luxury

Relais Oud Huis Amsterdam E4
Spiegelrei 3, t (050) 34 18 10, f (050) 33 88 91, e info@oha.be, w www.oha.be.
Four 17th-century mansions combined to offer idiosyncratic luxury, with antique-furnished rooms, many overlooking the canal or a garden. Feels like a large, grand but relaxed family home.

Moderate

Adornes E3
Sint Annarei 26, t (050) 34 13 36, f (050) 34 20 85, e hotel.adornes@ proximedia.be, w www.proximedia .com/web/adornes.html.
A cluster of softly coloured gabled 16th–18th-century houses, tastefully restored and overlooking the canal. Friendly and welcoming. Free bicycle rental. Some car parking.

Biskajer D4
Biskajersplein 4, t (050) 34 15 06, f (050) 34 39 11, e info@hotel biskajer.com, w www.hotel biskajer.com.
Quiet, cosy, personable hotel, a short walk from the Markt. Bright, modern furnishings.

Bryghia E3

Oosterlingenplein 4, t (050) 33 80 59, f (050) 34 14 30, e info@bryghia hotel.be, w www.bryghiahotel.be.
Central yet peaceful family-run hotel with traditional décor of exposed brickwork and beamed ceilings.

De' Medici E3

Potterierei 15, t (050) 33 98 33, f (050) 33 07 64, e demedici .brugge@flanderscoast.be, w www.goldentulip.com.
A sympathetic fusion of modern and traditional design. Gym, sauna, solarium, Turkish baths, jacuzzi. Lounge bar leading onto a Japanese garden, and excellent Japanese restaurant specializing in *teppanyaki*. Two rooms have wheelchair facilities. Part of the Golden Tulip group.

Ter Brughe D3

Oost-Gistelhof 2, t (050) 34 03 24, f (050) 33 88 73, e info@hotelter brughe.com, w www.hotelter brughe.com.
Renovated, typical 16th-century narrow Flemish mansion; breakfast in the vaulted medieval cellar. Overlooks the canal.

Ter Duinen E2

Langerei 52, t (050) 33 04 37, f (050) 34 42 16, e info@terduinenhotel.be, w www.terduinenhotel.be.
Welcoming, family-run hotel, with views over the canal. Conservatory, real open fire, air-conditioned rooms, heavily double glazed. Nothing too much trouble. Free car parking.

Ter Reien F5

Langestraat 1, t (050) 34 91 00, f (050) 34 40 48, e hotel.ter .reien@unicall.be, w www.hotel bel.com/terreien.htm.
Much praised, well-located small hotel, overlooking the Sint-Annarei canal. Excellent value for money. Recent pretty renovation. Public parking at 800m.

Wilgenhof Off maps

Polderstraat 151, 8310 Brugge (Sint-Kruis), t (050) 36 27 44, f (050) 36 28 21.
On the banks of the Damme canal outside the city centre. Attractive cottage-style hotel set amidst the green polders. Good opportunities for walking and cycling.

Inexpensive

Asiris E3

Lange Raamstraat 9, t (050) 34 17 24, f (050) 34 74 58, e hotel.asiris@ pandora.be.
Former aristocrat's home near Sint-Gillis church, colourfully renovated. Free car parking.

De Pauw E3

Sint-Gilliskerkhof 8, t (050) 33 71 18, f (050) 34 51 40, e info@hotelde pauw.be, w www.hoteldepauw.be.
Traditional, cosy, sturdy brick house in a quiet street.

Jacobs D3

Baliestraat 1, t (050) 33 98 31, f (050) 33 56 94, e hoteljacobs@ glo.be, w www.hotelbel.com/ jacobs.htm.
Comfortable quiet rooms in a gabled mansion house. Family-run for almost 50 years. Private garage for €5 per night.

Cheap

Bauhaus Budget Hotel G4

Langestraat 135–137, t (050) 34 10 93, f (050) 33 41 80, w www.bauhaus.be.
Bauhaus have recently introduced budget hotel rooms for doubles, triples or four people. Doubles cost €35 per room, with breakfast an additional €2. All rooms have private shower.

Western Bruges

Again the map will show that several of these hotels are very close to the centre. Hotels on 't Zand are a little further out, but are still within walking distance of the centre, along the main shopping street, Steenstraat.

Expensive

De Castillion C6

Heilige-Geeststraat 1, t (050) 34 30 01, f (050) 33 94 75, e info@r castillion.bt, w www.castillion.be.
Once a prince's residence. Opulent hotel-restaurant furnished with heavy turn-of-the-century grandeur. Near St-Salvators-kathedraal. Parking €10 per night.

Sofitel Brugge B7

Boeveriestraat 2, t (050) 34 09 71, f (050) 34 40 53, e H1278@accor hotels.com, w www.sofitel.com.
Comfortable modern hotel behind the façade of a 17th-century monastery. Swimming pool.

Moderate

Albert I B7

Koning Albertlaan 2–4, t (050) 34 09 30, f (050) 33 84 18, e hotel@ albert1.com, w www.albert1.com.
A warm red-brick building on the busy 't Zand, with pleasant rooms and hearty breakfasts.

Aragon C4

Naaldenstraat 24, t (050) 33 35 33, f (050) 34 28 05, e info@aragon.be, w www.aragon.be.
Spacious 18th-century noble's house, opposite the Hof Bladelin.

Azalea B5

Wulfhagestraat 43, t (050) 33 14 78, f (050) 33 97 00, e info@azalea hotel.be, w www.azaleahotel.be.
Very elegant, traditionally decorated central hotel with beautiful, sweeping wooden staircase. Private car park.

Boterhuis C4

Sint-Jakobsstraat 38, t (050) 34 15 11, f (050) 34 70 89.
Lovely, whimsical hotel with a turret in the old dairy market. Quirky charm and friendly welcome.

Grand Hotel du Sablon C5

Noordzandstraat 21, t (050) 33 39 02, f (050) 34 20 18.
Turn-of-the-20th-century décor with an Art Deco glassed cupola in the entrance hall. Handily placed for shopping.

Hansa D5

Niklaas Desparsstraat 11, t (050) 44 44 44, f (050) 44 44 40, e information@hansa.be, w www.hansa.be.
Elegantly restored 19th-century mansion with air conditioning,

fitness centre, sauna, steambath and sundeck for afternoon tea. Crisply efficient.

Kasteel Cateline Off maps
Zandstraat 272, 8200 Brugge (Sint-Andries), t (050) 31 70 26, f (050) 31 72 41, e cateline@xs4all.be, w www.conquistador.be.
Located on the outskirts of Bruges. Small, turretted castle in the middle of a pretty park. Inventive cuisine.

Navarra C4
Sint-Jakobsstraat 41, t (050) 34 05 61, f (050) 33 67 90, e reservations @hotelnavarra.com, w www.hotelnavarra.com.
Gleaming white hotel, recently renovated – once the medieval trading house of the merchants of Navarre. Wicker armchairs scattered in the lovely enclosed garden. Sauna, fitness area and indoor pool. On site parking.

Pannenhuis Off maps
Zandstraat 2, 8200 Brugge (Sint-Andries), t (050) 31 19 07, f (050) 31 77 66, e hostellerie@pannen huis.be, w www.pannenhuis.be.
Black and white gabled former notary's villa on the outskirts, near the Smedenpoort, 15 minutes' walk from the centre. Expansive terraced garden and good seafood restaurant.

Park Hotel B6
Vrijdagmarkt 5, t (050) 33 33 64, f (050) 33 47 63, e parkhotel @unicall.be, w www.parkhotel-brugge.be.
Comfortable modern hotel on 't Zand.

Portinari B6
't Zand 15, t (050) 34 10 34, f (050) 34 41 80, e info@portinari.be, w www.portinari.be.
Relaxed and comfortable hotel with excellent service and pleasant terrace.

Prinsenhof C5
Ontvangersstraat 9, t (050) 34 26 90, f (050) 34 23 21, e info@ prinsenhof.com, w www .prinsenhof.be.
Very plush, with antique-furnished rooms in the heart of the city. A Relais du Silence hotel.

't Putje B6
't Zand 31, t (050) 33 28 47, f (050) 34 14 23, e info@hotelputje.com, w www.hotelputje.com.
Central, well-run, clean and friendly modernized hotel.

Inexpensive

Cavalier D4
Kuipersstraat 25, t (050) 33 02 07, f (050) 34 71 99, e hotel.cavalier@ skynet.be, w users.skynet.be/ hotel.cavalier.
Just behind the theatre, with eight cosy rooms and a touch of 19th-century grandeur.

De Markies B6
't Zand 5, t (050) 34 83 34, f (050) 34 87 87.
One of the many commercially oriented modern hotels on the 't Zand, with its own bistro restaurant (Brasserie Leffe) spilling out onto the square, and a breakfast room on the top floor. Public parking on 't Zand.

Goezeput C7
Goezeputstraat 29, t (050) 34 26 94, f (050) 34 20 13.
A small, recently renovated hotel with 15 rooms, in a former 18th-century monastery, close to Sint-Salvatorskathedraal.

Groeninghe C6
Korte Vulderssstraat 29, t (050) 34 32 55, f (050) 34 07 69.
Small guesthouse with the atmosphere of a private home, not far from Sint-Salvatorskathedraal.

Hotel Ensor B5–6
Speelmansrei 10, t (050) 34 25 89, f (050) 34 20 18, e hotel_ensor@ unicall.be.
Small hotel with 12 pretty rooms overlooking the canal.

Imperial C6
Dweersstraat 24, t (050) 33 90 14, f (050) 34 43 06.
Tucked down a side street east of 't Zand, with gleaming stepped gables and flourishing window boxes. Friendly and comfortable.

Karos B5
Hoefijzerlaan 37, t (050) 34 14 48, f (050) 34 00 91, e hotel.karos@ compaqnet.be.

New, well-equipped hotel on a busy road near 't Zand. With Breton-style façade, a swimming pool, sauna and solarium.

Lucca C4
Naaldenstraat 30, t (050) 34 20 67, f (050) 33 34 64, e lucca@hotel lucca.be, w www.hotellucca.be.
Neoclassical building in the centre, on the site of the trading house of the merchants of Lucca. Breakfast in the 14th-century cellar. Friendly and relaxed. Rooms have heavy blinds which cut down on the street noise.

Montovani B5
Schouwvergersstraat 11, t (050) 34 53 66, f (050) 34 53 67, e info@ montovani.com, w www .montovani.com.
Near 't Zand. Family-run pension with patio and attractive interior veranda.

Olympia Off maps
Magdalenastraat 16, t (050) 39 05 78, f (050) 39 01 13, e info@olympia-hotel.com, w www.proximedia.com.
Modern, low-rise hotel, just outside the town ramparts, 15 minutes' walk from the centre, near the Smedenpoort. Thirty quiet rooms and cheerfully efficient approach.

Van Eyck C5
Korte Zilverstraat 7, t (050) 33 52 67, f (050) 34 94 30.
In a quiet yet central street. Businesslike, but comfortable.

Cheap

Hotel Gran Kaffee de Passage C6
Dweersstraat 26, t (050) 34 02 32, f (050) 34 01 40.
This hive of activity (youth hotel, lively restaurant) also has rooms with themed décor – Indian, Moroccan and so on.

Lybeer C6
Korte Vulderssstraat 31, t/f (050) 33 43 55, e hotel.lybeer@pandora.be, w www.hotellybeer.com.
Cosy, budget hotel with rooms for 1–4 people, some with en suite shower and WC. Well-placed, close to Sint-Salvatorskathedraal.

Apartments

Bruges tourist office has a list of holiday flats for rent (*see* **w** *www.brugge.be*). Flats for four people cost around €550 a week in the high season, and 20% less in low season. Here is just one example: the friendly café/bar Lokkedize (*see* p.183) has a range of well-presented and comfortable apartments on the premises, with one/two/three bedrooms, living rooms with cable TV and hi-fi, fully equipped kitchens and private bathrooms. Price depends on length of stay and season: a three-bedroom flat, sleeping five, might cost about €900 for a week in summer. Contact Eric Broos, *Lokkedize, Korte Vulderstraat 33*, **t** *(050) 33 44 50*, **w** *www .lokkedize.be*.

Bauhaus (*see* Bauhaus Budget Hotel, below) also has flats for families or groups of 4–12 people, rented for the weekend, or 3–4 days midweek, or by the week. Prices vary according to the size of the party, length of stay and time of year, but can work out at €10–40 per person, per day.

Youth Hostels and Youth Hotels

There are several *jeuglogies* in Bruges, where you can find cheap and cheerful accommodation – fine if you don't mind sleeping in a dormitory.

Bauhaus Budget Hotel G4
Langestraat 135–137, **t** *(050) 34 10 93,* **f** *(050) 33 41 80,* **w** *www.bauhaus.be*.
Room for 81 people, about 20 minutes' walk from the centre, or bus no.6 from the station. €8 per person. Facilities include a cyber-café, restaurants and neighbouring laundromat.

Charlie Rockets E5
Hoogstraat 19, **t** *(050) 33 06 60,* **f** *(050) 33 66 74*.
Funky and very central youth hotel in a converted cinema. Rooms shared by 2, 4 or 6. €13 without breakfast; €15 with.

International Youth Hostel Off maps
Baron Ruzettelaan 143, 8310 Assebroek, **t** *(050) 35 26 79,* **f** *(050) 35 37 32*.
The modern youth hostel, located in a suburb east of the city. Bus no.2 to the city centre, or from the station out to the hostel. €10–15 with a Youth Hostel card, €3 more without.

Passage C6
Dweersstraat 26, **t** *(050) 34 02 32,* **f** *(050) 34 01 40*.
Capacity for 50, a stone's throw from Sint-Salvatorskathedraal. Dormitories from about €10 excluding breakfast. Also double rooms from €36 with breakfast.

Snuffel Sleep In C4
Ezelstraat 47–9, **t** *(050) 33 31 33,* **f** *(050) 33 32 50,* **e** *info@snuffel.be,* **w** *www.snuffel.be*.
Cheap backpacker hostel close to the centre. Easygoing regime. Rooms for 4, 8 and 12 persons; doubles possible except in July/August. €11–15 per person without breakfast (€2).

Bed and Breakfast

The tourist office publishes a list of approved bed and breakfast accommodation with further details and Web links available on its Web site **w** *www.brugge.be*. Double rooms are available in central locations for €35–125 upwards, family rooms sleeping four for around €60–185. Contact the tourist office for more details and reservations (*see* p.65).

Camping

Memling Off maps
Veltemweg, Sint Kruis 109, **t/f** *(050) 35 58 45,* **e** *info@camping-memling.be,* **w** *www.camping-memling.be*.
Situated in a wooded parkland in the east of the city, 2km from the centre; has places for tents and caravans. Tents €3.30 per person; caravans €3.40 per person. Discounts in low season.

Sint-Michiels Off maps
Tillegemstraat 55, 8200 Brugge, Sint-Michiels, **t** *(050) 38 08 19,* **f** *(050) 80 68 24*.
Camp site located southwest of the city. From €3 per person.

Eating Out

*So prodigiously good was the
eating and drinking on board
these sluggish but most comfortable vessels [between Bruges and
Ghent], that there are legends
extant of an English traveller,
who, coming to Belgium for a
week, and travelling in one of
these boats, was so delighted
with the fare there that he went
backwards and forwards from
Ghent to Bruges perpetually
until the railroads were invented,
when he drowned himself on the
last trip of the passage-boat.*

Vanity Fair, William
Makepeace Thackeray (1847–8)

It is now a well-known secret
that Belgium's food ranks among
the best in Europe – even the
French are prepared to admit it. It
has an armful of garlanded
restaurants over which even the
most hardened international
gastronomes will coo, and, more
importantly, it is almost impossible to eat badly. Since virtually
every Belgian is an expert on food,
restaurants serving sub-standard
fare simply cannot survive.

Belgians have a great
enthusiasm for eating out: decent
restaurants are well patronized
and are able to keep their prices
competitive. Standards are invari-
ably high – in the humble chip-
stand on a street corner as well as
at the pinnacles of haute cuisine.

Belgian Specialities

Belgian food is solidly northern
European, hearty and copious –
with a touch of genius that lifts it
above the ordinary. Clearly it is
closely allied to French cuisine,
and even in Flanders French is the
language of food, but its most
famous dishes are still firmly
rooted in burgher traditions and
by and large the Belgians have
little patience with the over-
priced preciousness to which *la
haute cuisine française* can so
easily fall victim.

Steak and chips is virtually the
national dish. The steak will be

first class and the chips, of course,
have no rival in Europe. Mussels
and chips comes a close second:
no dainty soup bowls scattered
with mussels, but a kilo per
person, which comes in a casse-
role the size of a bucket. *Moules
marinière/gestoomde mossels* is
the standard preparation: cleaned
live mussels are cooked on a bed
of sweated celery, onion and
parsley until the shells open.
Few elaborations improve on
this formula.

Lighter dishes may include delicately flavoured soups, such as
soupe de cresson/waterkers soep
(watercress); excellent fish; tasty,
substantial salads, such as *salade
Liégeoise/warme Luikse sla* (a warm
salad of green beans or salade
frisée and bacon pieces); and *steak
à l'américaine* (or *américain pré-
paré*), raw minced steak with capers,
chopped raw onion, Worcestershire
sauce and a raw egg.

The most typically Belgian dish
is *waterzooi*, a soothing soup-like
creation in which chicken is
cooked with cream and vegetables. The *waterzooi* formula has
recently been applied to fish.
Other classic Belgian dishes
include *vlaamse stoverij*, or *stoof-
carbonaden*, a hearty, sweetly
flavoured beef stew cooked in
beer; and various vegetable and
meat purées known as *stoemp*. In
the spring, you can try Dutch-style
raw herrings, *maatjes*, held by the
tail and dropped into the mouth.
May time is the season of asparagus raised on the sandy polders,
and known locally as 'white gold'.

There is a wide variety of pork
dishes: *andouillettes* (rich
sausages made of offal) and the
excellent *boudin blanc* and *boudin
noir* (soft meat and blood
sausages). Game (*wild*) in season
includes pigeon, hare, pheasant
and venison, often with berries,
raisins or braised chicory. Look out
for unusual seasonal vegetables,
such as salsify and hop shoots –
served in spring with a peppery
cream sauce and poached eggs.

Chicory

The French-speaking Belgians
call them *chicons*, the French call
them *endives*, the Flemish call
them *witloof*, the English-
speaking world refers to them as
chicory in the UK and Belgian
endives in the US – a suitably
mysterious confusion for this
bizarre little vegetable. Chicory
consists of a head of firm, bullet-
shaped leaves – white, yellow and
pale green – with a crunchy
texture and a distinctive, bitter
flavour. It is often eaten raw, in
salads, but with simple cooking,
chicory is transformed into one of
the most delicious and surprising
of Belgium's foods. Melt some
butter in a saucepan, drop in a
handful of chicory, put on the lid
and cook very slowly until it has
collapsed into its own aromatic
juices and transmogrified into a
sweet, succulent delicacy. Chicory
wrapped in slices of ham and
baked in a cheese sauce (*chicons
gratin*) is a classic, warming
Belgian dish.

Chicory is essentially a winter
crop. The roots of the *chicorée*
lettuce are replanted and allowed
to shoot, but are kept in the dark
to make the shoots white. The
process was apparently discovered
by accident in about 1840 by the
head gardener at the botanical
gardens of Brussels, who was
simply trying to overwinter some
rootstock. He kept the shoots in
the dark by gently piling up the
earth over them, and this is the
method still used in the *potagers*
today. Commercial growers,
however, use darkened sheds and
hydroponics to maintain a
thriving export industry.

Chips

If you want a quick snack in
Belgium, you could do worse than
stopping at a *frituur* van and
ordering a cone of chips (French
fries). Belgian chips – *frietjes* – are
quite simply the best: no thicker
than your little finger, served
piping hot, golden brown and
crispy. The traditional

accompaniment is a dollop of heavenly Belgian mayonnaise. One of the reasons Belgian *frietjes* are so good is the choice of potato – usually a sweeter one such as Bintje, and old enough to have the right quantity of starch.

Belgians bring critical appreciation to their potatoes, just as they do to any other aspect of food: hang the shelf life. Take, for instance, the Saint-Nicholas, a delicious, waxy potato with a yellowish hue and an aromatic, nutty flavour; this is not just a lump of carbohydrate filler but a vegetable of distinction.

So what is the secret of making good Belgian chips? First select an appropriate potato variety; cut the potatoes to size, keeping them fairly thin. Lastly, fry them twice: the first time so that they are cooked but not brown; then, after allowing them to cool, cook them a second time until golden brown. They do not always have to be crispy, by the way: chips served with stews, such as *vlaamse stoverij*, are sometimes deliberately left soft – the better to soak up the sauces. Traditionally, *frietjes* were cooked in the rendered fat of beef kidneys; but if beef kidneys are hard to come by, sunflower or corn oil is a lighter, modern alternative.

Chocolate

When it comes to chocolate, 'Belgian' is synonymous with quality – so much so that unscrupulous foreign operators will use the term liberally as a sales tool when their product contains only the merest fraction of Belgian chocolate, or is simply prepared in Belgian style. Imitation may be a form of flattery, but do not be misled: only the Belgians produce the chocolates that are responsible for this reputation. This is partly because freshness counts: Belgian chocolates are sumptuous, fresh cream confections with a limited shelf life (three weeks or so in the fridge); furthermore, because the Belgians themselves are

enthusiastic consumers of hand-made chocolate, turnover is high and the price is remarkably low.

Three factors have given rise to the unassailable reputation of Belgian chocolate: the cream fillings, white chocolate, and – most important of all – the quality of the plain chocolate. The Belgians may not have been the first to put fresh cream in chocolates, but they pioneered fresh-cream fillings for the mass market. White chocolate is a comparative newcomer; in fact it is barely chocolate at all, but a milk-based confection mixed with cocoa butter and sweetener. The best plain Belgian chocolate contains a very high proportion of cocoa solids – at least 52 per cent, usually more like 70 per cent (90 per cent is the feasible maximum). These cocoa solids are the crushed and ground product of cocoa beans (usually from West Africa), from which some of the oily cocoa butter has been extracted. This valuable cocoa butter is later reintroduced to make high-quality chocolate (in poor-quality chocolate, vegetable fat is substituted for cocoa butter and there is also a much lower percentage of cocoa solids). Cocoa butter makes a significant difference, as any chocolate addict will tell you: the natural oils in the cocoa butter evaporate in your mouth, provoking a slight cooling, refreshing sensation.

Leonidas, Godiva, Corné de la Toison d'Or and Neuhaus are the most famous manufacturers in Belgium, but there are many more, some of them tiny individual concerns with just one outlet. Of the big names, Leonidas is probably the cheapest, but this has little bearing on quality: many Belgians actually prefer Leonidas and find the others too rich. Leonidas appears to produce chocolates on an industrial scale, and has numerous outlets. Some have large counters opening directly on to the street, so that the staff can shovel out boxes of

chocolates to passing custo[mers] with the minimum of delay. O[nly] in Belgium could chocolates be treated as a kind of fast food. Godiva, however, has the greater international reputation: the company now has 1,400 shops worldwide, selling 120 different kinds of chocolate at the luxury end of the market. Why, you may ask, is a Belgian chocolate company named after Lady Godiva, the nobleman's wife who rode naked through the streets of Coventry in the 11th century? The answer is simply that, in 1929, the founders of the business liked the image, which seemed to represent the qualities of their chocolates: elegant, rich, sensual and daring.

Other Sweet Treats

Belgian biscuits are almost as famous as their chocolates. *Speculoos*, a hard, buttery biscuit, is a well-known speciality of Flanders, but the Bruges speciality is *Brugge Kletskoppen*, 'lace cookies', which resemble the lace for which the city is famous.

At the other end of the scale, you can sink your teeth into a luscious, freshly cooked *wafel* (*gaufre* in French), the original Belgian holiday food, generously sprinkled with icing sugar. Waffles appear at country fairs, or by the sea, at street cafés, and in homes whenever there is something to celebrate. The waffle iron is brought out, polished up, and set to work to stack up piles of steaming waffles for hungry guests. *Koeken* are another Flemish favourite – sweet, buttery pastries flavoured with spices or drizzled with sugar or topped with raisins and nuts. They are eaten with pots of strong coffee in the afternoon, or as part of a lazy Sunday morning breakfast ritual.

Eating Out

The fame of Bruges's best restaurants has spread far beyond the borders of Belgium. It has some outstanding chefs working in beautifully decorated

...mers

...ly

...ensive

...its

prominent tourist restaurants on the main tourist circuit the fare can be decidedly mediocre. Plasticized, formulaic menus in four languages are a bad sign!

Restaurant hours are generally 12–2.30pm and 6–10.30 or 11pm, although many of the smaller bistros and brasseries serve nonstop from about 11am to midnight. Many restaurants are closed for Saturday lunch and on Sunday. It's advisable to make a reservation for the more upmarket and/or smaller establishments. There are restaurants to suit all palates and appetites; menus at the door will show what's on offer. The fixed-price *dagschotel/dagmenu* (menu of the day) is often a bargain, and you will find that even luxury restaurants usually feature a cheaper menu at lunchtime. Many cafés serve a limited range of light dishes for lunch and supper, and bars may offer snacks or sandwiches. Some food shops and pâtisseries have tables and chairs where you can sit and eat a snack.

All the more established restaurants take Visa and MasterCard; the more expensive restaurants also take American Express and Diners Club – but as always, if in doubt, check before you eat!

Value Added Tax (TVA/BTW) at 21 per cent is generally already included in the price of restaurant meals. A 16 per cent **service charge** is also usually included, so no further tipping is required. If in doubt, check the menu or ask.

Price Categories

Price for 3-course meal (without wine) for one person:
expensive over €40
moderate €15–40
inexpensive below €15

Central Bruges

Restaurants

Expensive

Den Braamberg E6
Pandreitje 11, t (050) 33 73 70. **Open** *Mon and Wed–Sat noon–2pm and 7–9.30pm; closed 2 weeks in July.*
Elegant restaurant in an 18th-century house, with award-winning cuisine. Lunch €45.

Den Dyver D6
Dijver 5, t (050) 33 60 69. **Open** *Fri–Tues noon–2pm and 6.30–9.30pm.*
Sumptuous historic backdrop: dishes cooked with beer; perfect for beer enthusiasts (*see* p.181).

Den Gouden Karpel E5
Huidenvettersplein 4, t (050) 33 34 94. **Open** *April–Sept Tues–Sun noon–9.30pm, Oct–March Tues–Sun noon–3pm and 6–9.30pm.*
Elegant and relaxed fish restaurant run by third-generation fishmongers, with a terrace outside in summer. A la carte menu of classic fish dishes, and a more inventive daily menu. Their fish shop next door (on the Vismarkt) will give you a flavour of what they can achieve.

De Visscherie E5
Vismarkt 8, t (050) 33 02 12. **Open** *Wed–Mon noon–2pm and 7–10pm; closed mid-Nov–mid-Dec.*
Fish gastronomy of high renown, overlooking the fish market. *Waterzooi van de Noordzee* especially recommended. €30 plus.

Die Swaene E5
Steenhouwersdijk 1, t (050) 34 27 98. **Open** *daily noon–2.15pm and 7–9.15pm.*
Elegant hotel-restaurant which prides itself on its French-style cooking, served in a plush, candlelit setting. All very romantic. Dresscode: jacket.

Duc de Bourgogne E5
Huidenvettersplein 12, t (050) 33 20 38. **Open** *Mon–Sat noon–2.30pm and 7–9.30pm.*
Classy hotel-restaurant in former palace gatehouse, overlooking the canal at the heart of the city. Gastronomic menus from €33.

't Pandreitje E6
Pandreitje 6, t (050) 33 11 90. **Open** *Mon–Tues and Thurs–Sat noon–2pm and 7–9.30pm.*
Louis XV décor, terrace and garden in one of Bruges's most fetching locations. Excellent wine list and inventive French cuisine.

Moderate

Bierbistro Erasmus D6
Wollestraat 35, t (050) 33 57 81; wheelchair accessible. **Open** *Tues–Sun 11am–midnight.*
Small and friendly bistro and bar, serving countless types of Belgian beer and an array of tasty Flemish dishes – many of them cooked in beer.

Bistro de Eetkamer E6
Eekhoutstraat 6, t (050) 33 78 86. **Open** *Fri and Sun–Tues noon–2.30pm and 6.30–11pm, Sat noon–2.30pm and 6.30–midnight.*
Rigorously good cooking in a neat, straightforward setting – the sort of place that locals are happy to eat in.

Breydel-De Coninck D5
Breidelstraat 24, t (050) 33 97 46. **Open** *Thurs–Tues noon–2.30pm and 6–9.30pm; closed June.*
Hearty portions of mussels, seafood and steak; easy-going, modern ambience. Very central, favoured by locals and extremely well priced.

Cornée D5
De Garre 2, t (050) 33 95 88. **Open** *Fri–Tues noon–2pm and 6–10pm, Thurs 6–10pm.*
Friendly, intimate restaurant down a tiny alleyway off Breidelstraat. French and Belgian cuisine (eels in green sauce, dishes with *witloof*). Lunch menu €25.

De Mosselkelder E5
Huidenvettersplein 5, t (050) 34 23 20. **Open** *Wed–Mon noon–2pm and 7–10pm.*
Specialist mussel restaurant beside the fish market, owned by the same people as De Visscherie (*see* above). Also serves light dishes such as omelettes, scampi and fish.

Den Amand D5
Sint-Amandstraat 4, t (050) 34 01 22. Open noon–2.45pm and 6–9.45pm; closed Mon and Wed eve in winter.
Tiny and charming restaurant, much rated locally, serving inventive international cuisine based on 'what is in the market' that day. Their menu for €25 changes monthly.

De Stove D5
Kleine Sint-Amandsstraat 4, t (050) 33 78 35. Open Fri–Tues noon–1.45pm and 6.45–9.30pm.
Small, husband-and-wife-run restaurant with a flare for both décor and cuisine, noted especially for its seafood.

L'Imprévu E6
Gevangenisstraat 1, t (050) 34 97 16. Open Fri–Wed 11.30am–2pm and 6pm–late.
Tiny but stylish little restaurant, with a modern flare, specializing in salads, tapas and Flemish dishes. Menu at €25.

Lotus D5
Wapenmakersstraat 5, t (050) 33 10 78. Open Mon–Sat 11.30am–1.45pm.
Relaxed, elegant vegetarian restaurant, with inventive and well-priced dishes, including some fish.

Sint-Joris D5
Markt 29, t (050) 33 30 62. Open Fri–Wed noon–10pm.
Locals will tell you that, if you must eat on the Markt, this is the place to go, because the food (standard Belgian dishes) is reliable and the service attentive.

't Dreveken E5
Huidenvettersplein 10, t (050) 33 95 06. Open Mon and Wed–Fri noon–2.30pm and 6–10pm, Sat and Sun noon–10pm.
Restaurant in a pleasantly cosy historic house on this pretty square. Specializes in standard Flemish dishes, such as *waterzooi* and rabbit cooked in beer.

't Voermanshuys D6
Oude Burg 14, t (050) 33 71 72. Open Wed–Mon noon–2pm and 6–10pm.
Robust grilled dishes and filling fondues in 16th-century cellars.

Inexpensive

De Beurze D5
22 Markt, t (050) 33 50 79. Open daily 9am–11pm.
Laid-back bistro with wooden tables and an open fire. Mussels, grilled fish and meat, light snacks.

Het Dagelijks Brood D5
Philipstockstraat 21, t (050) 33 60 50. Open Mon and Wed–Sat 7am–6pm, Sun 8am–6pm.
A branch of the successful Pain Quotidien chain. Bakery snacks and upmarket sandwiches. Seating around a big central table.

Le Panier à Salade D5
Philipstockstraat 27, t (050) 34 48 96. Open Wed–Sun noon–2pm and 7–11pm.
Excellent French cooking at attractive prices in a new, small restaurant – fetching deep-sea blues and terracotta.

Lijnwaadmarkt D5
Wollestraat 3, t (050) 33 43 13. Open Mon–Sat noon–3pm and 6pm–late.
Small, atmospheric, very Belgian restaurant on the site of the old linen market, close to the Markt. Serves simple three-course meals for €13.70, plus steaks, omelettes, mussels, and so on.

Taverne Curiosa D5
Vlamingstraat 22, t (050) 34 23 34. Open Tues–Sun 11am–1am.
Restaurant and tearoom serving good value snacks (omelettes, sandwiches, smoked eel) and more substantial Flemish dishes in an atmospheric vaulted crypt.

't Koffieboontje D5
Hallestraat 4, t (050) 33 80 27. Open daily noon–11pm.
Unpretentious, modern restaurant forming part of a hotel/bike-hire operation, offering good Belgian standards, such as steak, mussels and other seafood.

Tom Pouce D5
Burg 17, t (050) 33 03 36. Open daily 8am–11pm.
Right in the heart of the old centre, this is a large, unpretentious, business-like restaurant and tearoom with a view out over the

Vegetarian Food
Meat plays a central role in Belgian cuisine, but it would be wrong to assume that vegetarians are completely left out in the cold. Belgian chefs have become increasingly aware of the call for lighter dishes, and that sometimes means vegetarian. Even traditional Belgian cooking includes noted vegetarian dishes, such as *flamiche aux poireaux*, a kind of flan filled with leeks in a cream sauce. Egg dishes are excellent, and although vegetarians often get tired of being fobbed off with yet another omelette, omelettes in Belgium are actually extremely good. Asparagus, chicory and hop shoots often feature in meatless dishes. There are several dedicated vegetarian restaurants in Bruges, listed below. In non-vegetarian restaurants, you may fare better if you pick and choose from the edges of the menu, ordering two starters instead of a main course and filling up on delicious, substantial puddings. Try:
De Bron, *see p.176*; **Lotus**, *see p.173*; **Zen**, *see p.179*.

Burg. Recommended for a coffee or a light snack, such as freshly made waffles and pancakes. Despite its name (Tom Thumb), it has room for 200 diners.

't Voske Malpertuus D5
Eiermarkt 9, t (050) 33 30 38; wheelchair accessible. Open Mon–Sat 11.30am–3pm and 5.30–10.30pm.
Solid Flemish food, including rabbit dishes and delicious *waterzooi*, in medieval cellars which once formed part of a monastery. A stone's throw from the Markt.

Cafés and Snacks

Craenenburg D5
Markt 16, t (050) 33 34 02. Open daily 7.30am–late.
Café, with stained glass and heavy brass chandeliers, on the site where Archduke Maximilian was imprisoned for three weeks in 1488. Good snacks. (*See also p.72.*)

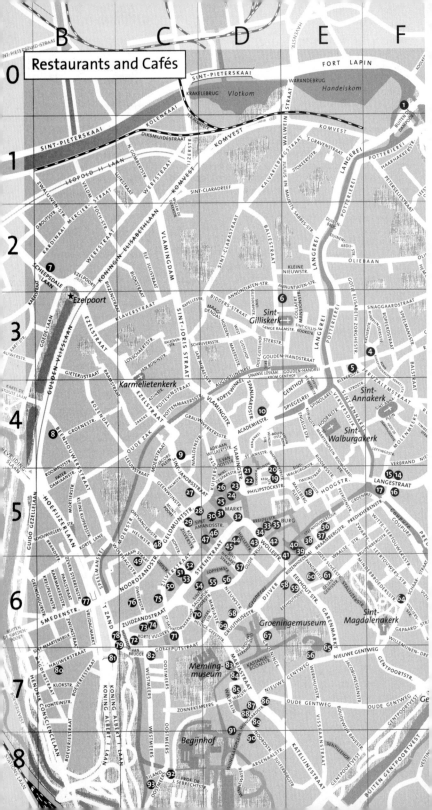

Restaurants and Cafés

Map Key

11	Bauhaus	19	Het Dagelijks Brood
13	Beenhouwerij De Leeuwebrug	92	Hotel-bistro Bruegelhof
55	Bhavani	71	Kardinaalshof
41	Bierbistro Erasmus	74	Lamourette
65	Bistro Christophe	19	Le Panier à Salade
59	Bistro de Eetkamer	42	Lijnwaadmarkt
63	Bistro De Schaar	61	L'Imprévu
1	Bistro du Phare	72	Lokkedize
4	Bistro 't Gezelleke	20	Lotus
9	Boterhuis Brasserie	68	Maria van Bourgondië
35	Breydel-De Coninck	69	Marieke van Brugghe
75	Cafedraal	91	Maximiliaan Van Oostenrijk
45	Café Hoegaarden	49	Pannekoekenhuisje/De Vlaamse Pot
37	Café 't Volkshuis		
5	Café Vlissinghe	50	Patrick Devos 'De Zilveren Pauw'
12	Celtica		
18	Charlie Rockets	27	Pietje Pek
81	Concertgebouw Brugge	22	Prestige
43	Cornée	33	Restaurant-Tearoom Hennon
87	Country Girl Sandwiches		
		15	Rock Fort
31	Craenenburg	88	Salade Folle
46	De Belegde Boterham	29	Sandwicherie St-Amandje
25	De Beurze	24	Sint-Joris
90	De Bron	88	Straffe Hendrik-De Halve Mann
70	De Castillion		
34	De Garre	86	Tanuki
56	De Gouden Zalm	21	Taverne Curiosa
53	De Hobbit	3	Taverne De Verloren Hoek
14	De Karmeliet		
82	De Lotteburg	6	Taverne Oud Handbogenhof
28	De Medici Sorbetière		
38	De Mosselkelder	85	't Begijntje
30	Den Amand	64	't Botaniekske
60	Den Braamberg	51	't Brugs Beertje
58	Den Dijver	39	't Dreveken
67	Den Gouden Harynck	17	Tearoom de Ijsbeer
38	Den Gouden Karpel	52	Tearoom 't Silversandt
84	De Proeverie	23	Tearoom Verdi
54	De Serre–Eetcaf 'De Vuyst'	83	The Coffee Link
		44	't Koffieboontje
66	De Snippe	62	't Nieuw Museum
47	De Stove	35	Tom Pouce
89	De Trog	73	Tout Paris
38	De Visscherie	16	't Paardje
93	De Watermolen	79	't Pallieterke
2	De Windmolen	61	't Pandreitje
10	De Witte Poorte	77	Traiteur de Poularde
88	De Zevende Hemel	7	't Stil Ende
36	Die Swaene	57	't Voermanshuys
40	Duc de Bourgogne	26	't Voske Malpertuus
32	Frituur Peter	78	Van Eyck
76	Gran Kaffee de Passage	48	Wijnbar Est
80	Het Andere Idee	8	Zen

250 m
220 yards

De Belegde Boterham D5
Kleine Sint-Amandsstraat 5, t (050) 34 91 31. **Open** *Mon–Sat noon–5pm.*
Bright, stylish and friendly lunch spot, with stripped pine tables and a beamed ceiling, and a terrace out front in summer. Soups, salads, freshly-made sandwiches, coffee and home-made cakes (from 2pm).

De Garre D5
See p.181.

Den Gouden Karpel E5
Vismarkt 10, t (050) 33 33 89. **Open** *Tues–Sat 8am–noon and 2–6.30pm.*
The place to stock up for a gourmet fish-based picnic: this is the shop of the restaurant of the same name, and sells wonderful fishy preparations such as smoked eel, *maatjes* herrings and salad preparations. They will provide forks.

Frituur Peter D5
Markt (at foot of the Belfort). **Open** *daily 10am–2am.*
Green-painted kiosks under the Belfort selling Belgian chips with a dollop of mayonnaise. The chips with *stoofvlees* (beef stew) is surprisingly good.

Prestige D5
Vlamingstraat 12–14, t (050) 34 31 67. **Open** *Tues–Sun 7.30am–6pm.*
The elegant tearoom of a master chocolatier-pâtissier (shop attached), serving good tea and coffee and cakes and other divine confections to set your taste-buds aglow.

Restaurant-Tearoom Hennon D5
Breidelstraat 16, t (050) 33 28 00. **Open** *Oct–March daily 9am–6pm, April–Sept daily 9am–10pm.*
Specialist in waffles, pancakes and ice cream, with a small but very presentable tearoom-cum-restaurant at the back, under beamed ceilings over 300 years old. Also serves snacks and light dishes (sandwiches, pasta).

Tearoom Verdi D5
Vlamingstraat 5, t (050) 34 42 43; wheelchair accessible. **Open** *Wed–Sun 9am–10pm, Mon 9am–2pm.*
Classic, sedate tearoom in a handy location, occupying one side of a tearoom-restaurant.

Southern Bruges
Restaurants
Expensive
Den Gouden Harynck D6
Groeninge 25, t (050) 33 76 37. **Open** *Tues–Sat noon–2pm and 6–9.30pm; closed 1st week after Easter and last two weeks in July.*
Elegant restaurant with antique furniture and an open fire. Inventive French cuisine with the emphasis on seafood and faultless service.

De Snippe E7
Nieuwe Gentweg 53, t (050) 33 70 70; wheelchair accessible. **Open** *Tues–Sat noon–2.30pm and 7–9.30pm, Sun and Mon 7–9.30pm.*
Hotel-restaurant with orangerie overlooking a garden. Superb *haute cuisine française* – such as *queues de langoustines à la ciboulette.* Lunch menu €38; four-course evening menu €71.

Tanuki D7
Oude Gentweg 1, t (050) 34 75 12. **Open** *Wed–Sun noon–2pm and 6.30–9.30pm.*
Teppanyaki, tempura, sashimi and sushi and a Japanese garden. Menus from €13 (lunch) to €50.

Moderate
De Watermolen C8
Oostmeers 130, t (050) 34 33 48; wheelchair accessible. **Open** *Thurs–Tues noon–9.15pm.*
Bistro with terrace, specializing in fish. Menus from €15.

Maria van Bourgondië D6
Guido Gezelleplein 1, t (050) 33 20 66. **Open** *Thurs–Tues 9am–11pm.*
Solid Belgian cooking (soup, ham, pâté, *vlaamse stoofkarbonaden* [beef stew in beer], *waterzooi*) in a comfortable and spacious townhouse with an open fire. 'Regional' lunch menu €16.

Marieke van Brugghe D6
Mariastraat 17, t (050) 34 33 66; wheelchair accessible. **Open** *daily 10am–10pm.*
Reminiscent of the galley of a Spanish galleon, with a modern designer twist. The *vlaamse*

stoverij met kasteelbier, a succulent stew, comes with delicious soft-fried chips, perfect for soaking up the juices. The all-in €25 menu is especially good value.

't Begijntje D7
Walstraat 11, t (050) 33 00 89. **Open** *Mon, Tues and Thurs–Sat noon–9.30pm, Wed and Sun noon–2pm.*
Minuscule and charming family-run restaurant serving good home-cooked Flemish food. Menus €25–40.

Inexpensive
Bistro De Schaar F6
Hooistraat 2, t (050) 33 59 79. **Open** *Fri–Wed noon–2.30pm and 6–11pm.*
Agreeable bistro with some tasty starters: fish soup, stuffed mushrooms with snails, and wholesome main courses of lamb, duck, monkfish, etc, produced on the wood-fired grill in the dining room.

Bistro Christophe E6–7
Garenmarkt 34, t (050) 34 48 92; wheelchair accessible. **Open** *Thurs–Mon 7pm–2am; closed Feb and July.*
An evening-only bistro that is popular with locals, where market-fresh fare is prepared in an open kitchen. Has an outdoor terrace in summer.

De Bron D7
Katelijnestraat 82, t (050) 33 45 26. **Open** *Tues–Sun noon–2pm.*
Agreeable vegetarian restaurant in an old town house built in 1647. Open for lunch only.

De Zevende Hemel D7
Walplein 6, t (050) 33 17 49. **Open** *Mon and Thurs 11am–6pm, Fri–Sun 11am–9.30pm.*
Friendly little restaurant and tearoom serving a variety of dishes and snacks such as omelettes, grilled meats and scampi.

Hotel-bistro Bruegelhof C8
Oostmeers 128, t (050) 34 34 28. **Open** *daily 9am–10pm; closed Wed in winter.*
Hearty menus of Belgian specialities to the sound of world music.

Northeastern Bruges   177

Maximiliaan Van Oostenrijk D7
Wijngaardplein 17, t (050) 33 47 23.
Open *Fri–Wed 10am–10pm.*
Straightforward Flemish food at
good prices in an attractive tavern.

't Nieuw Museum G5
Hooistraat 42, t (050) 33 12 80.
Open *Thurs–Mon noon–2pm and
5–11pm.*
A traditional-style *eet en drinkhuis*
much favoured by locals, specializing in grilled meats prepared in
an open hearth beneath a 17th-
century mantelpiece. The building
has been a tavern since the
18th century.

't Botaniekske F6
*Minderbroederstraat 26, t (050) 33
27 90.* **Open** *Wed–Sun 6–11.30pm.*
Small, old-fashion styled restaurant dating from 1612, with a snug,
relaxed atmosphere serving well-
prepared fare, some dishes with
an oriental touch, at accessible
prices. Always full, so reserve!

Cafés and Snacks

Café 't Volkshuis E5
See p.182.

The Coffee Link D7
*Oud Sint-Jan, Mariastraat 38,
t (050) 34 99 73, w www.thecoffee
link.com.* **Open** *Mon–Fri 10am–
9.30pm, Sat and Sun 10am–
8.30pm.*
Elegant cybercafé in the medieval
Sint-Janshospitaal complex
(which includes the
Memlingmuseum, *see* p.88).
Prides itself on the quality
of its coffee. (*See also* p.184.)

Country Girl Sandwiches D7
Katelijnestraat 44, t (050) 34 06 17.
Open *Thurs–Tues 8am–7pm, Wed
8am–3pm.*
Attractive shop selling freshly
made sandwiches: mini-
baguettes and toasted panini
with a choice of 24 fillings, as well
as local beers, to take out.

De Proeverie D7
Katelijnestraat 6, t (050) 33 08 87.
Open *daily 9am–6pm.*
A tastefully decorated tearoom
where you can try out a range of

chocolate goodies, or the house
speciality: real hot chocolate which
you make yourself from steamed
milk and a plate of melted chocolate. Also serves fine-quality teas
and coffee. Under the same
ownership as the Sukerbuyc handmade chocolate shop opposite.

De Trog D7
Wijngaardstraat 17, t (050) 33 31 37.
Open *Mon–Sat 8.30am–6.30pm.*
A good place to pick up a picnic: a
bakery of 25 years' standing,
offering a mouth-watering range
of organic bread, quiche, vegetarian
snacks and burgers, sandwiches
made to order, Belgian cheeses,
and traditional-style pastries.

Salade Folle D7
Walplein 13–14, t (050) 34 94 43.
Open *Mon–Sat 11am–6pm.*
Friendly, airy, freshly painted café
offering tasty open sandwiches,
pasta, salads and home-made
pastries, pancakes and waffles.

**Straffe Hendrik-De
Halve Mann** D7
See p.181.

Northeastern Bruges

Restaurants
Expensive
De Karmeliet F5
Langestraat 19, t (050) 33 82 59.
Open *Tues–Sat noon–2pm and
7–10pm, Sun noon–2pm; closed 2
weeks in June–July.*
Chic restaurant in patrician house
with terrace. Among the best
restaurants in Belgium, awarded
three Michelin stars in 1996. Dress
code: jacket and tie. Lunch €50.

De Witte Poorte D4
*Jan van Eyckplein 6, t (050) 33 08
83; wheelchair accessible.* **Open**
*Tues–Sat noon–2pm and 7–9pm;
closed 2 weeks in Feb and last 2
weeks in June.*
Specialists in Belgian cooking of
exceptional quality. Served in an
atmospheric arched and vaulted
dining room. Lunch €28.50.

Moderate
Bistro du Phare Off maps
*Sasplein 2, t (050) 34 35 90,
w www.duphare.be.* **Open** *Wed–
Mon 11.30am–late (kitchen open
11.30am–2.30pm and 7pm–
midnight, until 2am on Fri and Sat).*
Upbeat bistro set in the remains
of the Dampoort city gate, serving
succulent international dishes
(Thai, creole, chilli), salads and
snacks. Holds jazz and blues
concerts at least once a month.

Rock Fort F5
Langestraat 15, t (050) 33 41 13.
Open *Thurs–Sat, Mon and Tues
noon–2.30pm and 6–11pm, Sun
6–11pm.*
Small, stylish and new restaurant
offering modern brasserie cooking
with real flare: the talk of the
town. Also offers a selection of
vegetarian dishes.

't Paardje F5
Langestraat 20, t (050) 33 40 09.
Open *Wed–Sun noon–2pm and
6–9pm, Tues noon–2pm.*
Dependable and popular small
family restaurant, serving a
limited range of Flemish specialities, including eel, mussels, and
beef stew cooked in beer.

Inexpensive
Bauhaus G4
*Langestraat 135, t (050) 34 10 93,
f (050) 33 41 80 (for special group
prices).* **Open** *Sun–Thurs 6pm–
midnight, Fri and Sat 6pm–1am.*
Two student/youth restaurants
(the Local and Global) attached to
the youth hotel, and priding
themselves on wholesome value-
for-money. Serves good,
no-nonsense fare, including steak,
mussels, pizzas, salads, vegetarian
dishes, waffles and snacks to suit
all moods. Menus from €10.

Bistro 't Gezelleke E–F3
Carmersstraat 15, t (050) 33 81 02.
Open *Mon–Sat noon–2pm, Sat
6pm–2am.*
Agreeably wacky bistro-bar.
Pastas, salads and fish dishes.

Charlie Rockets E5
See p.183.

Couples' City

For a special evening out, when money is less of an object (or you'd like to pretend that it is), try one of the following restaurants, picked for their intimate atmosphere or stylish food and décor:

Die Swaene, see p.172; **Duc de Bourgogne**, see p.172; **De Snippe**, see p.176; **'t Pandreitje**, see p.172; **De Karmeliet**, see p.177; **Patrick Devos 'De Zilveren Pauw'**, see p.178.

De Windmolen G3
Carmersstraat 135, t (050) 33 97 39.
Open Sun–Fri 10am–9pm.
Charming, folksy, family-run bistro and bar. Pasta, sandwiches and garnaalkroketten (prawn croquettes).

Taverne Oud Handbogenhof D3
Baliestraat 6, t (050) 33 41 11.
Open Mon–Sat 6pm–late, Sun noon–2pm.
Good home-cooking in an authentic Flemish inn, serving traditional-style meat and seafood dishes.

Tearoom de Ijsbeer F5
Langestraat 8, t (050) 33 35 34; wheelchair accessible. **Open** Wed–Mon 10am–10pm; closed Mon mid-Sept–Easter.
Restaurant, tearoom and ice-cream parlour in an old maison de maître, also offering Flemish cooking and specialities from the grill. Has a canalside terrace.

Cafés and Snacks

Beenhouwerij De Leeuwebrug F4
Langestraat 61, t (050) 34 08 91.
Open Tues–Sat 8am–1pm and 2–7pm, Sun 8.30am–1pm.
A butcher's shop with 25 years' experience, offering home-made charcuterie and a long list of handsome sandwiches prepared while you wait.

Café Vlissinghe E3
See p.181.

Celtica F–G4
See p.182.

Taverne De Verloren Hoek G3
Carmersstraat 178, t (050) 33 06 98.
Open Thurs–Mon 10.30am–10pm.
Well-known bar and café, of a traditional kind, with Bruges beers on draught. Serves snacks, salads, as well as steaks and its speciality, smoked eel.

Western Bruges

Restaurants

Expensive

De Castillion C6
Heilige-Geeststraat 1, t (050) 34 30 01; wheelchair accessible.
Open Wed–Sat 11.30am–2pm and 6.30–10.30pm, Mon and Tues 6.30–10.30pm, Sun 11.30am–2pm.
Dignified and traditional hotel-restaurant serving rich, elegant French cuisine. Menus from €49.

De Lotteburg C7
Goezeputstraat 43, t (050) 33 75 35.
Open Tues–Wed, Fri and Sun noon–2pm and 7–9.30pm, Sat 7–9.30pm.
Regional specialities and delicious fish dishes at this elegant and intimate restaurant in an old maison de maître.

Kardinaalshof C6
Sint-Salvatorskerkhof, t (050) 34 16 91. **Open** Fri–Tues noon–2.30pm and 7–9.30pm, Thurs 7–9.30pm.
Attractively restored restaurant, relaxed and intimate; emphasis on seafood, imaginatively prepared.

Pannenhuis Off maps
Zandstraat 2, 8200 Brugge (Sint-Andries), t (050) 31 19 07. **Open** Thurs–Mon 11.30am–2pm and 6–9pm, Tues 11.30am–2pm (closed last 2 weeks of Jan and first 3 weeks of July).
A mock-Tudor stylish hotel restaurant on the outskirts. Delightful terrace and flower-filled garden; interesting French classics.

Patrick Devos 'De Zilveren Pauw' C6
Zilverstraat 41, t (050) 33 55 66.
Open Mon–Fri noon–1.30pm and 7–9pm, Sat 7–9pm.
Much-fêted restaurant in an elegant turn-of-the-century house with garden. Noted for French cuisine prepared with an ingeniously light touch. Lunch menu at a bargain €42, gourmet menu €59.50.

't Stil Ende B2
Scheepsdalelaan 12, t (050) 33 92 03. **Open** Tues–Fri noon–1.30pm and 7–9pm, Sat 7–9pm, Sun noon–1.30pm; closed last 2 weeks of July.
Crisp modern interpretations of classic French dishes served in a stylish setting.

Moderate

Bhavani D6
Simon Stevinplein 5, t (050) 33 90 25; wheelchair accessible.
Open daily noon–2.30pm and 6–10.30pm.
A well-run and elegantly exotic Indian restaurant, offering a broad range of classic dishes, including samosas, tandoori chicken, rogan josh, and vegetarian specialities.

Cafedraal C6
Zilverstraat 38, t (050) 34 08 45.
Open Tues–Sat noon–2.30pm and 6–11pm.
French brasserie and bar in a lovely 15th-century building (the Vasquezhuis). The house specialities include lobster and bouillabaisse.

Concertgebouw Brugge B7
't Zand 34, t (050) 47 69 99, w www.concertgebouw-brugge.be.
Café-restaurant still under construction as this volume went to press, but its position at the top of the 'Lantern Tower' in this prestigious new building, and the extensive views from the roof terrace, promise to make this a spot worth investigating.

De Gouden Zalm D6
Oude Burg 20, t (050) 61 59 87.
Open Mon–Sat noon–2pm and 7–9.30pm.
Fresh linen, fresh flowers and an unfussy atmosphere for nicely judged, inventive French-style cuisine: focusing on fish – plateaux de fruits de mer, fish soups, oysters, lobster and of course zalm (salmon). They also do steak. Lunch menu for €12.50.

Pietje Pek C5
*Sint-Jakobsstraat 13, t (050)
34 78 74.* **Open** *Thurs–Mon
5.30–11pm.*
Atmospheric bistro specializing in
fondues (meat, cheese); open
early to cater for families. 'Eat-as-
much-as-you-like' fondue €23;
children under 10 can share with
adults for free.

't Pallieterke B6
't Zand 28, t (050) 34 01 77.
Open *Wed–Mon 11.30am–9.30pm.*
Pleasant, friendly French-style
restaurant and tea room in the
west of the city, serving mussels,
game, fish and *waterzooi*. Menus
€13.50–25.

Zen B4
*Beenhouwersstraat 117, t (050)
33 67 02.* **Open** *Mon–Sat
noon–2pm.*
Inventive home-made vegetarian
cuisine dished up in suitably
minimalist surroundings.

Inexpensive

Boterhuis Brasserie C4
*Sint-Jakobsstraat 38, t (050) 34 15
11.* **Open** *daily 10am–1am.*
Warm welcome in traditional
brasserie with a real fire. Steaks,
brochettes, pasta and snacks.

De Hobbit C6
Kemelstraat 2, t (050) 33 55 20.
Open *daily 6pm–late.*
Relaxed, youthful and wacky
restaurant and bar specializing in
grilled meats and seafood, some
with a Thai touch, pastas, snacks
and sandwiches.

De Serre-Eetcaf 'De Vuyst' D6
*Simon Stevinplein 15, t (050) 34 22
31; wheelchair accessible.* **Open**
*Mon and Wed–Sat noon–3pm and
6–9pm.*
Friendly and bright. Quick lunch
menu €15.

Gran Kaffee de Passage C6
Dweersstraat 26, t (050) 34 02 32.
Open *daily 6–11.30pm.*
Flemish cooking in part of the
lively De Passage youth hotel
complex, with a funky low-light,
Edwardian feel.

Het Andere Idee B7
Hauwerstraat 9, t (050) 34 17 89.
Open *Wed–Fri 11.30am–1.45pm and
6.30–10.15pm, Sat 7am–1.45pm
and 6.30–10-15pm, Sun noon–
9.45pm.*
A little off the beaten track, but
worth the walk for a charming
and atmospheric 'pasta bistro'.
Candlelit warmth by night. Held in
high regard locally, and serves as a
market watering hole on Saturday.
Also offers vegetarian dishes.

**Pannekoekenhuisje/
De Vlaamse Pot** C5
Helmstraat 3–5, t (050) 34 00 86.
Open *daily noon–10pm.*
Recently renovated and extended
pancake house, now also offering
Flemish 'grandmother' cooking
based on local recipes and
produce. Intimate, cottage atmosphere inside, but also has three
terraces outside.

Van Eyck B6
't Zand 23, t (050) 33 41 48. **Open**
Wed–Mon 10am–10pm.
Tiny restaurant, brasserie and tea
room with vaguely Art Nouveau
décor, and well-priced menus.

Cafés and Snacks

Café Hoegaarden D5
See p.181.

De Medici Sorbetière C5
Geldmuntstraat 9, t (050) 33 93 41.
Open *Mon and Wed–Sat 8.30am–
6.30pm, Tues noon–6.30pm, Sun
3–6.30pm.*
Good coffee served with sorbets
and petit-fours in genuine Art-
Nouveau setting. Also does tasty
lunch dishes for €8–10.

Lamourette C6
Zuidzandstraat 29, t (050) 33 31 58.
Open *daily 7am–6.30pm.*
An outlet for picnic food: freshly
made sandwiches, quiches, tarts
and pastries.

Lokkedize C6
See p.183.

Sandwicherie St-Amandje C5
*Sint-Amandsstraat 38, t (050) 33 06
65.* **Open** *Mon–Fri 9.30am–
6.30pm, Sat 10am–6.30pm.*
Modern, purpose-built sandwich
shop. Sandwiches filled copiously
before your eyes, with a choice of
15 different fillings.

't Brugs Beertje C6
See p.182.

Tearoom 't Silversandt C6
Zilversteeg 33, t (050) 33 41 89.
Open *daily 8am–6pm.*
Tearoom located in the
Zilverpand shopping complex, also
offering light lunches, snacks,
pancakes and waffles, with a
large and pleasant terrace in
warm weather.

Tout Paris C6
Zuidzandstraat 31, t (050) 33 79 02.
Open *Fri–Wed 8am–7pm.*
Another delicatessen for picnic
purchases, with a dazzling selection of prepared foods, plus
cheeses, salads, quiches, cooked
meats, and a list of 25 sorts of
sandwiches made to order.

Traiteur de Poularde B6
Smedenstraat 14. **Open** *Wed–Mon
8am–7pm.*
Close to the Smedenpoort canal
walks and park, a delicatessen
offering a superbly presented
selection of prepared foods made
by people justifiably proud of their
craft. Ideal for a luxury picnic.

Wijnbar Est C5
See p.184.

Nightlife and Entertainment

Bruges is not a city famed for its throbbing nightlife – and no one would expect it to be otherwise. Sitting on a terrace at a café, or cradling a Trappist beer by a log fire in winter is perfectly sufficient night-time entertainment for many of Bruges's visitors, especially after a day of walking around the city's sights. There are no discos in Bruges: the young head off for the clubs of Antwerp, Ostend, Ghent and Brussels, leaving the city to its more sedate entertainments, although they can find some action in the youth-oriented bars of the Eiermarkt. That said, Bruges does provide a fair bit of fun after dark, ranging from friendly jazz bars to a couple of rock and jazz venues that attract highly respectable line-ups at weekends and during the summer season.

For listings, look for the free monthly newspapers called *Exit*, *Agenda Brugge* and *Brugge Cultuurmagazine*, available from the tourist office and many pubs, cafés, restaurants, shops and places of entertainment. The Bruges tourist office also has a leaflet about nightlife in Bruges, listing selected bars, published by Cart Idee. A special edition is being prepared for Bruges 2002. For tickets apply to the venue, or try at Music Cottage (Sint-Jakobsstraat 46, **t** (050) 33 70 37).

Bars

Bierbistro Erasmus D6
Wollestraat 35, **t** *(050) 33 57 81.*
Open *Tues–Sun 11am–midnight.*
Popular and friendly bar and bistro in a hotel, favoured by beer-enthusiasts.

Café Hoegaarden D5
Steenstraat 10, **t** *(050) 34 44 30.*
Open *Tues–Sat.*
Sleek, modern bar named after its main product, served on tap. Salads and sandwiches.

Café Vlissinghe E3
Blekersstraat 2, **t** *(050) 34 37 37.*
Open *Wed–Mon 11am–midnight.*
Artists apparently used to gather here to meet Van Dyck.

The Beers of Bruges
Beer is good for you. This was the message spread by St Arnold, who founded the Benedictine abbey of Oudenburg Abbey, to the west of Bruges, in the 11th century. During a bout of plague, he plunged his cross into a vat of beer, and told the people to drink it, instead of water. It was a miracle cure: people started getting better immediately, and St Arnold was made the patron saint of beer. There were sound scientific reasons for St Arnold's cure: beer was boiled and drinking water wasn't, but it took another eight centuries to discover how this worked, and the Belgians were prepared to take it on trust. To this day, Steenbrugge Abdijbier (abbey beer) features St Arnold himself on the label.

Before the First World War, there were 31 breweries in the city; today, there are just two: De Gouden Boom and De Halve Mann (Straffe Hendrik). Both produce excellent beers, and you can visit them to watch it being made. For sampling Bruges's beer, try one of the following:

Brouwerij 'De Gouden Boom' F5
Langestraat 47, **t** *(050) 33 06 99,* **f** *(050) 33 46 44.* **Open** *May–Sept Thurs–Sun 2–5pm;* **adm** *€3, including one free drink (guided tours for groups only).*
The name De Gouden Boom (The Golden Tree) recalls a trophy awarded in jousting tournaments held in the Markt. The brewery was founded in 1587, and moved to this site, called 't Hamerken (Little Hammer) in 1902. Today it produces several of Bruges's noted beers, such as Brugs Tarwebier, Brugse Tripel, and Abdij

Steenbrugge. The brewery museum is in the old malthouse (next door at Verbrand Niewlandstraat 10), which was used until 1976, while the brewery itself is on Langestraat. *See p.102.*

Den Dyver D6
Dijver 5, **t** *(050) 33 60 69.* **Open** *Fri–Tues noon–2pm and 6.30–9.30pm.*
An elegant restaurant whose speciality is dishes cooked in beer, served with beer of all kinds. This is a good place to discover the extraordinary range and nuances of Belgium's national drink. Some, like 'the red beers' of Rodenbach of Roeselare, edge decidedly towards wine.

Huisbrouwerij De Halve Mann 'Straffe Hendrik' D7
Walpein 26, **t** *(050) 33 26 97,* **w** *www.halvemaan.be. Guided* **tours** *April–Sept daily 10am–5pm, Oct–Mar daily 11am and 3pm;* **adm** *€3.70, including one free drink.*
Founded in 1856 beneath the sign of De Halve Mann (the Half Moon), this brewery was run by four generations of the Maes family, all called Henry. It now specializes in one brand called Straffe Hendrik (Strong Henry), with a picture of a cheery carouser on the label straining the beer through his copious moustache. The brewery has been developed with its own museum and tavern. *See p.91.*

't Brugs Beertje C6
Kemelstraat 5 (off Steenstraat), **t** *(050) 33 96 16.* **Open** *Thurs–Tues 4pm–1am.*
Stocks 300 sorts of beer, and is run by very knowledgeable enthusiasts. Follow their advice about what to drink on the day. You can even sign up for one of their seminars on beer.

Atmospheric, wood-panelled bar, with a cast-iron stove. *Boules* court in the garden. Soup, cheese, ham platters, pasta.

De Garre D5
De Garre 1, **t** *(050) 34 10 29.* **Open** *Mon–Fri noon–2pm, Sat and Sun 11am–1am.*

Cosy *staminee* (pub), in a passageway off Breidelstraat. Good beer and light snacks, including savoury tart.

La Plaza D5
Kuipersstraat 13, **t** *(050) 33 70 86.* **Open** *daily 11.30am–late.*

Beer

Belgian beer enjoys an unparalleled reputation. For beer-lovers, it is the object of pilgrimage and reverence. For others it can be a revelation. Belgium has some 400 different kinds of beers produced by 115 breweries (in 1900 there were 3223 breweries). Each has its own distinctive style, and even the ubiquitous Stella Artois (when brewed in Belgium) and Jupiler, made by the brewing giant Interbrew, are a cut above your average lagers.

A word first of all about how beer is made. The essential ingredient is grain – usually barley, but sometimes wheat. The barley is soaked in water to stimulate germination, then dried in a kiln to produce malt. The malted barley is then crushed and boiled before being left to ferment, during which process the natural sugars (maltose) and any added sugars are converted into alcohol. Yeast is the agent of fermentation. Some yeasts rise to the top of the brew, forming a crust that protects the beer from the air; this process creates a richly flavoured 'top-fermented' ale. Other yeasts sink to the bottom to make a lighter, clearer, lager-type 'bottom-fermented' beer. The choice of barley, the preparation of the malt, the quality of the water, and the type of yeast used all influence the final taste of the beer. Hops provide a spicy, bitter tang and may be added at various stages of brewing.

With Belgian beer there is no great concern about whether it is served from the keg or in bottles. The labels on the bottles give the vital statistics, including the all-important alcohol content. By and large Belgian beer has a higher level of alcohol by volume than equivalent British or American beers. Specialist bottled beers start at about 5 per cent; stronger brews measure 8 or 9 per cent.

The maximum alcohol content for beer is about 12 per cent – four times the strength of most lagers. Bush beer is one of several brands that claims to be Belgium's strongest beer: after two bottles you feel as though your knees have been hinged on backwards. Some breweries classify their beer as double/dubbel (dark and sweet, about 6.6 per cent) or triple/tripel (paler and lighter, but stronger, about 8 per cent). Labels also instruct you about the correct temperature at which to serve the beer and the shape of glass to be used. Every brew is assigned its own glass shape, from tumbler to goblet, and this is something that any bartender instinctively understands. Only in the appropriate glass can the merits of a particular beer be fully savoured.

The most famous bottled beers are those produced by the Trappists – the order of Cistercian monks which observes the strict (these days not quite so strict)

Extremely refined and elegantly comfortable bar, favoured by equally elegant ladies (and their consorts) who come to drink and snack on pasta, salads and light fish dishes for around €10.

L'Estaminet E6
Gevangenisstraat 5, t (050) 33 45 91. Open Tues–Sat 11.30am–late.
Famous Flemish pub with low-beamed ceilings: a trusty drankhuis since 1900. Also serves light pub snacks such as spaghetti, croque monsieur and pancakes.

The Snooker Palace C5
Noordzandstraat 4, t (050) 34 13 49; wheelchair accessible. Open Mon–Sat 11am–late, Sun 1pm–late.
Large first-floor bar with nine snooker tables, eight darts boards, a pool table and a large-screen TV. Also has an internet café with six screens (€2.60 per half-hour). Bar snacks include hotdogs and hamburgers.

Straffe Hendrik–De Halve Mann D7
Walplein 26, t (050) 33 26 97. Open Mon–Fri 10.30am–5pm, Sat and Sun 10.30am–6.30pm.
The brewery tavern. Snacks include beer soup (see p.181).

't Brugs Beertje C6
Kemelstraat 5, t (050) 33 96 16. Open Thurs–Tues 4pm–1am.
Mecca for beer-lovers (see p.181). Serves more than 300 beers, along with pâté and cheese snacks.

't Dreupelhuisje C6
Kemelstraat 9, t (050) 34 24 21. Open Tues–Sat 6pm–late.
Atmospheric (if noisy) local pub decorated by Bruegelesque murals: the place to try out jenever, the clear gin-type alcohol drunk very cold, in small glasses, often as a chaser with a glass of beer. Bruges has its own, called Oude Brugsche Graangenever, and the lemon-flavoured 't Brugs Dreupeltje Citroenjenever – but there are dozens of others.

Bars with Music

Café 'De Versteende Nacht' F5
Langestraat 11, t (050) 34 32 93.
Jazz (often free of charge) in the evenings in a friendly and lively bar. Bar meals include scampi, steaks and copious chips. Seems to appeal to all age ranges.

Café 't Volkshuis E5
Braambergstraat 11, t (050) 33 80 21. Open Fri–Wed 7.30am–late.
A traditional bar, proud of its cheap beer and good-value snacks, including its rich fish soup, omelettes and scampi (menu at €7.50). About twice a month on Saturday nights it becomes a café chantant, with a sing-along featuring Flemish and more current popular songs (free entry, starts 8pm, see listings magazines for details).

Celtica G4
Langestraat 121, t (050) 34 47 86; wheelchair accessible. Open daily noon–late.
Irish pub with snacks available.

order of silence. In the 19th century the monasteries produced beer for the consumption of the monks, but then they began to sell it to the outside world in gradually increasing quantities. Trappist beer has become a major income-earner for the monasteries, nowadays produced largely by lay workers rather than monks.

Nonetheless, the monasteries retain strict control over their product and have resisted offers of expansion into the large-scale export markets, which would rapidly lap up any increased production. These Trappist beers are top-fermented ales, with extra yeast added at bottling to produce a second fermentation in the bottle. Allow the beer to stand to let the sediment settle, then pour the entire contents off all at once to avoid disturbing it (it's not harmful, just rather yeasty).

The most famous Trappist beer is probably Chimay, produced by the abbey of Notre-Dame de Scourmont, the first to release its beers to the public. Today Chimay is available as 7, 8 and 9 per cent alcohol by volume. Kept for several years, Chimay Bleu (9 per cent) becomes ever richer, its flavour drifting towards port.

For a refreshing change, try the remarkable 'white' beers – witbier – made with wheat. De Gouden Boom Brewery in Bruges produces a fine witbier called Brugs Tarwebier, but the most famous is produced at Hoegaarden, to the east of Brussels. Hoegaarden (also a brand name) is a wheat beer flavoured with a touch of coriander; it has a delicious peppery tang and a modest alcohol content (5 per cent) – excellent for that jaded moment in the late afternoon. Some witbier-drinkers even add a slice of lemon to their glass. It is often a little cloudy – don't send it back: that is how it should be!

One of the most unusual of all Belgian beers is lambic, a wheat beer unique to the valley of the River Senne. What makes lambic so special is that it is 'spontaneously' fermented by the agency of naturally occurring airborne yeasts – tiny fungi called Brettanomyces that are found only in Brussels itself and in the countryside to the west. Fermentation begins within three days, but the beer is allowed to age for a year or more. Lambic is a fairly strong (about 5.5 per cent), still beer with a distinctive sour, winey flavour – something of an acquired taste. Cherries (formerly from the Brussels suburb of Schaerbeek) may be macerated in lambic to produce the fruity beer called kriek; raspberries are added to make framboise; and sugar and caramel are added to make faro. Blended lambic of different ages is allowed to ferment a second time in bottles to become the slightly fizzy sour beer called gueuze.

Celtic Ireland D5
Burg 8, t (050) 34 45 02. **Open daily 11am–late.**
Irish pub offering regular free live music, usually along the Celtic theme. Also has a moderate-priced restaurant featuring Irish fare (noon–10pm).

Charlie Rockets E5
Hoogstraat 19, t (050) 33 06 60. **Open daily 8am–4pm.**
Lively, relaxed, fun bar attached to a youth hotel. Loud music. Tex-Mex dishes, nachos, burgers.

De Kogge E5
Braambergstraat 7. **Open daily 7pm–late.**
Built in 1637 as a trading house for fish porters and little changed.

Grand Café du Théâtre D5
Kuipersstraat 14, t (050) 33 45 36. **Open Mon–Fri 4pm–late, Sat and Sun 2pm–late.**
Smart but relaxed bar featuring 'round' (easy-on-the-ears) pop and rock music of all decades back to 1960s, with DJs of similar tastes at the weekends.

Jazz-Club 'The Duke' C5
Hotel Navarra, Sint-Jakobsstraat 41, t (050) 34 05 61. **Open daily 3pm–midnight.**
Occasional jazz, gratis, in sedate surroundings. Look out for announcements.

Joey's Café C6
Zilverpand, t (050) 34 12 64. **Open Mon–Sat noon–late.**
Atmospheric, warm and sociable bar, with comfortable seating, low lights, exposed brickwork and wooden flooring. Serves light, home-made snacks and dishes. Plays singer-songwriter music, and hosts live, free concerts once a month (see listings magazines).

Lokkedize C6
Korte Vuldersstraat 33, t (050) 33 44 50; wheelchair accessible. **Open Tues–Thurs 7pm–late, Fri–Sun 6pm–late.**
Warm and friendly bar for relaxed evening rendezvous, tastefully renovated in exposed brickwork, and stripped pine. Offers value-for-money snacks and meals of salads, lasagne, moussaka, all home-made, served until 1am. Features singer-songwriter music, and hosts the occasional live concert.

Taverne Ambiorix D5
Eiermarkt, t (050) 33 74 00. **Open Mon–Fri noon–late, Sat and Sun 2pm–late.**
Self-proclaimed 'pre-eminent student café since 1982', a lively and loud traditional-style bar named after the Celtic chieftain who wiped out a Roman garrison in 54 BC. (Some clients attempt to live up to this reputation at the happy hour every Wednesday evening.)

The Crash F5
Langestraat 78, t (050) 34 70 81. **Open Tues–Thurs and Sat 9pm–late, Fri 5pm–late.**
Dingy and loud rock bar, with inexpensive drinks (one pint €1, three pints €2.15). Easy-going hangout for the 18–30 crowd. Happy hour 10–11pm.

Wijnbar Est C5
*Noordzandstraat 34, t (050) 33 38
39; wheelchair accessible.* **Open**
*Mon, Tues, Thurs and Sun 5–
11pm, Fri and Sat 3–11pm.*
Traditional-style bar offering an
extensive choice of wines, plus
cheese platters and raclette. Also
the venue for occasional
blues/jazz/jive concerts.

Contemporary-music Venues

There are also two festivals of
contemporary music each
summer, the Cactusfestival (2nd
week of July) and the month-long
Klinkers Festival (late July–Aug).
See p.198.

Bistro du Phare F1
*Sasplein 2, t (050) 34 35 90,
w www.duphare.be.* **Open** *Wed–
Mon 11.30am–late; kitchen open
11.30am–2.30pm and 7pm–
midnight (until 2am on Fri and Sat).*
Jazz and blues concerts are held at
least once a month at this upbeat
bistro on the northern perimeter
of the town. See listings magazines for details.

Cactus Club C4
*Sint-Jakobsstraat 36, t (050) 33 20
14, e info@cactusmusic.be,
w wwwcactusmusic.be.* **Open**:
*depends on performances, phone
to check.*
Part of the Sint-Jakobsstraat/
Boterhuis complex. Interesting
line-ups for music, including world
music, rock, jazz and folk, usually
on Saturday evenings. The club
also organizes the Cactusfestival
of music in the Minnewater Park
in mid-July.

The Coffee Link D7
*Oud Sint-Jan, Mariastraat 38,
t (050) 34 99 73, w www.thecoffee
link.com.* **Open** *Mon–Fri 10am–
9.30pm, Sat and Sun 10am–
8.30pm.*
This cybercafé occasionally hosts
small-scale contemporary
music/blues/jazz/folk concerts.
See listings magazines for details.
(*See also p.177.*)

De Werf C1
*Werfstraat 108, t (050) 33 05 29,
e info@dewerf.be, w www
.dewerf.be.*
Venue for cutting-edge jazz, as
well as theatre. Also has its own
record label.

Snuffel Sleep In C4
Ezelstraat 47-49, t (050) 33 31 33.
Open *daily 5pm–midnight.*
This youth hotel holds regular
concerts of jazz, jam sessions,
drum 'n bass nights, usually on
Saturday evenings. See listings
magazines for details.

Theatre

Stadsschouwburg D4
Vlamingstraat 29, t (050) 44 30 60.
The premier city theatre, offering
mainstream or highbrow plays,
usually in Dutch. Also the venue
for dance and classical music
concerts, including ones by international touring companies and
the occasional sedate rock event.

Theater Het Net C4
*Sint-Jacobsstraat 36, t (050) 33
88 50.*
Mainly contemporary Dutch-
language drama, at part of the
Sint-Jakobsstraat Boterhuis
complex.

Theater De Werf C1
Werfstraat 108, t (050) 33 05 29.
Part of the De Werf complex, for
jazz and contemporary theatre.

Cinema

Foreign films are almost always
played in the original language,
with Dutch and French subtitles.

Ciné Liberty D5
Kuipersstraat 23, t (050) 33 54 86.
Stylish movie house for general-
release films.

Cinema Lumière C4
*Sint-Jakobsstraat 36, t (050) 34
34 65.*
Bruges's best cinema, an 'art-
house' with three screens. Rolling
agenda of impressive, upmarket
and current films as well as
archive and classics from Europe
and the USA.

Classical Music

The high season of classical
music is the Flanders Festival (two
weeks in late July/early August;
see p.198). As well as at the
following venues, concerts also
take place from time to time in
the Provinciaal Hof (D5; see p.71),
Sint-Salvatorskathedraal (C6; see
p.110), Sint-Jakobskerk (C4; see
p.115), Kapel 't Keerske and the
Sint-Walburgakerk (E4; see p.98).

Concertgebouw Brugge B6
*'t Zand, t (050) 47 69 99. For
details, ask at the tourist office or
see w www.brugge.be.*
The brand-new concert venue,
built to coincide with Brugge
2002, with two concert halls, the
larger one seating 1,200, the
smaller Chamber Music Room
seating 300. This is set to become
Bruges's cultural centrepiece.

Joseph Ryelandtzaal C3
*Achiel van Ackerplein (off
Ezelstraat).*
Converted church, now a stylish
municipal concert hall for classical
music. Reservations are made
through the various organizing
bodies.

Stadsschouwburg D4
Vlamingstraat 29, t (050) 44 30 60.
See 'Theatre', above.

Historical Banquets

**Brugge Anno 1468/
Bruges Celebrations** D4
*Vlamingstraat 86, t (050) 34 75 72,
f (050) 34 87 28; wheelchair accessible.* **Open** *Nov–March Sat
7.30–10.45pm, April–Oct Thurs, Fri
and Sat 7.30–10.45pm;* **adm**
*€52–67, discounts for children.
Advance booking essential.*
The extravagant marriage festivi-
ties of Charles the Bold and
Margaret of York in 1468 provide
the theme for ye olde four-course
medieval feast (with beer and
wine included), accompanied by
minstrels, jesters, fire-eaters,
falconers, sword fights, set in a
neogothic former Jesuit church.

Shopping

The shops in Bruges are excellent: stylish, enticing, competitively priced. You can buy anything you like, from a new outfit to a Tintin watch, designer shoes to Trappist beer – all elegantly displayed in individual shops, most run by knowledgeable experts.

The main shopping streets are to the west of the Markt: Steenstraat, which leads into Zuidzandstraat, and Noordzandstraat, which continues into Smedenstraat. These are all good for clothes, shoes, designer household wares and mouth-watering specialist food shops.

Between Zilverstraat, Zuidzandstraat and Noordzandstraat there is a warren of shops called the Zilverpand, a mixture of covered arcades and pedestrianized courtyards (mainly clothes boutiques).

Katelijnestraat also has plenty of shops but, as this is a major tourist thoroughfare, many of them sell chocolates and other goods to appeal exclusively to the tourist trade.

Most shops are open from about 9 or 10am to 6 or 6.30pm, closing later in summer. Many however close for an hour for lunch from 12.30 or 1pm. A fair number of shops in the main shopping areas are open on Sunday too, especially during the summer. The late-night shopping day is Friday. Supermarkets tend to be open later, 9am–8pm, and 9am–9pm on Friday. For information on Value Added Tax and reclaiming on purchases in excess of €175, see p.62.

Antiques

There are some forty or so antique shops scattered around the centre of Bruges. Here are just four of them:

Artifex E5
Predikherenstraat 2, t (050) 33 49 22. Open Tues–Sat 10am–noon and 2–6pm, Sun 2–6pm.
Paintings (including ones of Bruges) by 19th- and 20th-century

artists, plus furniture and *objets d'art*.

Chronos Antique Gallery E5
Braambergstraat 12, t (050) 34 11 64. Open Wed–Sat 2–6.30pm.
Splendid grand-style furniture (bombé chests, ormolu clocks, tapestry) from the 17th and 18th centuries.

Kasimir's Antique Studio E6
Rosenhoedkaai 3, t (050) 34 56 61. Open Mon–Sat 10.30am–noon and 1.30–6pm.
Interesting selection of fine antique furniture, toys and dolls, paintings, figurines and domestic ware.

Pollentier-Maréchal C6
Sint-Salvatorskerkhof 8, t (050) 33 18 04. Open Tues–Fri 2–6pm, Sat 10am–noon and 2–6pm.
Dealer and framer of antique prints, many of them illustrations of Bruges.

Artists' Materials

Bruges attracts a large number of artists each year, lured by the ravishing visual beauty of its medieval streets and skyline, the canals, the Begijnhof and much else. With excellent art suppliers like the three below, they need never run short of materials.

De Schacht D7
Katelijnestraat 49, t (050) 33 44 24. Open Mon–Sat 8am–noon and 1–7pm.
Paper, canvas, paints of all kinds, pastels, brushes, modelling materials – they stock everything.

Huis de Meester E6
Eekhoutstraat 14, t (050) 68 00 05. Open Mon 1.15–6pm, Tues–Sat 10am–6pm.
Comprehensive range of artists' materials, as well as a small gallery upstairs. The owner also runs art classes on Saturday afternoons.

Huis Van Locke D–E5
Philipstockstraat 24, t (050) 33 50 17. Open Mon–Sat 9.30am–noon and 2–6pm.
Full range of artists' materials offered by a shop established 80

years ago and now run by the third generation of the founding family.

Beer

Good bottled beers (and wines) are widely available in supermarkets and food shops. Here are two specialist beer outlets:

The Bottle Shop D5
Wollestraat 13, t (050) 34 99 80. Open daily 10am–7pm; closes at 6.30pm Jan–Feb.
All-Belgian beer shop: some 120 brands altogether, including the famous Trappist and abbey beers, Bruges beers and a few rarities. Some are conveniently packed in cartons to carry away; large orders can be delivered to your hotel.

Brugs Bierpaleis D7
Katelijnestraat 25–27, t (050) 34 31 61. Open daily 9am–8pm.
Comprehensive selection of Belgian beers, as well as other beer-drinking accoutrements: correctly shaped glasses for each brand, and T-shirts with beery slogans.

Books

De Meester E6
Dijver 2, t (050) 33 29 52. Open daily 8.30am–noon and 1.30–6.30pm.
Good range of books, including books on Bruges, as well as cookery, gardening, history, etc. Also, international newspapers and magazines.

De Reyghere Boekhandel D5
Markt 12, t (050) 33 34 03. Open Mon–Sat 8.30am–6.15pm.
A fine shop with good books on Bruges and Belgium. Also has English-language books and newspapers.

Marechal D7
Mariastraat 10, t (050) 33 13 05. Open Mon–Sat 10am–12.30pm and 1.30–6pm.
Large bookshop-cum-toyshop with illustrated books about Bruges, interesting cards and postcards, prints of Bruges, toys and printed T-shirts for kids.

Chocolates

Belgian chocolates are of course world famous, and Bruges has a long list of shops run by cottage-scale manufacturers, plus outlets selling the more famous national brands, such as Godiva, Leonidas and Neuhaus. Don't leave Bruges without some!

Chocoladehuisje D5
Wollestraat 15, t (050) 34 02 50.
Open *daily 9.30am–6pm.*
Outlet for quality chocolates, hand-made in Bruges, in all price ranges, plus some inventive and seasonal shapes (angels, Father Christmas, Valentine's hearts, Carnival masks, breasts and underwear). Also a good place to discover the wonders of proper ground-almond marzipan, Belgian-style. 500g box of pralines for €10.20.

The Chocolate Line D6
Simon Stevinplein 19, t (050) 34 10 90. **Open** *Mon 10am–6.30pm, Tues–Sat 9.30am–6.30pm, Sun 10.30am–6.30pm.*
Specialists in handmade chocolates of every imaginable kind, enticingly presented in an olde-worldy style.

Godiva C6
Zuidzandstraat 36, t (050) 33 28 66.
Open *April–Sept daily 9am–7pm, Oct–March daily 10am–6pm.*
Leading name in Belgian luxury chocolates, sumptuously rich. Over twice the price of Leonidas (*see below*).

Honfleur C5
Noordzandstraat 31, t (050) 36 24 02. **Open** *daily 9am–6.30pm.*
Traditional artisan-style chocolates and delicious hand-made biscuits.

Leonidas D7, D5
Katelijnestraat 24 (also at Steenstraat 4), t (050) 34 69 41.
Open *April–Sept daily 9am–7pm, Oct–March daily 10am–6pm.*
A comprehensive selection of the excellent and good-value Leonidas brand, conveniently located on the route to the main out-of-town coach- and car-parks. Box of 250g

of pralines for €3.40; 500g for €6.80; 1 kg for €13.60.

Neuhaus C6
Steenstraat 66, t (050) 33 15 30.
Open *April–Sept daily 9am–7pm, Oct–March daily 10am–6pm.*
Up-market and pricey – almost three times the price of Leonidas (*see above*).

Sukerbuyc D7
Katelijnestraat 5, t (050) 33 08 87.
Open *daily 8.30am–6.30pm.*
Fine handmade chocolates made on the premises. Their speciality is 'chocolate lace' – disks of very thin chocolates sold in elegant long boxes. The same owners run the De Proeverie tearoom opposite (*see p.177*).

Sweertvaeglier D5
Philipstockstraat 29, t (050) 33 83 67. **Open** *Tues–Sun 9.30am–6.15pm.*
Praline makers since 1933: filled chocolates made with fresh butter and cream. Superb truffles, and a craftsman's presentation to remind you that you have something special. Box of 500g of pralines for €12.15.

Cigars

Havana House D5
Sint-Amandsstraat 14, t (050) 33 14 99. **Open** *Mon–Sat 10am–12.30pm and 1.30–6.30pm.*
Belgium's only purely Cuban cigar store, stocking all the leading brands, expertly kept in a room-sized humidor. Useful for US cigar-lovers while the embargo on Cuba lasts.

Clothes and Accessories

Bishop Tailors D5
Vlamingstraat 16, t (050) 49 04 64.
Open *Tues–Sat 10.15am–6pm.*
Traditional men's outfitters, specializing in classic-style suits and jackets. Tailors since 1898.

InWear/Matinique C–D6
Steenstraat 42, t (050) 33 12 19.
Open *Mon–Sat 10am–6pm.*
Smart off-the-peg clothes for men and women. Part of a large chain.

Lodge D6
Dijver 3, t (050) 33 32 42.
Open *Tues–Sat 10am–noon and 1.30–8pm, Sun and Mon 1.30–6.30pm.*
Stylish sports and leisurewear featuring in particular the brand Peak Performance.

Meire C5
Geldmuntstraat 6, t (050) 33 32 90.
Open *Mon–Fri 9am–noon and 2–6.30pm, Sat 9am–noon and 2–6pm.*
Long-established shop selling women's and men's clothes and accessories of classical elegance by labels such as Burberry, Barbour and Daks.

Morgan C6
Steenstraat 60, t (050) 34 98 49.
Open *Mon–Sat 9.30am–6.30pm, Sun 11.30am–6.30pm.*
Outlet for this fashionable French label, offering young high fashion that – at the current exchange rate – costs as much as 40 per cent less than in Britain.

Newport C6
Zuidzandstraat 14, t (050) 34 15 50.
Open *Mon–Sat 9.30am–6.30pm, Sun 2–6pm.*
Men and women's clothes shop, carrying a broad range of fashionable, down-to-earth brands. Specializes in the rugged, outdoor look.

Olivier Strelli (for women) D5
Eiermarkt 3, t (050) 34 38 37.
Open *Mon–Sat 10am–6.30pm.*
Very elegant, youthful high fashion by a respected Brussels-based label.

Olivier Strelli (for men) C5
Geldmuntstraat 19, t (050) 34 38 37.
Open *Mon–Sat 10am–6.30pm.*
A smaller outlet of the above label, for menswear.

Quicke C6
Zuidzandstraat 21, t (050) 33 23 00. **Open** *Mon–Sat 9.30am–6.30pm.*
One of the leading shoe shops of Bruges, featuring many of Europe's top *haute-couture* brands. From chunky to super-dainty to medieval-revisited.

Rex C5
Geldmuntstraat 18, t (050) 34 66 50. *Open Mon–Sat 9.30am–7pm.*
Graffiti-decorated clothes-store for the young: sweatshirts, T-shirts, jeans, heavy-duty shoes, etc, from brands such as Diesel.

Shoes in the Box D5
Steenstraat 18, t (050) 33 47 00. *Open Mon–Sat 9am–6pm, plus Sun in Dec.*
Large range of fashionable shoes, trading on quality and good value-for-money. The shop is part of a major Belgian retail chain.

Zazou C5
Sint-Amandsstraat 19–20, t (050) 33 46 27. *Open Mon–Sat 10am–12.30pm and 2–6.30pm.*
Specialists in contemporary designer jewellery in silver, steel and resin. Their interesting selections, relaxed and arty approach and low prices make this a popular place among the local young. Also sells bags and scarves. Cash only: no credit cards.

Crafts

Argus D7
Walplein 18, t (050) 34 44 32. *Open daily 10am–7pm.*
Attractive hand-made and painted ceramic tiles featuring views of Bruges.

Käthe Wohlfahrt D7
Walplein 12, t (050) 34 63 71. *Open Feb–Dec Mon–Thurs, Sat and Sun 10am–6pm, Fri 10am–7pm.*
A Christmas shop, selling beautifully made German decorations, many of them in wood – angels, candle-holders, incense burners, tree decorations and nutcrackers. Also has a range of decorations and gifts for Easter.

La Casa Mexicana D7
Mariastraat 24, t (050) 34 47 76. *Open Mon–Sat 10am–6.30pm, Sun 12.30–6.30pm.*
Imaginative selection of pottery and metalwork from Mexico (and some from Indonesia) – fish, monkeys, suns, Aztec heads, transformed into ornaments, lamps, mirrors, candleholders.

Department Stores

Hema D5
Steenstraat 73, t (050) 34 96 56. *Open Mon–Sat 9.15am–6pm.*
Clothing, housewares, toiletries.

Inno D5
Steenstraat 11, t (050) 33 06 02. *Open Mon–Sat 9.15am–6pm.*
Large, upmarket department store, with clothes, luggage, household goods, toiletries, etc.

Design Products

B D5–6
Wollestraat 25, t (050) 49 09 31. *Open Mon 2–6pm, Tues–Sat 10am–noon and 2–6pm.*
A shop specializing in Belgian design goods, including furniture and furnishings, jewellery, toys, household wares, chocolates and strip-cartoon books.

Diamonds

Bruges lays claim to being an old centre for diamond-cutting and polishing. It does not have the reputation of Antwerp, but diamond-lovers might like to check out the wares and prices in Bruges's diamond outlets.

Brugs Diamanthuis D5
Cordoeaniersstraat 5, t (050) 34 41 60. *Open Mon–Sat 9am–noon and 2–6.30pm.*
An old *maison de maître* provides the suitably elegant setting for this diamond-jewellery shop.

Het Brugs Diamantmuseum D7
Katelijnestraat 43, t (050) 34 20 56. *Open daily 10.30am–5.30pm.*
The museum (*see p.92*) has a shop with an extensive range of diamond jewellery.

Jewellery Quijo D5
Breidelstraat, t (050) 34 10 10. *Open Mon–Sat 9am–noon and 2–6.30pm.*
The shop of local jewellery designer Peter Quijo, presenting original, stylish and pleasurably

chunky work incorporating diamonds cut to his own formula.

Flowers

Flowers are almost as much a part of Belgian life as chocolates, chips, beer and *pâtisserie*. Florists conjure up spectacular displays with flowers and plants – more like sculpture than flower arrangements. Here are two, for flowers real and deceptively artificial:

De Binnentuin D5
Philipstockstraat 16 (at No. 9 after July 2002), t (050) 34 61 26. *Open daily 9.30am–6.30pm.*
If you can't take fresh flowers home, try these: top-quality silk flowers beautifully presented in magnificent arrangements.

De Vier Seizoenen E2
Langerei 65, t (050) 34 61 14. *Open Tues–Sat 9am–12.30pm and 1.30–7pm, Sun 9am–12.30pm.*
Inventive flower-arranging, combining nature and artifice to spectacular and surprising effect.

Food

There are numerous specialist food shops in Noordzandstraat, Zuidzandstraat and Smedenstraat, selling hams, sausage, smoked eels, cheese. Even the vegetable shops take trouble to put on a show to gladden the eye.

De Brugse Kaashove D5
Eiermarkt 2. *Open daily 9am–6.30pm.*
A good selection of cheeses, including many of Belgium's finest such as Herve and Limburger.

Deldycke D5–6
Wollestraat 23, t (050) 33 43 35. *Open Wed–Mon 9am–2pm and 3–6.30pm.*
High-class delicatessen and caterers, offering specialist foods from Belgium and around the world – fresh foods, cheeses, biscuits, chocolates, wines and much more, all enticingly presented.

Javana D5
Steenstraat 6, t (050) 33 36 05.
Open Mon–Sat 9am–6.30pm.
Aroma-rich shop offering freshly
ground coffee from around the
world, on a site where coffee has
been roasted for over 50 years.

Lace

Breidelstraat (linking the Markt
to the Burg) is virtually a lace alley,
but there is not much to choose
between the shops here (they
double up as souvenir shops).
Those listed below are all serious
outlets, reinforced by expert
knowledge and good displays. If
you want proper handmade lace,
be sure to ask for a certificate of
authenticity. For details about
lace-making *see p.99.*

Kantcentrum F4
Peperstraat 3a, t (050) 33 00 72.
Open Mon–Fri 10am–noon
and 2–6pm, Sat 10am–noon
and 2–5pm.
The shop in the Lace Centre, with
fully authenticated handmade
lace, plus everything for the lace-
maker: bobbins, cushions, yarn,
work stands.

The Little Lace Shop D5
Markt 11, t (050) 34 54 26. Open
daily 10am–6pm (closes at 7pm
Easter–Sept).
The oldest lace shop in Bruges,
founded in 1923 and still run by
the same family four generations
on; also, as its name implies, the
smallest.

The Little Lace Shop D8
Wijngaardstraat 32, t (050) 33 64
06. Open daily 10am–6pm.
Another, larger branch of the
above. Also has lace-making
demonstrations.

Selection D6
Dijver 4, t (050) 34 72 23. Open
daily 10am–6pm.
Fine lace, sold as table linen, cushions, ribbons, blouses, beautifully
laid out for display and admiration
in deep shop windows. Also sells
tapestry.

't Apostelientje F4
Balstraat 11, t (050) 33 78 60. Open
Mon, Tues and Thurs–Sat 9.30am–
6pm (to 5.30pm Dec–Feb), Wed
9.30am–12.30pm and 1.30–6pm,
Sun 10am–noon and 1.30–4pm.
New and antique handmade lace,
along with lace-making equipment. The owners make wooden
bobbins, you can even buy chocolate bobbins as well.

Markets

Bruges's main markets sell fruit,
vegetables, flowers, cooked meats,
cheeses, fresh fish and household
wares. They are visually ravishing
– worth sampling for the ambience and the sales folks' cries. The
main markets are in the Markt
and 't Zand.

Christmas Market: Markt D5
Held first week Dec–first week Jan.
During this period the Wednesday
market shifts to the Burg.
Festive stalls selling Christmas
goods around an open-air
skating rink.

Dijver D6
Fleamarket. Held mid-Mar–mid-
Nov Sat and Sun afternoon.

Markt D5
Held Wed 8am–1pm.

't Zand B6
Held Sat 8am–1pm.

Vismarkt E5
Fresh fish. Held Tues–Sat 8am–1pm.

Music

Compact 500 D5
Steenstraat 10, t (050) 34 53 33.
Open daily 10am–6.30pm.
The place to buy your CDs: pop,
rock, jazz, world music, even
Belgian music. Also stocks DVDs.

Rombaux E5
Mallebergplaats 13, t (050) 33 25 75.
Open Mon–Fri 9am–12.30pm and
2–6.30pm, Sat 9am–6pm.
Old-style music shop, selling a
broad range of CDs (classical, pop,
jazz, world), as well as musical
instruments and printed music.

Soap

Soap Bar D5
Wollestraat 21, t (050) 61 52 71.
Open daily 9.30am–7pm.
Instead of a box of chocolates,
how about a box of little chunks
of soaps in a range of exotic perfumes and flavours? Stocks wacky,
fun soaps of all shapes and sizes.

Supermarkets

There are a few small supermarkets within the city – good for
finding basic items, plus a fairly
wide range of Belgian specialities.
For a more substantial stock-up
(with a car), the out-of-town
supermarkets offer a broader
range. One of these is listed
below, but your hotel will be able
to give you local advice.

Delhaize Off maps
Junction of the Expressweg (main
road linking Zeebrugge to the E40)
and Exit Sint-Andries/Olympia
stadion. Open Mon–Sat 9am–8pm.
One of several large out-of-town
supermarkets, conveniently placed
en route to the Channel ports.

Profi F5
Langestraat 55 (also at Oude Burg
22). Open Mon–Thurs 9am–
12.30pm and 1–6.30pm, Fri
9am–12.30pm and 1.30–7pm, Sat
9am–12.30pm and 1.30–6pm.
Medium-sized, but with a full
range of food, drink, toiletries,
stationery, etc.

Tapestry

Mille Fleurs D6
Wollestraat 33, t (050) 34 54 54,
w www.millefleurstapestries.com.
Open daily 10am–6pm (closes at
7pm April–Oct).
Ready-made tapestry woven on
looms (mechanically or by hand)
in Flanders: wall-hangings,
cushion covers, upholstery mate-
rial, handbags – with a price range
from a few euros to €3,200 for a
major wall-sized tapestry.

Sports and
Green Spaces

Most visitors to Bruges spend all their time within the ring of canals that bounds the old city. To some degree this is a world apart from the extensive suburbs where everyday European lives are led. In no field is this more noticeable than in the provision of sports facilities. With the exception of a few hotel swimming pools and fitness suites there are virtually no sports facilities in the old city. There are, however, numerous clubs and public facilities in the suburbs and beyond, offering tennis, squash, golf, skating, horse-riding. In other words, keen sports players are unlikely to find facilities on their doorstep, and will have to make a special effort to seek them out.

The fact is, visitors to Bruges are not really expected to play sports. For one thing, most visitors do not stay long enough to consider packing their sports kit. In addition, visiting Bruges can in itself be a fairly physical activity, and most people will find themselves well enough exercised staying within the old city limits – by just walking the streets, or climbing the 366 steps of the Belfort. The more energetic may hire bicycles.

For those in search of green spaces to walk in, there are a few very small parks within the city limits, and an extensive ribbon of green spaces along the canals at the perimeter. But again, the most extensive parks lie in the suburbs, particularly to the southwest.

Sports
Cycling

Along with football, cycling is the nation's favourite sport. The Tour de France sometimes cuts through Belgium; otherwise the annual highlight is the **Ronde van Vlaanderen** (Tour of Flanders), which takes place on the first Sunday of April.

That said, the city of Bruges is not well-suited to sports cycling.

The streets are narrow and often cobbled. Nonetheless, it's a good place for some gentle cycling, and for thousands of Bruges's citizens, young and old, this is their preferred means of getting about. And for visitors, sightseeing by bicycle adds novelty. See p.55 for bicycle hire, and for organized tours by bicycle.

Football

Bruges is not all history: it also has a famous football club, Club Brugge, champions of the Belgian league in recent years. Support incites great passions, and at the time of crunch matches the gentle streets of Bruges are occasionally the scene of skirmishing fans and riot police anxious to put their training to good use. In February 1999 rioting fans of the Brussels club Anderlecht ran amok during a match against Club Brugge, hurled seats on to the pitch, caused play to be suspended, and did an estimated one million BF (€250,000) damage.

In fact Bruges has two teams: Club Brugge and Cercle Brugge. **Club Brugge** (the blue-and-blacks) was founded in 1890 and had links with the Socialists, still maintaining strong working-class support today. **Cercle Brugge** (the green-and-blacks) was founded in 1899 by old boys of the Xavier Institute, a Jesuit school (close to the Gruuthusemuseum), which had a strong British contingent from the 1860s. They are arch-rivals, though currently separated by being in different divisions. Club Brugge is a leading club in the first (top) division (called the Jupiler League), and was four times champion in the 1990s. The glory days for Cercle Brugge were the 1920s, but it now hovers around the middle of the second division, where it has been for the past five years.

Since 1975 the two teams have shared the new **Jan Breydel Stadium** (Olympiapark; see below) in Sint-Andries, a western suburb

of Bruges (the only stadium in Flanders to host the European Championship in 2000). When the two teams clash for a local derby (as they could do in principle in the FA cup) all the emotions of football tribalism emerge, demonstrating that Bruges is, after all, a European city just like any other. For more information (in English) on Belgian football go to w *www.footbel.com*.

Club Brugge KV Off maps *Olympialaan 74, 8200 Sint-Andries*, t (050) 40 21 21, w *www.clubbrugge.be.*

KSV Cercle Brugge Off maps *Olympialaan 74, 8200 Sint-Andries*, t (050) 38 92 57, w *www.cercle brugge.be.*

Jan Breydel Stadium (Olympiapark) Off maps *Leopold II-laan, 8200 Sint-Andries*, t (050) 40 21 21; *bus No.25 from Biekorf; car via the Tourhout road (Tourhoutsesteenweg).*
The Jan Breydel Stadium, to the west of the old city, is Bruges's prestige soccer venue. Attached to it is a sports centre which includes an Olympic-sized swimming pool (*see* 'Swimming' p.192).

Golf

For reviews of the courses, and further details, *see* w *www.golf europe.com.*

Damme Golf-Club Off maps *Doornstraat 16, 8340 Sijsele-Damme*, t (050) 35 35 72. *Open April–Oct 8.30am–6pm, Nov–March 9am–5pm.*
Located about 10km to the east of Bruges, close to Sijsele, this offers the 18-hole 'Damme' course, plus a 9-hole short (3-par) course. The Damme course is particularly enjoyable – challenging, well-kept and pretty. The green fee is €45 for the 18-hole course, and €18 for the short course. Visiting players must present their golf-club membership cards and/or handicap certificates to gain access. Telephone ahead for a start-time, particularly in summer.

Royal Zoute
Golf-Club Off maps
Caddiespad 14, 8300 Knokke-le-Zoute, t (050) 60 16 17.
A club course in the upmarket coastal resort of Knokke-Heist, 20km north of Bruges. It has two 18-hole courses, one par 64, the other par 72. These are both highly regarded, particularly the latter; but the green fee of €90 reflects the prestigious Knokke-Heist location.

Horse-riding

There are a large number of riding stables and schools around Bruges. The following stable has broad local approval, and is based in the pretty polder country near Damme. For alternatives, enquire at the tourist offices at Bruges (see p.65) or Damme (see p.126).

Manège 'De Blauwe Zaal' Off maps
Blauwezaalhoek 2, 8310 Sint-Kruis, t (050) 36 10 08.
Located just to the south of the Bruges-Damme Canal, about 2km from the Dampoort. Pony and horse-riding for children and adults: €25, including lunch. Telephone for appointment.

Skating

Boudewijnpark Off maps
A. Debaeckestraat 12, Sint-Michiels, t (050) 40 84 08; bus No.7 or 17 from Bierkorf or the station.
Rollerskating: Wed, Sat and Sun 2–6pm; adults €3.80, children under 12 €2.50; rollerskate hire €2/hour; rollerblade hire €2.50/hour. Ice-skating: Oct–mid-April, Wed–Fri 2–5.30pm and 7–9pm, Sat 10–11.30am and 4–5.30pm and 7–9pm, Sun 10–11.30am and 2–5.30pm; €3.80/session; skate hire €2.20/hour.
The Boudewijnpark theme park, 1.5km from the southern perimeter of the city, has facilities for both ice skating and roller-skating/rollerblading.

Snooker

The Snooker Palace C5
Noordzandstraat 4, t (050) 34 13 49. Open Mon–Sat 11am–late, Sun 1pm–late.
Bar with nine snooker tables, eight darts boards, a pool table and a large-screen TV (see p.182).

Swimming

Olympiabad Off maps
Doornstraat 110, 8200 Sint-Andries, t (050) 39 02 00. Open Tues–Sun 5–9pm.
Olympic-sized indoor public swimming pool, part of the Jan Breydel Stadium (Olympiapark) complex. Fun-swim on Sundays, with slides and floats. Costs €2.30 for adults, €1.60 for under-14s.

Zwembad Jan Guilini A3
Keizer Karelstraat 41, t (050) 31 35 54. Open Mon, Tues and Sat 7–8.30am and 4–6pm, Wed and Fri 7–8.30am, 2–5pm and 7–9.45pm, Thurs and Fri 7–8.30am and 2–5pm.
A straightforward indoor public pool located just beyond the city limits, to the northwest, between the Smedenpoort and Ezelpoort. €1.75 for adults; €1.10 for under-14s.

Tennis and Squash

Brughia Tennis and Squashcenter Off maps
Boogschutterslaan 37, 8310 Sint-Kruis, t (050) 35 34 06. Open daily 9am–11pm. Costs vary according to time of day: tennis courts €12–16 for one hour; squash courts €5–8 for half an hour.
Club to the east of the city, 1km from the Kruispoort, with seven indoor tennis courts, two squash courts and a fitness centre with the usual machines.

Tennis De Blauwe Reiger Off maps
Oude Oostendsesteenweg 87, t (050) 32 09 36. Open daily April–Sept 9am–midnight. €10 per hour.
A club with 9 courts (4 of them brand new), outdoor but floodlit.

Green Spaces

Arentshof D6
A tiny park beside the Arentshuis (see p.83) dotted with bronze sculptures. The sculptures, depicting the Knights of the Apocalypse (1987), are by the contemporary Neoexpressionist sculptor Rik Poot. Note also the pillars standing in the park – the last surviving remnants of the Waterhalle (see p.71).

Begijnhof D8
The Begijnhof (see p.89) is one of the city's best-known green spaces – particularly beautiful in spring, when daffodils pierce the lawn beneath the trees. Pleasant for a gentle amble along the pathways.

Brugse Vesten and Kruisvest
Paths lead around much of the outer ring of canals that define the egg-shaped limits of old Bruges. Particularly attractive sections include the Kruisvest, with its windmills (see p.104) and the Boeverievest and Smedenvest, to the north and south of the Smedenpoort (see p.114).

Koningin Astridpark E–F6
The prettiest of the city parks, Koningin Astridpark has been thoroughly overhauled in preparation for Brugge 2002 (see p.92).

Minnewater D8–9
Tree-hung pathways lead along Minnewater Lake (see p.90) and the line of the old ramparts (the Begijnenvest) to the south.

North Side of the Burg D–E5
Once the site of the city cathedral, Sint-Donaaskathedraal (destroyed by the French in 1799), this tree-lined square provides pleasant breathing space in the centre of town. It has a new addition for Bruges 2002, the Pavilion on the Burg (see p.76). Another feature is the modern statue entitled *The Lovers*, featuring a couple on their way to their marriage in the Stadhuis. It is a self-portrait by the local artists Stefaan Depuydt and

(Italian-born) Livia Canestraro, also the creators of the remarkable set of statues on 't Zand (*see* p.112), along with numerous other sculptural works in the city.

Sebrechtspark B–C5
Closes before dusk.
Like the Koningin Astridpark, this was formerly the site of a convent, destroyed by the French in the 1790s. Dedicated to St Elizabeth, it was run by the Grauwzusters (Grey Sisters) as a mental hospital. It was later bought by a Professor Sebrechts, and became a pleasant little walled municipal park in 1981.

Outside the City

Three adjoining parks (divided by roads), formerly the estates of castles, fill much of the area to the southwest of the city, in the suburbs of Sint-Andries and Sint-Michiels. Extensive, wooded, with paths and various incidental features (notably the castles), they provide pleasant open spaces for walking, cycling and picnicking – although the proximity of the A10–E40 motorway doesn't go unnoticed.

Provinciedomein 'Tillegembos' Off maps
Tourhoutsesteenweg, Sint-Michiels, **t** *(050) 38 02 96;* **bus** *No.25 from Biekorf;* **car**: *via the Tourhout road (Tourhoutsesteenweg).* **Open** *daily dawn to dusk.*
A large park (107 hectares) with marked walks, and a rustic *estaminet* (pub/cafeteria) called De Trutselaar (**t** *(050) 38 98 10*). Domain of a fine old moated castle dating from the 16th century, renovated in neogothic style in the 19th century, and now the seat of the West Flanders Tourist Office.

Stedelijk Domein 'Beisbroek' Off maps
Zeeweg 96, Sint-Andries, **t** *(050) 31 98 03;* **bus** *No.793 from 't Zand and Station;* **car**: *via the Tourhout road (Tourhoutsesteenweg).* **Open** *daily dawn to dusk.*
A 99-hectare park with picnic areas, a deer park and cafeteria. The castle is now used as a Nature Centre (**open** *April–Nov Mon–Fri 2–5pm, Sun 2–6pm; March Sun 2–6pm*). There is also an observatory and planetarium (**observatory open** *Fri 8–10pm all year; March–Nov also Sun 2–6 pm,* **t** *(050) 39 05 66*).

Stedelijk Domein 'Tudor' Off maps
Zeeweg 147, Sint-Andries, **t** *(050) 31 98 03;* **bus** *No.5 from Biekorf.* **Car**: *via the Tourhout road (Tourhoutsesteenweg).* **Open** *daily dawn to dusk.*
Smaller park between Provinciedomein 'Tillegembos' and Stedelijk Domein 'Beisbroek' (*see* above) with gardens, picnic area and a cafeteria in the Kasteel Tudor (**t** *(050) 38 05 28*), a Tudor-style mansion built in the early 20th century.

Children and Teenagers' Bruges

Children

Children seem to like Bruges. In truth, there is not a great deal to do that is specifically designed for them apart from the Boudewijnpark (see p.196), but they seem to respond to the historical magic of the place – its twisty streets, its medieval spires and towers, the canals and bridges. They are also made to feel welcome, in hotels, in restaurants and in museums. This is because Belgian children are by and large well integrated with society as a whole. For the Belgians, children are what society is about.

The first thing you notice about Belgian children is how well behaved they are. Belgium has a comparatively close-knit society, where traditional values are maintained not only by parents but also through the kindly guidance of ever-present older cousins, aunts, and grandmothers. Just about all children go to the local state-run school, which therefore has the strong backing of Belgium's mighty middle classes. If a child is unacceptably disruptive, the parents will soon be under pressure to do something about it. For all that, this is a child-friendly society, where children are broadly welcomed and generally well catered for.

The knock-on effect of this is that you do not have to worry about children being well provided for in Bruges. Shops sell all the necessities, from disposable nappies and powdered milk to delightful designer clothes. Pharmacies will be able to diagnose minor ailments and provide remedies. The hospital system is admirable. Hotels are used to installing cots and extra beds to make up family rooms, if requested – but always telephone first to check.

Eating Out

Restaurants happily accommodate children. If in doubt try the fondue restaurants, such as Pietje Pek (see 'Eating Out', pp.169–79), where they actually cook the food themselves; this will keep them entertained.

Snacking is no problem. There are plenty of outlets selling sandwiches, pastries, ice creams and soft drinks. For a properly Belgian experience, try some chips and mayonnaise from an outlet like Frituur Peter (see p.176) on the Markt, or waffles from Hennon in Breidelstraat.

If you must, there is a fast-food burger restaurant on the Markt: Quick (Markt 14, t (050) 33 19 79).

Entertainment

There is no regular form of children's entertainment in Bruges (apart from television in the hotel rooms), but keep an eye out for one-off events, announced in the tourist office and listings magazine, especially in summer.

Older children may enjoy the swashbuckling medieval banquets laid on by **Brugge Anno 1468/Bruges Celebrations** – a five-course meal accompanied by minstrels, jesters, fire-eaters, sword-fights and other riotous fun (see p.184).

Festivals

Most of the festivals listed on p.198 will delight children, particu-

Some Things to Do

Here are some ideas to keep your children amused:

A ride in a **horse-drawn carriage**, or the **Peerdentram** (see p.56)

A **boat-tour** on the canals (see p.56)

A **city tour** (with headphones) on one of the little Sightseeing Line buses (see p.56)

A **bicycle tour** of the city (see p.55)

Just **walking around the city centre** can be fun. Make the children map-read for you – a challenge they usually seem delighted to accept.

Magical Mystery Walk

The centre of Bruges, particularly the area just to the north of the Markt, is a wonderful network of alleys and streets, many of them off the usual beaten track. Try this game. Find four identical pieces of paper and write one of the following on each: Left, Right, Straight Ahead, Backwards. Take these with you on a walk: as you go, get a child to select unseen one of these pieces of paper. All the others in the party must then follow the direction it gives at the next junction – until the next junction, when someone picks another instruction. It's amazing the places you end up!

larly the major costume parades (the **Heilig-Bloedprocessie, Reiefeest** and **Praalstoet van de Gouden Boom**).

Christmas is enchanting, kicking off with the **Feast of Sinterklaas** on 6 December, when St Nicholas roams the streets. All the shops are decorated in greenery and gold, giving a glowing, candlelit effect that spells Christmas-how-it-should-be. The Markt is converted into a **Christmas market**, complete with skating rink.

Museums

You will have to work quite hard to keep children interested in Bruges's museums, unless they happen to like paintings, bits of medieval furniture, lace, silverware and beer-brewing equipment. Still, it can be done. The task is perhaps easiest in the following two museums:

Groeningemuseum D6
Dijver 12, t (050) 44 87 11. Open Wed–Mon 9.30am–5pm; adm adults €7, 13–16s €4, under-13s free. How about a gallop through the medieval art (much of it spectacularly grisly – saints being tortured, or pulled apart by horses – that kind of thing)?

Museum voor Volkskunde F3
Rolweg 40. Open April–Sept daily 9.30am–5pm, Oct–March Wed–

*Mon 9.30am–5pm; **adm** adults €2.50, 13–26s €1.50, under-13s free.*
Children may enjoy the jumble of exhibits at the Folklore Museum which provide a vivid, texture-rich and sometimes alarming, picture of life in times past.

Outside the Centre

Boudewijnpark and Dolphinarium Off maps
*A. Debaeckestraat 12, 8200 Brugge (Sint Michiels), **t** (050) 40 84 08.*
*You can reach the park by **bus** (nos. 7 and 17) from Biekorf and Kuipersstraat in Bruges city centre. **Open** May–Aug 10am–6pm; Easter and Sept 11am–6pm; **adm** adults €16, children under 12 €13.*
Just off the A17 to the south of Bruges, an entertaining amusement park with a big wheel, water chutes, crazy golf, etc. The dolphinarium (*June–Aug daily at 11.15am, 2pm and 4pm; April–May daily at 11.15am and 4pm; Oct daily at 4pm; Nov–Jan Sat and Sun at 4pm*) presents a show that demonstrates the remarkable intelligence and agility of these creatures. Boudewijnpark also has iceskating and rollerskating/rollerblading rinks.

Domein 'Zeven Torentjes' Off maps
*Canadaring 41, Assebroek, **t** (050) 35 40 43. **Open** Mon–Fri 8.30am–noon and 2–4pm. By **bus** No.2 from Biekorf; by **car** via the General Lemanlaan.*
Children's farm to the east of the city, in a former feudal estate.

Other Attractions
Belfort (*see p.70*). 366 steps up a tight spiral staircase, leading to a view over the city and deafening bells.
Stadhuis (*see p.73*). The Town Hall is spectacular: there should be enough here to keep children interested for at least 10 minutes.
The **windmills** on the Kruisvest (*see p.107*). Actually, kids tend to prefer just running down the hill.
See also 'Sports and Green Spaces', pp.190–3.

De Toverplaneet Off maps
*Lege Weg 88, Sint-Andries, **t** (050) 31 89 50. **Open** Wed 1–8pm, Fri 3.30–8pm, Sat and Sun 10.30am–8pm.*
Romp-about indoor playground for toddlers and young children, with sea-of-balls, slides and chutes, rope bridges and ladders.

Parks and Playgrounds

The Koningin Astridpark (close to the city centre) has a children's adventure playground at its southern end. *See* the section on 'Green Spaces' on pp.192–3 for other options.

Shopping
Babies and Toddlers
Bert D7–8
*Katelijnestraat 74–76, **t** (050) 33 28 44. **Open** Mon–Sat 9am–noon and 1.30–6.30 pm.*
Everything for the baby, a delightful and thoroughly modern shop with a flare for well designed products, clothes and toys.

Clothes for Children
Belgium does some fabulous ranges of children's clothes. Why do they have to grow so fast?
Folieke C6
*Steenstraat 98, **t** (050) 33 26 95. **Open** Mon–Sat 10am–6.30pm.*
Very stylish casual high fashion for children (0–12), particularly strong in cottons and linen in tasteful pastel shades. Part of a Flanders-based chain.

Toys
Krokodil C4
*Sint-Jakobsstraat 47. **Open** Mon–Sat 10am–12.20pm and 2–6.30pm.*
Part of a chain of up-market toyshops, specializing in attractive toys and games of the old-fashioned kind, many of them made of wood.

Tintin D5
*Steenstraat 3, **t** (050) 33 42 92. **Open** Mon–Sat 10am–6.30pm.*
The little Belgian hero and his pals in figurines, towels, postcards, posters, chess sets, cutlery – and books, of course.

Teenagers

Many teenagers just don't get the point of Bruges. Lace museums, horse-and-carriage rides and convents just don't turn them on. But the situation is not hopeless; there are things to do that even picky teenagers might enjoy.

Sights and Attractions

The Belfort (*see p.70*) has a tight spiral staircase and is a quite scary and challenging, while the Groeningemuseum (*see p.82*) and Memlingmuseum (*see p.88*) have images of unspeakable things medieval artists have inflicted on the saints. For the more active, it might be worth trying a cycling tour of the city (*see p.55*) or there's always rollerblading or iceskating at Boudewijnpark (*see p.192*).

Entertainment

Older teenagers might enjoy hanging out at Charlie Rockets (*see p.183*) or Bauhaus (*see p.168*). It's also worth checking out the listings magazines to see what concerts are on at Cactus Club and De Werf (*see p.184*) or what films are showing at Cinema Lumière and Ciné Liberty (*see p.184*).

Shopping

It is impossible to predict what teenagers will find acceptable, but try the streets to the west of the Markt, around Steenstraat, Sint-Amandstraat, Geldmuntstraat, Noordzandstraat and Zilverstraat. There they'll find shops (*see p.188*) like Rex (for clothes), Shoes in a Box (for shoes, obviously) and Zazou (for jewellery).

Festivals

Belgium has an extensive calendar of events: some are age-old ceremonies and pageants, widely advertised and drawing large crowds; others are religious festivals, including some of disturbing fervour; others still are entirely local excuses for an annual knees-up and binge. Bruges is no exception: it holds one annual pageant of national importance, the Heilig-Bloedprocessie, and has a busy timetable of other cultural events.

March

Cinema Novo Film Festival

3rd week in March

This film festival is dedicated to film making in Asia, Africa and Latin America. Founded in 1983 as the 'Third World Film Festival', it has grown to become one of Belgium's most important film festivals, featuring over 60 films and attracting audiences totalling over 15,000 from Belgium and far further afield. The focus of events is the Cinema Lumière (see p.184). For more information visit **w** *www.cinemanovo.be*.

May

Heilig-Bloedprocessie (Procession of the Holy Blood)

Ascension Day, 40 days after Easter, a Thursday, usually in May

Bruges's principal festival takes place annually on Ascension Day. Following an 800-year-old tradition, the holy relic is paraded through the streets, accompanied by medieval interpretations of biblical scenes, which were traditionally presented by the city's craft guilds and trading associations. Tickets (about €12) for the grandstand are available from the tourist office from 1 March onwards.

July

Cactusfestival

2nd weekend (Fri–Sun) in July

This three-day open-air rock concert held annually in the Minnewater Park (*see* p.90) attracts a range of interesting, medium-ranking bands. More details are available on the Web site **w** *www.cactusmusic.be*.

July

Nationale Feestdag België (Belgian National Holiday)

21 July

A public holiday is celebrated with such events as a Big Band concert and shows in the parks.

July/August

Klinkers Festival

Late July–Aug

The month-long Klinkers Festival, a '*culturele zomer happening*' of world music, jazz and cinema takes place in the parks and other open-air venues. For details check **w** *www.cactusmusic.be*.

Flanders Festival

End July–early Aug

For about two weeks, the celebrated Flanders Festival of classical music comes to Bruges as part of its six-month round of Flemish cities. Concerts take place in the Concertgebouw Brugge, Provinciaal Hof in the Markt, and the Ryelandtzaal, as well as several of the churches. For details, and tickets in advance, contact the tourist office (*see* p.65). Or visit **w** *www.festival-van-vlaaderen.be*.

August

Blindekensprocessie

15 Aug

In a solemn, and touching procession, a large candle (16kg) is taken from the chapel of Onze-Lieve-Vrouw van de Blindekens (*see* p.115) to Onze-Lieve-Vrouw ter Potterie (*see* p.96), fulfilling a pledge made in 1304 to the Madonna of the Blindekens to deliver the menfolk home safely from the Battle of Pevelenberg.

The Reiefeest (Festival of the Canals)

Last 10 days in Aug

The Reiefeest takes place once every three years (next in 2004). From about 9pm, spectators walk between various points on the illuminated canals to see a series of historic tableaux.

The Praalstoet van de Gouden Boom (Pageant of the Golden Tree)

Late Aug

This festival takes place every five years (next in 2006). A huge costumed procession, first held in 1958, tells the story of Bruges up to the 15th century, its myths and legends, culminating in a re-enactment of the spectacular parade for the marriage of Charles the Bold to Margaret of York in 1468. (The Golden Tree was a bejewelled trophy awarded at jousting tournaments held in the Markt.)

September

Open Monumenten Weekend (Heritage Weekend)

2nd weekend in Sept

A range of historic houses, private collections, gardens and businesses throw open their doors for a day. Ask for details at the tourist office (*see* p.65).

December

Christmas Market

About 2 Dec–2 Jan

Over the Christmas period, a market takes place in the Markt (*see* p. 70) in the centre of town, beside a temporary open-air ice rink.

Feast of Sinterklaas

6 Dec

St Nicholas, aka Santa Claus, walks the streets and markets and enters schools in his guise as the Bishop of Myra. He is usually accompanied by his jolly sidekick, the blacked-up and decidedly un-PC Zwarte Piet. Many Belgian children receive their main Christmas gifts, as well as traditional *speculoos* biscuits.

Language

Belgium has two main languages: Dutch and French. (The third official language is German, which is spoken on the eastern border.) Dutch is the language of Flanders, the provinces that stretch across the north of Belgium, which includes Bruges. In the past, people referred generally to this language as Flemish (Vlaams); there are broadly varying dialects within Flanders, but the basic standard language, taught in schools – and shared with the people of the Netherlands – is Dutch (Nederlands), and this has now become the preferred name for the language of Flanders.

The Flemish are generally reluctant to use French. There are strong historical and emotional reasons for this. French, the language of southern Belgium, was imposed as the language of the ruling classes by the Burgundians in the 14th century, and by the 19th century the French-speaking population held political and economic sway over the Flemish to a degree that can justifiably be called oppression. French, therefore, became the language of oppression, an issue that is still deeply resented to this day. As it happens, the language boot is now definitely on the other foot: Flemish and Dutch are in the ascendant, partly as a result of the decline of heavy industry in the French-speaking south and the growing strength of modern light industries and ports in the Flemish-speaking north, and partly because to succeed in administration it is now essential to be bilingual.

Remarkably few French speakers have made the effort to be conversant with Flemish, while a larger proportion of the Flemish have learned French. The result is that the Flemish have now gained the upper hand in the civil service in central government, as well as in public services such as the post office and railways. But they are not inclined to be magnanimous to the French-speakers in victory.

So there is no point brushing up your French for a visit to Bruges. The locals might know some French, but will only use it as a last resort, and speak it as though they have some unpleasant taste in the mouth. English, by contrast, is widely spoken. Most people connected to the tourist industry will speak it a bit, and many speak it very well indeed. That said, some knowledge of Dutch will come in handy, if only to read signposts and decipher labels. Also, a little Dutch, even if just in an exchange of greetings, is almost always appreciated: few visitors make the effort.

A Guide to Dutch Pronunciation

Two main problems confront anyone trying to learn even just the rudiments of Dutch. One is the grammatical structure – although if you know German you will be familiar with the broad pattern of the postponed verb. The other is pronunciation. It is a phonetic language, but you have to begin by shedding any preconceived notion about how written vowels should be pronounced. A, e, i, o and u are pronounced in a broadly similar way to English – although the 'a' is much throatier and ends up more like the 'o' in the English 'odd'. When it comes to combination vowels, however, any attempt to interpret them in an English or, worse, a French manner, will end in failure. Wipe the slate clean and relearn! Names of places, or familiar words, will often provide useful aids to memory. For instance huis sounds similar to the English word 'house', which is what it means (although the 'ow' sound is more complex, making it more like 'ah-oohss').

Combination Vowels

aa like aa in the English 'aardvaark'; e.g. *waar* (= where; pron. 'wahr')

ae like ar in the English 'part'; e.g. Verhaeren (Belgian poet; pron. 'Verharen')

au like ow in the English 'cow'; e.g. *kabeljauw* (= cod; pron. 'cabbelyow')

ee like ai in the English 'hail'; e.g. *een* (= one; pron. 'ayn')

ei like ij (see below); e.g *trein* (= train; pron. 'trayne')

eie like ay in the English 'say'; e.g. Reie (name of a river; pron. 'Ray')

eu like the English 'err'; e.g. Leuven (place name; pron. 'Lerven')

eeu ay-ooh; e.g. *leeuw* (= lion; pron. 'lay-oohv')

ie ee in the English 'three'; e.g. *drie* (= three; pron. 'dree')

ieu ee-oo; e.g. *nieuw* (= new; pron. 'nee-oo')

ij like ay in John Wayne; e.g. *wijn* (= wine; pron. 'wayne')

oe like oo in the English 'pool'; e.g. *soep* (= soup; pron. 'soup')

oo like oa in the English 'boat'; e.g. Te koop (= For sale; pron. 'Te cope' or 'Te cohp')

ou like ou in the English 'out'; e.g. *zout* (= salt; pron. 'zout')

ui like ow in the English 'house'; e.g. *huis* (= house; pron. 'ouse' or 'ah-oohss')

uu like oo in the English 'hoot'; e.g. Te huur (= For rent; pron. 'Te ooer': but round your lips, or you risk enquiring about a *hoer*, a prostitute)

Consonants

Most consonants sound the same as they do in English, although some combinations present their own difficulties. Here are some of the more troublesome ones:

ch pronounced like the ch in the Scottish 'loch'.

g pronounced like a gutteral h – something similar to the h in 'hotel' or (again) like the ch in the Scottish 'loch'.

j pronounced like the English y.

v closer to the English f.

w in Dutch is like a soft English w.

sch at the end of a word is pronounced s. At the start of the word it sounds more like sr, with a bit of gutteral throat-clearing.

Basic Vocabulary

Numbers
0 *nul*
1 *een*
2 *twee*
3 *drie*
4 *vier*
5 *vijf*
6 *zes*
7 *szeven*
8 *acht*
9 *negen*
10 *tien*
11 *elf*
12 *twaalf*
13 *dertien*
14 *veertien*
15 *vijftien*
16 *zestien*
17 *zeventien*
18 *achttien*
19 *negentien*
20 *twintig*
21 *een en twintig*
22 *twee en twintig*
30 *dertig*
31 *een en dertig*
40 *veertig*
50 *vijftig*
60 *zestig*
70 *zeventig*
80 *tachtig*
90 *negentig*
100 *honderd*
101 *honderdeen*
200 *twee honderd*
thousand *duizend*
million *miljoen*
first *eerste*
second *tweede*
third *derde*
half *een half*
a third *een derde*
a quarter *een kwart*

Useful Words
very *erg/zeer*
much/too much *veel/te veel*
little/few *weinig*
enough *genoeg*
expensive *duur*
cheap *goedkoop*
old *oud*
new *nieuw*
little *klein*
big *groot*

quickly *snel*
slowly *langzaam*

Days of the Week
Monday *maandag*
Tuesday *dinsdag*
Wednesday *woensdag*
Thursday *donderdag*
Friday *vrijdag*
Saturday *zaterdag*
Sunday *zondag*

Shopping and Services
open/closed *open/gesloten*
entrance *toegang/ingang*
exit *uitgang/uitrit*
No smoking *Niet roken*
shop *winkel*
bakery *bakkerij*
cake shop *banketbakkerij*
grocer *kruidenierswinkel*
bookshop *boekhandel*
pharmacy *apotheek*
clothes *kleding*
shoes *schoenen*
lace *kant*
bank *bank*
post office *postkantoor*
postage stamp *postzegel*
letter *brief*
postcard *ansichtkaart*
air mail *luchtpost*

Time
What is the time? *Hoe laat is het?*
today *vandaag*
yesterday *gisteren*
tomorrow *morgen*
morning *morgen/ochtend*
afternoon *namiddag*
evening *avond*
night *nacht*
day *dag*
week *week*
month *maand*
year *jaar*
century *eeuw*
early/late *vroeg/laat*

Directions and Transport
Where is...? *Waar is...?*
left/right *links/rechts*
straight on *vooruit*
near/far *dichtbij/ver*
airport *luchthaven/vliegveld*
railway station *station*
platform (five) *spoor (vijf)*
ticket *kaartje*
single/one way *enkel*
return/round trip *heen en terug*

car *auto*
car hire *auto verhuur*
driving licence *rijbewijs*
petrol *benzine*
petrol station *benzinestation*
unleaded *loodvrij*
car park *parkeerplaats*
bicycle *fiets*

Emergencies
police *politie*
doctor *dokter*
dentist *tandarts*
ill *ziek*
I'm not feeling well.
  Ik voel niet lekker.
ambulance *ambulance*
hospital *ziekenhuis*
medicine *geneesmiddel*

Greetings, Responses and Getting By
I am... *Ik ben...*
Britain/British
  Groot Brittannië/Brits
America/American
  Amerika/Amerikaan
Canada/Canadian
  Canada/Canadees
Australia/Australian
  Australië/Australisch
yes/no *ja/nee*
please *alstublieft (abbrev. a. u. b.)*
thank you (very much)
  dank u (wel)/bedankt
hello, good day
  goedendag, or simply *dag*
good morning
  goedemorgen
good evening
  goedenavond
good night (at bedtime)
  goede nacht
goodbye *tot ziens*
How are you? *Hoe maakt u het?*
Very well, thank you.
  Goed, dank u.
My name is...
  Mijn naam is...
mister/sir *mijnheer*
mrs/madam *mevrouw*
how much? *hoeveel?*
I can't speak Dutch
  Ik spreek geen Nederlands.
Do you speak English?
  Spreekt u engels?
a little *een beetje*
I do not understand.
  Ik begrijp het niet.

I don't know. *Ik weet het niet.*
Go away! *Ga weg!*
Where is the toilet?
Waar is het toilet?
ladies/gents
damestoilet/herentoilet
Watch out! *Pas op!*
Sorry! *Sorry!/Het spijt me.*
Cheers! *Gezondheid!/Proost!*

Eating Out

The language of cuisine in Flanders is traditionally French, and in restaurants French terms are still often used for the dishes, although this is changing. Dutch terms are used in food shops. Both Dutch and French versions are given here.

General

to eat *eten*
to drink *drinken*
the bill *de rekening*
breakfast *ontbijt*
lunch
middagmaal/noenmaal
dinner *avondeten*
beer *bier*
a bottle of wine
een fles wijn
red/white wine *rode/witte wijn*
glass *glas*
tea/ coffee *thee/koffie*
milk *melk*
soft drinks *limonaden*
orange juice *sinaasappelsap*
mineral water
mineraalwater
soup *soep*
starter *voorgerecht*
main course *hoofdgerecht*
dish of the day
dagschotel/dagmenu
bread *brood*
butter *boter*
cheese *kaas*
egg *ei*
filled chocolates *pralinen*

Fish (*poisson/vis*)

cod *cabillaud/kabeljauw*
haddock
aiglefin/églefin/schelvis
lobster *homard/kreeft*
mussel *moule/mossel*
oyster *huître/oester*
salmon *saumon/zalm*
scallop *coquille Saint-Jacques/Sint-Jacobsoester/ Jacobsschelp*
shrimp/prawn *crevette/garnaal*
squid *calamar/calamar/inktvis*
trou *truite/forel*
tuna *thon/tonijn*

Meat (*viande/vlees*)

game *gibier/wild*
beef *boeuf/rundvlees*
chicken *poulet/kip*
duck *canard/eend*
ham *jambon/ham/hesp*
lamb *agneau/lamsvlee*
pork *porc/varkensvlees*
snails *escargots/slakken*
venison *cerf/chevreuil/ree(bok)*
leg *gigot/bout*
sausage *saucisse/saucisson/worst*

Vegetables (*légumes/ groenten*)

asparagus *asperges/asperges*
Belgian endive/chicory
chicon/witloof
carrots *carottes/worteltjes*
cauliflower *choufleur/bloemkohl*
chives *ciboulette/bieslook*
garlic *ail/knoflook*
green beans *haricots princesse/princesbonen*
leek *poireau/prei*
mushroom
champignon/champignon
onion *oignon/ui*
peas *petits pois/erwten*
potatoes *pommes de terre/aardappelen*
potato chips/french fries
frites/frieten
rice *riz/rijst*
spinach *épinards/spinazie*

Fruit (*fruits/fruit/ vruchten*)

apple *pomme/appel*
banana *banane/banaan*
cherry *cerise/kers*
chestnut *marron/kastanje*
orange *orange/sinaasappel*
peach *pêche/perzik*
pear *poire/peer*
pineapple *ananas/ananas*
plum *prune/pruim*
raspberry *framboise/framboos*
strawberry *fraise/aardbei*

Dessert (*dessert/ nagerecht*)

cake *gâteau/koek*
cheesecake
tarte au fromage/kaastaart
tart *tarte/taart*
whipped cream
crème Chantilly/slagroom
ice cream *glace/ijs*
pancake *crêpe/pannekoek*
waffle *gaufre/wafel*

Preparation

rare *saignant/rood*
medium *à point/half doorbakken*
well done *bien cuit/gaar*
plain (without sauces)
nature/natuur
minced *haché/gehakt*
stuffed *farci/gevuld*
grilled *grillé/geroosterd*
steamed *à la vapeur/gestoomd*
smoked *fumé/gerookt*

French/Walloon Dishes and Specialities

à l'ardennaise cooked with Ardennes ham (and sometimes cheese)
à la liégeoise cooked or prepared with strips of bacon
à la nage (fish) served in a delicately flavoured stock
andouillettes rich sausages made of offal
anguilles au vert eels in green herb sauce
assiette anglaise a selection of cold meats
boudin/boudin noir sausage/black pudding
boulettes meatballs
carbonnades flamandes beef stew cooked with beer
civet (de lapin, etc.) game stew enriched with blood and red wine
cramique raisin bread
cuisses de grenouille frogs' legs
entrecôte à l'os a huge rib steak
(poissons) en escavèche (cold fish) cooked in a jellied stock flavoured with herbs
jets de houblon hop shoots
navarin d'agneau lamb stew

oiseaux sans tête slices of beef rolled around a meat stuffing

plateau de fruits de mer platter of mixed cold shellfish and other seafood

quenelles (de brochet) rolls of poached pasta flavoured with pounded fish (pike)

salade liégeoise green salad made with green beans and bacon pieces

steak à l'américaine raw minced steak

steak tartare raw minced steak (*steak à l'américaine* is the usual term)

tartare (de thon) raw and minced (tuna)

tourte savoury pie made with meat and vegetables

Flemish Dishes and Specialities

boterham a slice of bread and butter (for open sandwich)

fricandel meatballs

garnaalkroketten potato croquettes with shrimps inside

Gentse stoverij rich beef stew from Ghent cooked with beer and mustard

gueuze beer made from matured and blended lambic (see below)

hutsepot hearty stew (perhaps oxtail or pig's trotters) with root vegetables

paling in 't groen eels in green herb sauce

speculoos hard biscuits made with butter, brown sugar and spices

karbonaden braised beef with onions, usually cooked in beer

koeken pastries

lambic beer brewed in the Senne Valley, fermented by natural yeasts (*see* p.183)

Noordzee vissoep thick fish soup, with North Sea fish and vegetables

rijstpap rice pudding flavoured with cinnamon

stoemp mashed potato mixed with vegetable and/or meat purée

waterzooi chicken (now also fish) cooked in a soup-like cream sauce

Place Names

Many places in Belgium have two versions of their name: Dutch and French. Signposts tend to be based on the assumption that you know both. Below is a list of the principal cities and towns in Belgium (and France) where the two versions are noticeably different and might cause confusion.

Dutch/English/French

Aalst/Alost
Antwerpen/Antwerp/Anvers
Bergen/Mons
Brugge/Bruges
Brussel/Brussels/Bruxelles
Doornik/Tournai
Furnes/Veurne
Gent/Ghent/Gand
Ieper/Ypres
Kortrijk/Courtrai
Leuven/Louvain
Mechelen/Malines
Namen/Namur
Oostende/Ostend/Ostende
Rijsel/Lille (in France)
Zeebrugge/Zeebruges

Index

Numbers in **bold** indicate main references. Numbers in *italic* indicate maps.

Bruges Street Maps

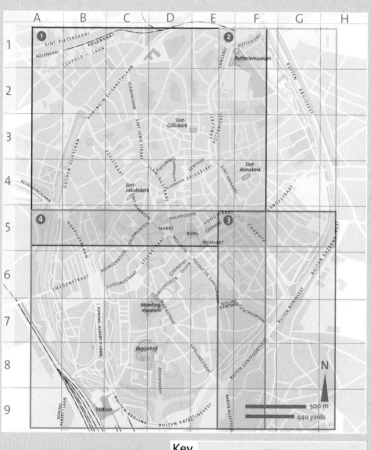

Key

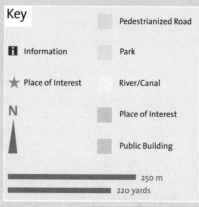

i Information

★ Place of Interest

N

Pedestrianized Road	
Park	
River/Canal	
Place of Interest	
Public Building	

250 m
220 yards

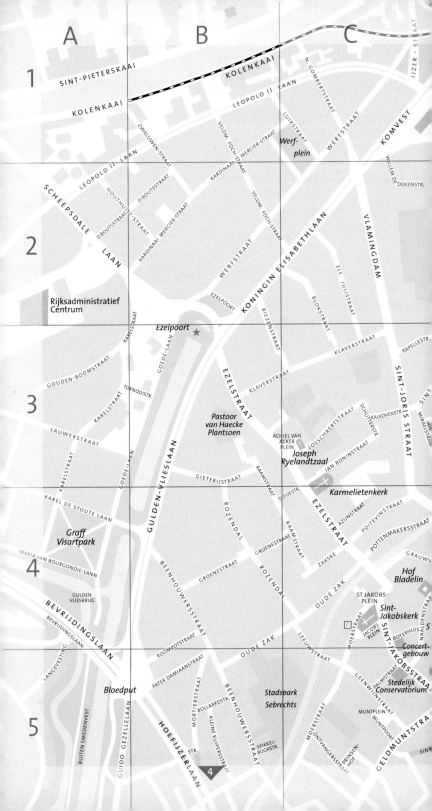

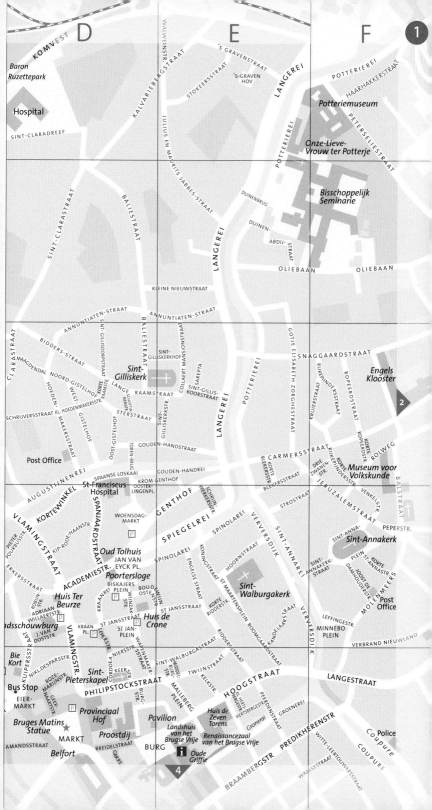

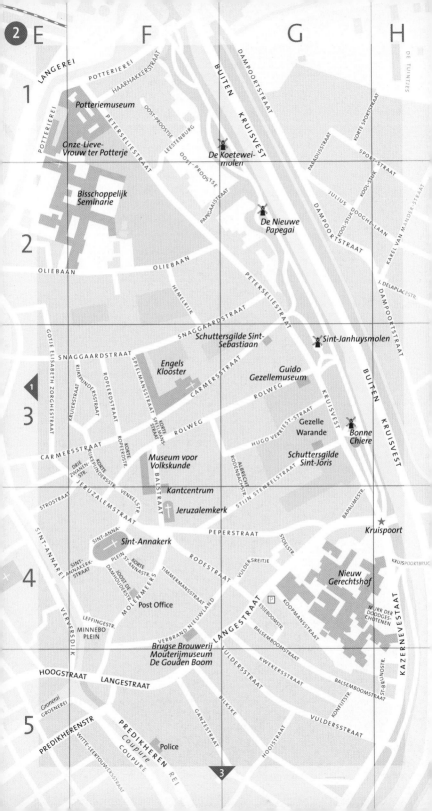

E

F

G

H

2

1

LANGEREI

POTTERIEREI

HAARHAKKERSTRAAT

BUITEN

DAMPOORTSTRAAT

KRUISVEST

Potteriemuseum

OOST-PROOSSE

LEESTENBURG

POTTERIEREI

PETERSELIESTRAAT

Onze-Lieve-
Vrouw ter Potterje

OOST-PROOSTSE

De Koetewei-
molen

PARADIJSSTRAAT

KORTE SPORTSTRAAT

SPORT-STRAAT

DE TUINTJES

2

Bisschoppelijk
Seminarie

PAPEGAAISTRAAT

De Nieuwe
Papegai

JULIUS DOOGHE-LAAN

KOOL-STUK

KOOL-STUK

DAMPOORTSTRAAT

KAREL VAN MANDER-STRAAT

OLIEBAAN

OLIEBAAN

HEMELRIJK

SNAGGAARDSTRAAT

PETERSELIESTRAAT

J. DELAPLACESTR.

DAMPOORTSTRAAT

3

GOTJE ELISABETH ZORGHESTRAAT

SNAGGAARDSTRAAT

KRUISERSTRAAT

RIJKEPIJNDERSSTRAAT

ROPEERDSTRAAT

SPEELMANSSTRAAT

KORTE
SPEELMANS-
STRAAT

SNAGGAARDSTRAAT

Schuttersgilde Sint-
Sebastiaan

CARMERSSTRAAT

Engels
Klooster

ROLWEG

Guido
Gezellemuseum

ROLWEG

Sint-Janhuysmolen

KRUISVEST

BUITEN

KRUISVEST

1

CARMERSSTRAAT

DRIE
ZWANEN-
STR.

KORTE
RIJKEPIJNDERSTR.

KORTE
ROPEERDSTR.

VENKELSTR.

Museum voor
Volkskunde

BALSTRAAT

HUGO VERRIEST-STRAAT

ALBRECHT
RODENBACHSTR.

Gezelle
Warande

STIJN STREUVELSTRAAT

Schuttersgilde
Sint-Joris

Bonne
Chiere

4

STROSTRAAT

JERUZALEMSTRAAT

SINT-ANNA-
STRAAT

Kantcentrum

Jeruzalemkerk

SINT-ANNA-
PLEIN

Sint-Annakerk

KORTE ST-ANNASTR.

SINT-ANNAKERK-
STRAAT

OOST DE
DAMHOUDERSTR.

MOLENMEERS

Post Office

PEPERSTRAAT

RODESTRAAT

TIMMERMANSSTRAAT

VERBRAND NIEUWLAND

LANGESTRAAT

VULDERSREITJE

STOELSTR.

ESSEBOOMSTR.

KOOPMANSSTRAAT

BAPAUMESTR.

Kruispoort

KRUISPOORTBRUG

Nieuw
Gerechtshof

MUUR DER
DOODGES-
CHOTENEN

KAZERNEVESTVAAT

SINT-ANNAREI

VERVERSDIJK

LEFFINGESTR.

MINNEBO
PLEIN

Brugse Brouwerij
Mouterijmuseum
De Gouden Boom

BALSEMBOOMSTRAAT

KWEKERSSTRAAT

BALSEMBOOMSTRAAT

ST-BRUNOSTR.

KONFIJTSTR.

5

HOOGSTRAAT

Groenerei
GROENEREI

LANGESTRAAT

PREDIKHERENSTR

WITTE-LEERTOUWERSSTRAAT

PREDIKHEREN
Coupure
COUPURE

Police

GANZESTRAAT

BILKSKE

PREDIKHEREN
REI

COUPURE

HOOISTRAAT

VULDERSSTRAAT

VULDERSSTRAAT

3

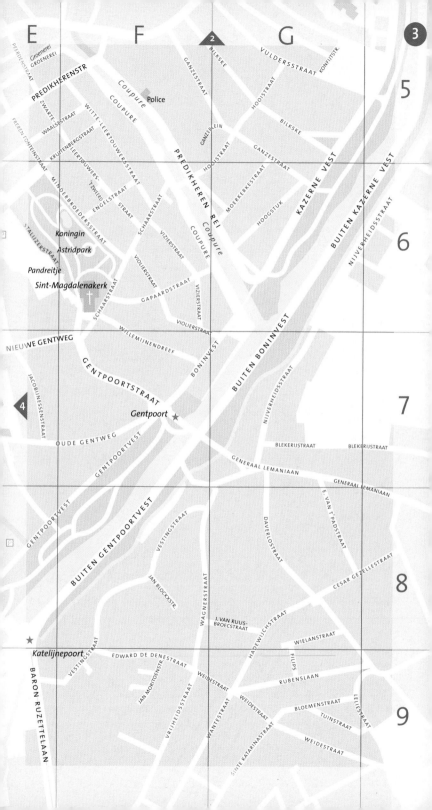

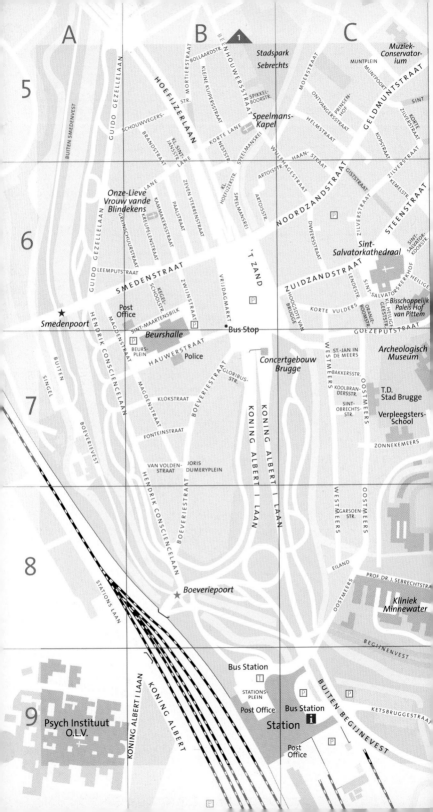

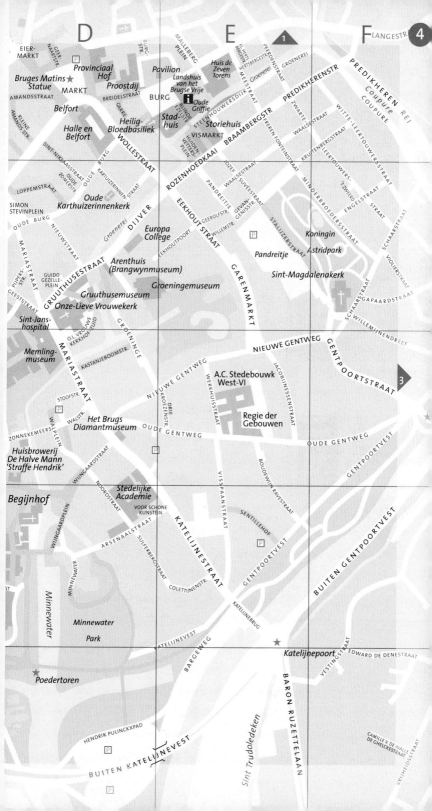

BRUSSELS

Antony Mason

CADOGANguides

PARIS

Dana Facaros & Michael Pauls

AMSTERDAM

Rodney Bolt

CADOGANguides

CADOGANguides

Cadogan City Guides...
the life and soul
of the city

CADOGANguides
well travelled **well read**